THE DECLINE OF MALES

The Imperial Animal *(with Robin Fox)*

Optimism: The Biology of Hope

The Pursuit of Pleasure

Men in Groups

Women in the Kibbutz *(with Joseph Shepher)*

The Manufacture of Evil: Ethics, Evolution, and the Industrial System

Female Hierarchies *(editor)*

Man and Beast Revisited *(co-editor with Michael Robinson)*

China's Food *(with photographs by Reinhart Wolf)*

THE

DECLINE

OF

MALES

LIONEL TIGER

ST. MARTIN'S PRESS NEW YORK

Design by Richard Oriolo

Library of Congress Cataloging-in-Publication Data

Tiger, Lionel
  The decline of males / Lionel Tiger.
    p. cm.
  Includes bibliographical references and index.
  ISBN 1-58238-014-7 (alk. paper)
  1. Men—Social conditions. 2. Sex role. 3. Man-woman relationships.
  I. Title.
HQ1090.T52   1999
305.3—dc21   98-27743
                               CIP

First published in the United States by Golden Books Publishing Co., Inc.

10 9 8 7 6 5 4 3 2 1

To Rose Ravid and Joyce Ravid

CONTENTS

THE DECLINE OF MALES

Love, Money,
and the Future

T H E   B O D Y   S H O P   is a self-conscious international retailer of cosmetics. It prides itself on environmental commitment, wholesomeness of commercial purpose, and thoughtfulness about securing products from benign suppliers. So it was startling to see a window ad in one of its Manhattan stores featuring a photo of a woman holding a small mammal, with the text: "Why test on poor defenseless little animals when they could use my husband?" Imagine if the ad had said "wife" instead.

The telephone repair trucks of NYNEX carry ads on their walls, one of which in 1996 displayed a pay telephone and the text: "You were wrong. Call her."

* * *

During a stupifyingly narcissistic performance at Madison Square Garden in New York in 1995, among other memorabilia Barbra Streisand projected photos of her son at various stages of his life. Was a new religion founded on virgin birth emerging before our eyes? At no time did the mother note that the child had a father—who was, after all, a non-anonymous film star.

The film *The First Wives Club*, an enormous commercial and popular success, featured a lively trio of women seeking revenge against their errant ex-husbands using a variety of ruthless means, including the involvement of the Mafia. The interplay of ex-wives with husbands who have moved out and perhaps on to other women represents an archetypically bitter struggle between men and women. Of sharp interest was the unquestioned desirability and even moral virtue of any effort to vilify males. The film ends with the establishment of a center for battered women. Battered by whom is obvious. The automatic and virtually universal assumption is that the source of evil is male. As Molly Haskell has so astutely described, films provide serious scripts not only for actors but for the millions of women and men whose lives are expanded or undermined or challenged by the hazily potent cinematic art form.[1]

In *The New York Times*, September 30, 1998, in a firmly negative review of a network series called "The Secret Lives of Men," critic Anita Gates puzzlingly concluded her comment with, "Still, it's good to see male characters played as vulnerable and insecure."

This book is about an emerging pattern. Men and women may not discern it clearly, but the pattern underlies their experiences in industrial society. It is a pattern of growth in the confidence and power of women, and of erosion in the confidence and power of men.

What follows is a chronicle of the decline of men and the ascendancy of women. More women are having children without men, and therefore more men are without the love of families. Women as a group are working more and earning more. Men are working less and earning less. In 1998, for the first time in the United States, "young women are completing high school and graduating from college at higher rates than their male peers," which yields clear impact on the future of employment.[2] For the first time since women acquired the right to vote they have begun to vote decisively differently from men. Whether or not they are the principal politicians themselves—and ever more women are—they are changing the rules and dreams of politics.

Finally, this book is about ideas. The body of social knowledge and conjecture conforms more and more to the female shape. An imprecise but effective group called "feminists" has redefined how words may be used or forbidden to be used in discussing sex. They have become allergens, evasions, and statements in themselves. Women have appropriated and renovated public dialogue. They own a certain echelon of discourse the way medieval churchmen governed Latin or Microsoft's MS-DOS became the modern universal language of computation and, in effect, of nearly all formal communication.

A fundamental change in the lives of men and women has flowed from a striking new reality. It has overtaken us altogether. Once upon a time many, if not most, women could expect to secure some education, then perhaps work for a few years. Thereafter they would marry and have children. Forever after they would be part of a family supported by a husband who would supply virtually all his earnings until he died. The young men and women in my college classes in the 1950s scarcely questioned this plan. We expected to follow it, more or less, if we were lucky and we behaved. There was no thought that men were being exploited because they had to work or that women were being deprived because they didn't. It was life's deal. Dwellings, time, resources, and a sense of life's meaning were shared.

This was a remarkable transfer payment, as the economists call this kind of movement of money between people. Once upon a time the pattern predominated in North American society. In 1955 in some 60 percent of American families, Dad worked, Mom stayed home, and there were two to three children. Thirty-one years later barely 4 percent of families boast this form.[3]

There are several factors in the shift that I will suggest flow from the

underlying forces surrounding human biology. As influentially reflected
in the 1953 publication of Simone de Beauvoir's *The Second Sex*, the
overwhelming image of our society was that it was dominated by men.
The women in the picture were restricted and subservient. The
prevailing ethic was patriarchal, of political, religious, and economic life
supported and justified by the interests of men.[4] Men had, or were
thought to have, personal and public control. They had the most
opportunities to have the most colorful and explicit fun. They appeared
to be clearly and firmly in the driver's seat. Even the postman was an
automatic autocrat.

But the college-educated male associated with this family form, at
least in stereotype, has seen his income decline by 20 percent over a
quarter of a century.[5] There is a relatively common divorce rate of up to
50 percent in many places. There have been profound changes in notions
of female personal autonomy. There have also been major changes in the
sources of women's self-respect and sense of adeptness. Employment and
fulfillment in the public sphere loom larger than ever in the life plans of
women. "Housewife" and "mother" have become uncomfortable and
even embarrassing answers to the ubiquitous and quintessential twentieth century question: "What do you do?"

Private domestic experience has become associated with long-
standing inequality of women. Even intimacy and the emotions that swirl
around it are questioned and under the suspicion of oppression while
experience in the public sphere is clean, crisp, and privileged.

The cold stigma of the "old maid" that females have had to endure
has in a curious way returned. But now the stigma flows from a *job* they
don't have, not a husband. It appears to have become more controversial,
or at least more questionable, to be unemployed than unmarried.

Nor do many have the choice or desire to remain jobless. Now both
men and women are equally obligated to work in the money economy.
The practical and possibly psychological effects on children are enormous
and complex when Mommy and Daddy are at work at the same time, in
different places. Some couples must arrange for one partner to work at
night and the other in the daytime to cover housekeeping responsibili-

ties. In the late 1990s, despite enormous prosperity by international standards, North Americans spend more time at work than they did in the 1950s, particularly those with postsecondary education.[6] The average commute—23.6 miles to work and 23.6 miles back—consumes yet more time, making it unavailable for personal enjoyment and domestic experience. Auto manufacturers have had to supply cup holders in their vehicles so that people can consume breakfast en route. Surely car microwaves will follow so that people can eat food while they talk on car phones or read the faxes they receive when engulfed in traffic.

Presumably, they would prefer more graceful conditions of life. But they appear to be too committed to the norms of industrial economy and too hard-pressed to choose which assets and forms of consumption they are prepared to forgo. Can they do without a second twenty-seven-inch television set or a power riding mower? In 1996, 59 percent of Americans saw themselves as short on time and long on responsibilities.[7]

All told, there is a significant shift from the past in the relative power of men and women. In the United States productive system in the mid-90s women earned 7.6 percent more than they did in 1979, while men earned 14 percent *less* than they did then. Women earn 40 percent of family income. In the early 1990s at least one of six wives earned more than her husband; in 1968, it was one in eighteen.[8] According to Gail Sheehy, by 1996 nearly one of three wives earned more than her husband.[9]

Meanwhile, increases in female income and the relative decline in male income have had an impact on reproductive opportunities for both, but especially for females—who have usually focused on the drama and obligations of love and money for at least twenty years of their lives.

Doing public work to earn money is more prestigious for women than private activity founded on affection, such as staying home to take care of children, which bears a real if tacit stigma of personal inferiority. It is a relatively rare contemporary woman who relies comfortably on the traditional pattern. Those who choose it may feel apologetic and that they must justify themselves. In the words of one lawyer who resigned as the executive of a writers' organization, "While I tried to plan my legal career so that I would eventually be able to be of use to writers, the decision to leave a job that I love to spend more time with my family was one that I never thought I would want to make; the strength of my desire to spend more time at home has caught me (and my family) completely off guard."[10] She has had to question her elemental passion for domestic life against the unquestionable meaning of a job. Simone de Beauvoir once remarked that women shouldn't have children because they would want too much to be with them, which in her opinion would interfere with desirable social change.

The one undisputed power of females, fertility, has always been acknowledged in the arts and in religion—from the prehistoric Venus excavated in Willendorf to the Madonna portraits of Renaissance Siena to the power of childbirth in virtually any play, film, or other dramatic representation. But in the late twentieth century, fertility has lost its explicit primacy. Babies have become instigators of the dual threats of pollution and population. One feminist called childbirth "shitting pumpkins."[11] Fertility itself has ceased to be an irrefutable human value. Serious demographers even ponder why people want children at all, as if there was a genuine mystery about it.[12]

Virtually everyone in the industrial world has come to accept that the planet is overpopulated. The industrial countries are barely replacing themselves demographically, if that. Countless individual decisions to restrict pregnancies have been made, partly justified or at least colored by a sense of human excess, degraded environments, and ebbing resources. Any man or woman concerned, uncertain, or fearful about becoming a parent could claim the high moral plateau—*they*, at least, were not contributing to overpopulation. And not only has there been a strong influence from the social consensus on the practical and moral dangers of overpopulation but also new and effective contraceptive technology, controlled by women, has governed the inside of the body and provided safe and excellent means to avoid pregnancy. It will become clear later in this book how extraordinary, indeed revolutionary, this is.

Yet at the very time that countless women can control their fertility, a turbulent paradox remains: Many members of a population as healthy as any in history and far more robust than most experience great difficulty with the core challenge of biology—having babies. Fertility clinics are overpopulated with deeply troubled applicants. Celebrated fertility doctors arrange their appointment lists months in advance. With new drugs, a few women have given birth to five or more children at once. With startling new techniques, unprecedented arrangements have been struck for insemination, conception, implantation, frozen embryos, adoption, and surrogate mothers. Adoption has become an international trading pattern as infertile nationals of one country import the children of other countries with more children and fewer resources to care for them.

Meanwhile, men fade out of the picture. Each instance of a single mother implies a father without a live-in child. Although the situation is changing, post-divorce child custody is still overwhelmingly awarded to mothers. Divorce usually leaves men without their children, which causes many of them unexpected anguish. According to Sylvia Hewlett and Cornel West, 38 percent of absentee fathers may have neither custody nor visitation rights to their children, and it is scarcely surprising they will fail to cheerfully provide support to children they are forbidden to see.[13] Hence, men are severed from the skein of ongoing family life. Whether they want it or not, they are outlaws, not in-laws. Consider what this means in a country such as Iceland where 60 percent of infants are born to single women.[14] And when we reflect on the Million Man March of African-American males in Washington in 1995, it becomes plain that with a single-motherhood rate of 66 percent in their community, some 660,000 men were in effect absentee fathers.

These changes have also disenfranchised men from traditional social roles but have not offered men many new opportunities. Even the most traditional male specialty—warfare—has been aggressively opened to women, with complicated results for everyone. Perhaps their apparent explosion of interest in sports and pornography means that men are trying to find new outlets to express their inherent maleness, which they may feel otherwise obligated to repress.

And, come to think of it, does an ambient acrimony between men and women, inaccurately attributed largely to feminism, actually reflect female resentment and disillusion about male helplessness in supporting family life?

I don't want to oversell the extent of change or the meaning of its intensity. Much remains how it was. Many people conduct their lives the way their parents did. The problems they face and the solutions they produce are more or less the same. Yet, while the emergent pattern may not directly involve most people, it *indirectly* affects nearly all people. The social climate changes. When nearly one-third of babies born in industrial communities are born to single mothers, as was the case in the late 90s, married mothers and non-mothers are affected, too. When divorce rates rise to roughly half of marriages, as they have in the United States and in urban centers such as Paris, the other half cohabits in historically new uncertainty. When 55 percent of college students in the United States and 60 percent in Canada[15] are women, and education is having more influence over people's economic and social destinies, the potential long-term impact on men affects everyone. Yes, there is consistency, but even change at the margins affects and challenges the behavioral heartland. And what is afoot is more than a skirmish at the border.

In the inexplicit and undeclared war between the sexes, women are on the way to winning, but the conditions of victory may not be agreeable. The armistice agreement may contain conditions no one wanted or expected. At the very least, the contestants don't have separate countries to which to return. Men and women have to remain involved in complicated ways. Men may not yet perceive that they have been bested in a confusing war, though they may be vaguely aware that they are uncomfortable. They may fail to understand and may experience greater perplexity: What does a woman—what do women—want? While there are some wispy attempts at a "men's movement" in an effort to turn private feelings into public action and comment, nothing has emerged among men in groups as efficient and ambitious as among women.[16] Even one of the men's groups that was temporarily effective in attracting attention and adherents, the Promise Keepers, had to dismiss its entire staff in 1998 because of lack of support.[17] There is an effectiveness gap as well as a gender gap. In the United States, apart from some affably cooperative men's studies programs in universities, there are no effective national entities comparable to the National Organization for Women that reflect the interests of men. Meanwhile, well-schooled graduates of activist programs of women's studies migrate onto the staffs of politicians and other decision-makers, which they will become in due course.

There appears to be an irresistible trend toward blurring the lines between public and private lives, between personal emotions and their public evaluation and significance. What has been called political correctness is in large measure about personal demeanor and private experience. The personal has in fact become the political. Local notions of social change are ratified firmly in such international forums as the Conference on Women, sponsored by the United Nations in 1995 in Hairu, China. There, the word "marriage" scarcely appeared in the manifestos issued by delegates. At least since the publications of John Stuart Mill there has been considerable criticism of traditional female roles, but now the issue preoccupies not only scholars and journalists but also a broad coalition of politicians and their supporters. They confront the issues actively and at the level of explicit consciousness. Serious social activism has continued nationally and internationally. Consciousness has been raised. The once-idealized appeal of real and metaphorical suburban and bourgeois motherhood and wifeliness has declined in a remarkably steep trajectory—if not in the experience of most people, then certainly in public dialogue.

Modern feminism of the 1960s and 1970s was first an expression of this change and then an astonishingly effective catalyst for it.[18] There was a massive program of lectures, rallies, and workshops on gender. Commentators wrote shelves of books and urgent manifestos. Reading and discussing them avidly was a central feature of a sea change in knowledge and consciousness about sex and gender in industrial countries. Public controversy erupted, revealing the enormous interest of women—much more than men, who had and still have little idea of what is happening to them—in directly reassessing their circumstances when their deepest interests are challenged.

Whether or not it was clear to them or anyone else at the time, women were identifying and responding to an array of new conditions in industrial life that would eventually affect their productive and reproductive lives. Feminism was not the self-evident revelation of scientific truth that some of its supporters claimed, but unquestionably it became an effective instrument of public power. It is almost as if a new continent has been discovered. Its intrepid explorer heroines return with news, and revised maps begin to appear. The latest textbooks of sexual geography describe a new land populated by sexually liberated, economically industrious, and cooperatively independent women.

But the inequalities have not disappeared. In particular, multitudes of women in non-affluent countries, as well as poor ones in rich countries, have not experienced the shifts achieved by those in industrial countries. Here, they must continue to endure the deep abrasions of polygamy, and there, the literal cuts of genital mutilation. They may be barred from education and scorned when they venture to comment about public matters. A decent job remains a dream. Their reproductive lives may be coerced by priests or politicians or both. But there *is* a substantial underlying change in industrial societies in the experience of women, despite the resistance that may exist.[19] It is not yet wholly clear-cut and is very much a work and struggle in progress; however, it will animate all of us for the next decade or two at least.

As the twentieth century comes to an end, sex and its expressions in gender are the most engrossing of public and private subjects. Matters that once were not discussed in public—such as female orgasm, male impotence, anal and oral intercourse, and the morality of infidelity—are featured on the front pages of newspapers. They spice hours of television. The United States spent at least half a year talking about the sexuality of the dominant male, the president. The very personal has become political; the private, very public. Intimacy is for broadcasting. Gender is an act of political registration. Acts of erotic power flood all media, from home computers to stadium concerts. Sex is as environmental as it had been when on the walls of Pompeii and in the phallic sculpture gardens of ancient India.

Trying to Understand

A startlingly new politics defines the dialogue about what is right, wrong, good, and bad, and about a whole new array of issues. Single motherhood, gender styles, infertility, government food for babies, sexual harassment, homosexual infantry, women in combat, abortion, clitoridectomy, human breeders under contract—these are issues undreamed of by writers of political science textbooks five or even two generations ago. There are brawls over whether or not it is fair to infants to leave them with paid employees of varying skill, away from their parents and especially their mothers, who bear the brunt of guilt associated with surrogate childrearing. Raising boys and girls has become a battleground of conflicting views and values of the nature of human sex.[20] Even the most elemental of mammalian episodes, breast-feeding, has become a focus of dispute.[21] Men and women have become members of often bitterly hostile groups defined by increasingly precise and draconian laws. A combative situation is nourished by feminist ideology, fueled by moral outrage, and roiled by confused male isolation.

No man or woman could have foretold the swift collapse of male public dominance in symbol and, increasingly, in practice. No one could possibly have foreseen the new directions that men and women have taken singly as members of their sex and together as members of families. Men and women appear to have been cast in a new play that has stage directions so general and so subtle that they are useless. Neither players nor critics nor audience is certain what the turbulent pageant is about.

Many experts, from politicians to social scientists to theologians, have offered explanations for the changes in social and family matters. The explanations are often far-reaching and passionate, but largely incomplete and insufficiently searching. Let's examine them anyway. There have been numerous specific social, economic, and moral explanations, such as feminist thought, lapsed morality, and the imperatives of work, but these are more symptoms than explanations. They reflect the problem but don't parse it. They're comfortably simple but beside the point. They remain too conventional for a new environment.

One helpful but partial explanation is that the changes we confront have been caused by the power of feminist thought, by legislation associated with the ongoing emancipation of women, and by a general enhancement in awareness of the sexual morality of communities. New laws range from denying sexual or reproductive discrimination in work and government to sharpening definitions of rape and other kinds of sexual exploitation. Underlying much legal change is a largely ideological insistence that boys and girls are roughly the same, and therefore in perfectly equitable communities they will have similar goals, opportunities, and lives.

Another explanation rests on a claim of lapsed morality: Traditional values based on Christianity, Judaism, Islam, and Buddhism have been eroded by the crass mass media and assisted by secularist ideologues and courts of law. Ethically lazy families and schools don't bother to or can't counter the godless rules of the day. The result is a widespread morass of worsening sinfulness. Classical verities of sexual conduct and social propriety have dramatically lost their grip. It will take a major religious or messianic renovation to recapture what was best and is lost, and a good deal of contemporary religious energy is expended to this end.

Previously the reason offered for lapsed morality was godless Communism, but Communism has deteriorated both as a discredited source of morality and a practical guide to effective socioeconomic behavior. In Euro-American communities, the widespread replacement of religious norms by psychological ones means that more people are focusing on what they should feel, not on what they should do. The discipline of therapy has become the basic sauce in a menu of various modes of private experience. People shed the rules of society and migrate to what I have called "psychiety," where private experience, not social action, is the basic unit of human value.[22]

Finally, the most obvious and least controversial explanation for the changes is economic. People work to acquire money to afford the means to live and obtain material goods. Over several million years at least, until about ten thousand years ago, human beings evolved as hunters and gatherers. With new and almost dizzyingly perfect symmetry the industrial way of life allows us to make and do things *for* money and then hunt and gather them *with* money. The industrial way of life has proselytized and colonized the planet more successfully than any religion or political creed. Nearly everyone appears to want to join industrial society. They may endure privation and expense to immigrate illegally to rich countries. If they remain in a poor one, their home is likely to be in an amazingly squalid slum such as those outside Jakarta or Hydrabad. The industrial society has had an almost fierce impact on families and friends; like air it is everywhere and always.

But populations take industrialism for granted; people don't think consciously about it, as they have learned to do about polluted air. It is so pervasive and seemingly inevitable that few people realize it is barely ten generations old. But the nature of industrialism is sharply different from the nature in which we evolved that produced our human nature— which, remarkably and recklessly, we no longer seem to consider important.

The social, economic, and moral explanations fail because they are not deep enough. They are of inadequate practical use or psychic comfort when people seek social change or remedy, or when they confect the dream of voyaging back to the good old days.

How are we to understand these convulsive social, sexual, and familial changes if so much of the conventional explanations for them is insufficient? Instead of examining them as closely as has been done in the past, we need to change the level of the discussion. Before we can even talk about economic, political, psychiatric, or feminist theories, we have to talk about our human nature. Only a perspective that takes human nature into account can encompass and help evaluate all these other, more limited theories.

For example, one hugely ambitious attempt to explain large social changes was Marxism. Karl Marx proposed that men were "alienated from the means of production," means that are central to our evolution as a species committed to the importance of work and economic organization. His colleague Friedrich Engels even wrote on the role of labor in what he saw as our transition from ape to man.[23] At the beginning of the century Marx was clearly the leading accountant of the major issues that gripped leaders and citizens, such as labor unions, restrictions on capital, child labor, worker safety, and the fairness of receiving holidays. People were preoccupied with the impact of the industrial system as the old rural environment disappeared and new ways of earning a living had to develop. The goad of scarcity and the lure of equity fueled the impact of Marx's analysis of what was wrong and what could be right. The world was literally convulsed and eventually was split in two belligerent blocs, each linked by some common interest and guided by ideology and moral urgencies.

But even an ambitious and global theory like Marxism is too narrow to explicate the roots of what is changing. We have at once to look more broadly and yet peer more deeply to a frankly fundamental view of human nature. The broadest and most comprehensive answer to the puzzle posed by what is happening is to be found in biology. After all, what is happening is not only self-evidently related to biology but is also profoundly biological.

Charles's Big Idea

Biology—unexpected, labyrinthian, colorful, direct, unclear, demanding, chronic—is the most reliable and fundamental source of explanation for the decisive changes people have experienced in social, sexual, and family matters. It animates the whole system, sets its limiting conditions, and also carries a burden of swirling emotion as an irrepressible indicator of its ongoing role. Of course, biology does not completely determine anything other than the boon of birth and the gravity of death.[24] But in between it is always a subtext and often the story itself. Religions have often tried to create categories of experience for souls separate from bodies, while philosophers frequently announce an *apartheid* between mind and body. But this cannot be done without violence to the facts and without disregarding the elegant unity of nature.

Social scientists work in a different neighborhood of the university from natural scientists and have for many years largely imposed the same duality on their analysis of the wellsprings of human behavior. But they, too, fail when they skip biology to illuminate the part of the human story that remains ever compelling. These social scientists are to basic science about human nature as Christian Scientists are to medicine. We may respect their goals and their ardor but decide to seek help elsewhere when there are harsh emergencies to confront. This is especially so where love, marriage, and baby carriages are involved or, as the case may be, when they are absent or excluded from people's lives.

Homo sapiens is a species designed to live in a zoo very different from the one on which it is currently the leaseholder.

An Irish poet once said, "To the blind, everything is sudden." But our existence is not a sudden event. One reason our communities struggle so with the new conditions of life is that we confront them with an instrument—our species—which was formed unimaginable years ago. Our human genome—which is only now being aggressively explored—was formed in evolutionary conditions far different from those in which we live, differences reflected in both our physical and behavioral natures. Our biology at once is extraordinarily old and reflected anew in each newborn child. As Darwin theorized, what created our nature today was the sexual behavior in which we engaged over countless yesterdays, and that behavior remains at the behavioral core of the abiding preoccupation with sexual matters people experience throughout their lives. Sex may be banned, curtailed, legislated, scorned, admired, creative, cruel, or obsessive—but it always has an impact.

In spring, flowers bloom because of pollination and the sexual urgency of plants. All year long babies are born, a remarkable triumph for the human sexual system. After nine months, couples become servants of a wet stranger a minute old. People spend five decades associating with the new human they made in five seconds. What a force!

As the twentieth century closes and seems ever more removed from nature, it is essential to understand biology's ramified and complicated impact on social and family matters.

Not Logical — Biological

Biology centrally informs all my work in this book. It is the most useful point of departure to understanding matters that Darwin showed us are at the very core of social life—*sexual selection* and *natural selection*. It was not only Darwin but a cavalcade of researchers and theorists since his time who have identified unexpected and often thrilling regularities in nature and emphasized the ongoing links between an animal in the present and its evolution in the past. It is no more possible to avoid biology in analyzing sex than it is to ignore chemistry as a factor in photosynthesis. The contemporary illusion that fundamental sexuality derives mainly from cultural episodes is unsustainable in the face of a library of knowledge about the roots of sexuality in the prehistoric genetic past and its role in creating the future of species, including our own.

I focus necessarily on sexual selection because natural selection happens so slowly that we can largely ignore it for our purposes. I would repeat the last sentence in another form were it not already so clear. I will focus instead on whether, if, how, and who people choose as mates and what reproduction ensues if any. Of course with humans, and indeed the primates overall, the story is not as clear as with fish, birds, elephant seals, or bison. But this just means the work of understanding the sexuality of humans is more difficult and more subtle, and requires many kinds of information. It should proceed at once.

The result cannot be neatly linear, a straight historical narrative, a crisp picture of cause and effect. We are dealing with a process that is not logical; it is biological. The comparison may sound glib, but it reveals an important difference in analytical technique. Biological thinking is circuitous, indirect, multifaceted, almost *pointillistic* in its approach. It does not depend on clear-cut models such as rational choice, which economics has (very imperfectly) sought to use. It cannot scrutinize voting patterns alone to learn what people think about power, their futures, and their leaders. It cannot embrace unifactor schemes such as Freudian drive theory or Skinnerian conditioning or Marxist money causation.

No, we have to know about a host of diverse matters: the endocrines, the cortex, neurotransmitters, regulations about maternity leave, symbolic concepts of masculinity, the sexual schemes of monkeys and apes, religious rules about touching people's bodies, sterilization and contraception, laws about inheritance, the astonishing behavior of spermatozoa, the link between owning property and the right to vote, the role of beauty and the body in the workplace—many things but probably not enough. Therefore, do not expect here the precision of math or the confident forms of engineers. We are confronting the most intricate of living systems. We are just learning for the first time about the interdependence of many of its components.

Deconstructing Nature

Nature is a tease. Scientists are its lovers and admirers but also its opponents. The history of science is the quest for ever more intimate, ever more improbable, and ever grander understanding of the planet around us and its life-forms.

Nearly all of human history elapsed before we understood what water was made of: two H's and an O. Objects fell to earth both before and after Newton extracted the secret scheme that governed their relationship to Earth. And it took until Charles Darwin and the nineteenth century to comprehend these elementary questions: Why are there males and females? Why do they mill about with such urgency and colorful clatter? Do they follow any plan? If they do, what is it?

A main job of science is to reveal how what first seems to be just random circumstance is actually organized. Scientists can tell us that we are in the thick of an extensive pattern even if we don't know it. Over nearly all our history as a species we have barely known the regularities of our existence, where we came from, and by which forces we are gripped. For nearly the entire history of our species we have not known why it evolved, what governs it in the present, and what is likely to define our future. Every year it seems we learn that we are another fifth of a million years older than we thought. "To the blind, everything is sudden." We are no longer blind, but much seems sudden still, every morning.

Now we know very much more about sex, about men and women, about work and babies. Thousands of scientists and chroniclers have described those most basic arrangements of everybody's detailed daily lives, formerly the province of novelists such as the Brontës, Henry James, Charles Dickens, and Balzac. In comparison with our great-grandparents, we know astonishingly more about our evolution, our bodies, our inner chemistry, and the stew of thinking, feeling, and communicating from which our social behavior emerges.

How useful is this knowledge? Does it help us live our lives with more skill? Not necessarily. People are knowledgeable about psychology and sex to an unprecedented degree, but the divorce rate is nonetheless higher than ever. With effective contraception controlled by women, there are still more abortions than ever. A high, and in some places ever higher, percentage of all births are to single mothers. With ever greater personal freedom, there is still a high level of public and private anxiety about restrictions on individual happiness. Why, why, and why?

Contemporary science has given us ways of understanding changes so general that they seem like weather. In fact, there is more sophistication about weather patterns themselves. Even if they remain largely impossible to control, we nevertheless want to and should want to know as much as we can about them. At least we can respond prudently to an analysis of the weather. This book is a psychosexual weather report and a forecast. Satellite pictures afford new perspectives, and so has biological science—which has also instructed us about our antiquity and the unfolding of the genetic information that guides us. We are ancient, a model millions of years old. We are our own antiques but carry the instructions for assembly in our genome.

Everyone acknowledges that these issues are all chronically and significantly controversial. Perhaps poets and magicians are committed to "the willing suspension of disbelief." But in this venture we should commit to the suspension of belief—not judgment, but belief. When I first involved myself with these matters thirty-five years ago, I neither expected nor could have predicted events now taking place, such as the burgeoning of the single mother, women in the army, the gender gap in politics, and the approach to sexual parity in the labor force. Events have far overtaken the boldest of expectations. Perhaps this is because the analysis of them has been wrong or incomplete. It has to be the working principle of intellectual workers that research and reflection provide optimal opportunities for genuine understanding. To comprehend what has happened and what may happen next appears to require both passion about "getting it right" and compassion about the events that human beings are experiencing.

Whatever their explanation, the conditions that face us are dramatic.

The traditional struggle of economic classes that Marx chronicled at the beginning of the century has been replaced on center stage as it ends by the natural interaction of sexual classes—sexual selection in all the variety that Darwin defined. And it's the Darwinian lens that we'll peer through here, not only because sexuality is a Darwinian process but because, as I have claimed, the other participants in the battle to explain what has been happening have failed to do the job.

The Plot

The relations between males and females have changed and ramified in complicated ways, in large measure because through effective contraception—for the first time in natural history—one sex can control the reproductive process. The result is a profound and probably enduring alteration of family patterns. In our minds we may continue to assume that families are as they were in the 1950s and in earlier real or imagined

Golden Ages, but they are increasingly different for growing numbers of people. Perhaps the stereotypical family of conventional sentiment has been a historical blip of some several hundred years of industrial life.[25]

Millions of years of evolutionary regularity have been altered in a very brief period. A relatively few but profound features of the industrial way of life have produced a sea change, actually an ocean change. One of the most fundamental and important is reliable contraception privately controlled by women either with drugs or devices. For the first time in human experience, and perhaps in nature itself, one sex is able to control making babies. With the condom, once the most employed contraceptive, there was always a conscious or tacit collaboration between men and women. But with the pill that is no longer true.

One result is that women can have sexual experiences without fear of pregnancy. Another is that they can plan when and with whom they will bear children if they want. Because of changed mores, many more now have babies without husbands. Reproductive technology permits them to have babies without lovers and even without sexual congress of any kind. Still another result is that men have sharply reduced confidence in who their children are—what biologists call "paternity certainty." This is a central and poorly understood feature of the changes under way, and we will return to explore it fully in chapter 2.

Consequently, feminist politics have generated alterations in public ideas about male entitlement and about special support for women in the economy and politics. While equality has been by no means achieved, more women earn more money than ever. More men earn less. We see that women can and do have children, even on their own. Men cannot. Women have hired on to the workforce with increasing success. More often than men they become successful small employers themselves.

Men have been decreasingly successful in the labor force. Partly for that reason, many have been "fired" as potentially useful fathers by women who expect that as mates they will be a burden, not a help. They will consume resources, not bring them in. They will import problems, not defend against them. They may well be nothing but chronic trouble. Who needs them? Why bother?[26]

But it is difficult to raise a child oneself. When men can't or won't help out or are not asked to, the state does. As a result, a remarkable new family pattern has emerged. I call it bureaugamy. A new trinity: a woman, a child, and a bureaucrat. Not monogamy. Not polygamy. Bureaugamy. Much more about this later.

Our species seems to be leaping back in time to the more basic mammalian system that was the core of our evolutionary history, one founded on the primacy of the unit of the mother and child. More and more we appear to resemble the other primate species whose communi-ties are focused on *females and their young*, with males scuffling for reproductive access to females and a place in the political sun. While the males seem to and usually do dominate primate politics, predation on other species, and defense, nonetheless the ongoing central group of females and their young remain the most identifiable and persistent social unit in the system. Over time the interests of this core unit must be served by males; otherwise, they will fail to achieve and maintain their positions of apparent power. To be crass, they have to kiss baby primates and impress their mothers. This is not for moral reasons but rather because the essential reproductive obligations of any community are necessarily served by healthy females raising capable offspring. This is the existential bottom line among numerous mammals, and especially in primatology.

Now this is becoming clearer among human groups as well. The shift is often puzzling and may also be very strenuous. To the extent that commentators confuse this fundamental turbulence with moral struggles about "family values" they miss the importance of what is happening. They will be ill-equipped to prepare effective social policies to help create the kind of community people want. (One of the most effective rituals that illustrates the issue is Christmas, to which we will return.)

First, it is essential to remember that we are mammals—creatures who receive their first food from the bodies of the mothers who give birth to them. This has enormous consequence. One of the most basic is that the mother and offspring must be protected and provisioned. For an essential period the mother is inhibited from full adult action, and for a longer one the youngster is wholly dependent on adults. In the fox family, the mother and young are supported by the father for one year, which is the fox family cycle. In the human species the time period may be decades, a very different and complex cycle.

There is an irreducible requirement. The species has to protect its mothers and their offspring until the youngsters can manage on their own. Every mammalian species has to try to protect mothers and babies from whatever dangers, insecurities, and shortages afflict the community. Some form of metaphorical eggshell must be built around the central vital unit.

In light of this demand, when the systems of human kinship are analyzed, it turns out that *their bedrock function is to protect the link between babies and mothers from the frailty and volatility of the bond between men and women.*[27] The obligation to raise children is long-term. It may last decades. Somehow it has to be separated from the impulsive power of the sexual desire that brings the parents together in the first place. After all, men and women remain wired up for sex for the rest of their lives. They may turn to someone else and disrupt that family bond. More often than not when people in a marriage fall out of love, it is because one partner has found a new one. To a person in the clutches of love, little else may matter except the next meeting—even if it is not with a current spouse but with the next. Therefore all communities try to control the potentially antisocial passion of sex with some cold-hearted admonition such as the stark commandment "Thou shalt not commit adultery."

How societies protect the mother and child varies a great deal. In some societies, such as those in much of Europe and America, the father of the baby is legally supposed to support the mother and infant. This is an especially clear responsibility for husbands or ex-husbands. When you renew a New York driver's license, you have to provide your Social Security number "to invoke driver license sanctions for delinquent support payments."[28]

In Israel there have been cases of women who had intercourse with men for the purpose of getting pregnant and then had babies about which the particular partner was unaware and unprepared. Later the men were sued for child support on the basis of DNA testing. The situation has become so common, or at least prominent, that a group has been formed to protest it—the Fathers Against Their Will Association—and in July 1998 a bill was introduced into the Israeli Knesset to change the law that made DNA paternity an unequivocal basis for child support, whatever the conditions or agreements surrounding conception.[29]

As we have seen, in 38 percent of American child support orders the fathers expected to supply the funds may have neither visitation nor custodial rights.[30] There certainly exists the possibility that some proportion of these fathers assumed or were led to assume that contraception was employed by their partner and that they were not planning to become pregnant. As governments become more stringent about capturing resources from non-residential parents, it is inevitable that some men will be obligated to supply funds for children whom they did not want to have or suspect are not theirs. Professor Ira Ellman of Arizona State University Law School described to me the case of County of San Luis Obispo v. Nathaniel J.—57 Cal.Rptr.2d 843 (App. 1996)—in which a fifteen-year-old boy was seduced by a thirty-four-year-old woman, who was convicted of statutory rape for the event. After the woman gave birth to their daughter, the District Attorney's office sued the boy and his family for reimbursement of the costs for Aid to Families with Dependent Children for which the mother applied. The Court upheld the claim against the boy. This is not to suggest this child and other children involved in involuntary or unexpected paternity do not need suitable support. However, as we will see, the issue of confidence about paternity is both volatile and fundamental. Current legal practice exacerbates the tension surrounding it.

The current arrangement for supporting children may appear problematic, but it is only one of a great variety of systems. In much of traditional West Africa, the mother's brother is responsible for her children. At least the genetic lines are clear. Elsewhere, the mother's father or family is responsible. There, inheritance flows through the female line, not the male. This pattern has surfaced in Europe and America where unmarried mothers live in their childhood homes with their parents, even in traditionally staid blue-collar families. Or the mother alone is responsible for helping her daughter and her child. This is a common route followed in African-American communities in which two-thirds of babies are born to single women. Some industrial communities adopt the bureaugamy plan, either by intent or happenstance. One word they use for it is "welfare."[31]

So human communities acknowledge this recurrent and fundamental issue of providing for mother and child even if they don't articulate it clearly.

If people do not explicitly define what they do and what preoccupies them, their religious and ritual observances do so for them. Christmas certainly does, with emotional grandeur and clarity. The enormous power of Christmas reveals the undercurrent of strength of the mammalian program.

Let's set aside the religious feature of the celebration. That's about a different genre of experience and conviction. Let's restrict our focus to how Christmas reflects the human life cycle, not the larger issues of belief, divinity, and the meaning of experience. Along with everything else it is, Christmas is a story about mammalian bedrock, about the foundation event of human experience. Apart from its religious meaning, that is why it is perhaps the most successful holiday in the world. That is why it is one of the most reliably positive and is biased toward the lustrous possibility of human generosity, not the meanness of Charles Dickens's Scrooge.

Consider it with the fresh innocence that can be so illuminating to people who live in a tribe and who take its rigmarole for granted. Pretend you came upon it after sailing a catamaran for a month in uncharted tides.

Christmas is in essence about the care of mothers and infants. Mary bears a child. She possesses no housing, no resources. There are evidently no available family members—no sisters, cousins, aunts, brothers—to call on for shelter and succor. She has to confront alone the central mammalian struggle for assistance at a crucial time. There is a physiological analogue of this. The epic difficulty of childbirth itself reflects a compromise between the size of the pelvis and the mother's birth canal with the amount of developed brain tissue packed into the newborn's skull. In the same way, the social trauma of birth reveals the capacity of a community to turn away from private matters to the needs of others.

Mary seeks room at the inn. There is none. She finds no relief from the emergency that she and her child face. Finally she turns to the stable, where she is welcomed. Symbolically and in practice, this is where mammalian life is maintained. What could be more revealing? Bear in mind the importance of shepherds and other caretakers of animals in the pastoral and agricultural life of that part of the world at that time.

They have been sheltered, at least. But mother and child need more. They require active care and resources. Here the miracle of the three wise men reveals a classic solution to the new mother's problem, which is also the equivalent of modern-day welfare. They arrive with gifts. In colorful symbolic terms they represent the community's general decision to respond to the basic mammalian challenge. Consider the elements of the story: the event of the birth; the plight of Mary and Jesus; the providence of the wise men and hence of the community at large.

The legacy to us of this is an unexpected celebration of great generosity and conviviality. This is the character of the secular element of the holiday. People give gifts both to family members and others. They provide the highest level of hospitality during the whole year. The events of the Nativity stimulate an unusual episode of life's reaffirmation at its most elemental and profound. Birth and generosity unite at a glad and assertive party. Forty percent of all alcohol sales, the principal social drug, surround the Christmas and New Year fetes.

But what of Joseph?

Here the brilliance of effective religious symbolism is at its most thrilling. Mary is a virgin. Therefore, Joseph is not the father. Therefore, at a fundamental level, he is not responsible for caring for the child and its mother. Therefore, he is not a "deadbeat dad." He is not specifically required to pay child support. He is not biologically responsible for the birth. No, the community is responsible. It accepts the responsibility with gifts, lights, and an extended hand. The human power of the religious celebration is untrammeled by paternal delinquency. The link between the birth and the community is pure and clear.

The peripheral role of that long-ago Joseph prefigures in troubling clarity the emerging plight of an ever-increasing group of contemporary men.[32] He suddenly becomes an important ancestor, if not a genetic one, for an unexpected reason.

We don't know why some celebrations remain meaningful and others flow and ebb and finally become at best routine. Certainly they are subject to local conditions and ongoing invention—as was Christmas itself, especially in the United States. But as a holiday Christmas reaches deep into areas of the foundation of human emotionality.

Back to Basics:
Feminism Is Female-ism

Humankind in the industrial world is returning to this most basic mammalian model. We are returning to the deepest taproots of our system of life. We are returning to our fundamental biology. Females are the consistent and robust basis of the most effective and central social action—reproduction. Females have the most responsibility, the most enduring burdens, and the most complex alloy of experience surrounding love and money, family and work.

Modern feminism is a sign and symptom of *female-ism*. Despite its relatively sharp emphasis on matters of work and power and bias toward earned money, the issue of mothers raising their young is at center stage and drives the broad effort to revamp social arrangements. Numerous feminist theorists vigorously dispute the role of biology in influencing social and family patterns. But much feminist action reflects the elemental undertow influencing the events of life that constitute our central biological nature. The leading lady in the story, the mother, inherits tens of millions of years of practice at making life continue, with a focus on the bond between child and mother. Her pregnancy, her milk, her hormones, her behavior, her emotions—positive, sullen, or varied— are astonishingly intricate legacies from the experience of nature's most complex social species.

At the same time a large and increasing number of men are redundant and peripheral. Marx said about the industrial system that people are profoundly alienated from the means of production—jobs. Political and social radicalism was one response to that. If Darwin were alive today, he might comment that men are profoundly alienated from the means of *reproduction*—women. The response to that is the opposite of petty, and we are in the midst of it.

We are embarking on a social change as important as the shift from hunting and gathering to agriculture, or from agriculture to industry. It is a shift from male-centered production to female-centered reproduction.

The subject and focus of this book is the walnut of interaction of the human genome with the myriad forms of industrial society. I explore the critical issue of how reproductive technologies affect matters from contraception to fertility to employment. I show how effective contraception *causes* abortion; how new conditions of male and female independence influence issues such as moral codes about intercourse and pornography; how academic ideas about boys and girls may determine the personnel of combat groups; why welfare for mothers and children is at once a sign of mammalian responsibility and Judeo-Christian ethics; how a new kinship system called *bureaugamy* has been emerging, featuring a mother, a baby, and a government official; and how and why the human species may be returning to the basic mammalian system revolving around mothers and children, with ever more peripheral and confused males puzzled about their loneliness.

The briefest of words about two questions: Why me? And why this book? My interest in the biology of human social life was reflected in my first book, *Men in Groups*, in 1969. It explored what we knew about human evolution, our biology, and our arrangements of male behavior in various cultures. It was an effort to define what males did and why. I developed the idea of male bonding to describe a basic male-male interaction. The term has proved widely durable because it refers to a real phenomenon. People understand that it describes something tangible about human nature. The impact of new contraceptive technology, especially the pill, also seemed to me of watershed consequence, and I examined the role of medication on primate sexuality. Combined with new understanding of male reproductive behavior in other species as well as our own, this presented the possibility that our species has entered a new phase of sexual experience.

It is no longer a possibility but a reality. Charles Darwin had a remarkable insight. He identified the link between the private sexual choices that individuals make and the nature of the offspring that emerge as a result of these choices. He showed the direct connection between the general and the particular. The largest group, the species, is generated by the smallest and most intense unit of interaction, the act of love.

That is still true. But technological and other factors have scrambled the situation. Like a bag of marbles that falls and bursts, the options run every which way. The impact of expanded personal choice emerges more quickly than ever, but the new rules of conduct are unclear. In the absence of a referee or synod or Vatican or politburo or family council accepted by everyone, it is difficult to know what is a win and what is a loss, who is a player or an exile or a fool or a master or a chump.

The result is private perplexity and public tumult. The result is a human zoo in which robust well-fed inmates eagerly, even angrily, post their grievances on the cage bars. However, the bars are still invisible to the naked eye. Their effect on males will be unprecedented and a sharp departure from everything we take for granted about our society and its history. *The Decline of Males* tells the story.

CHAPTER TWO

The Industrialized Body

THERE IS AN UNDERSTANDABLE con-
cern with one's roots and enduring values in a contemporary
world marked by colorful human variety and palpable social change. One
result is an often fierce assertion of the moral importance of ethnic and
cultural origins. School systems and national political factions commonly
enshrine differences proudly and stubbornly sustained by groups with
various ethnic and religious traditions. The melting pot has been retired
to the storage room.

However, the most important human roots are often ignored or even
actively rejected. These are the real links to the past that all people share
as common members of the species *Homo sapiens*. We ignore or dismiss
these roots at our peril. Each new generation of babies reflects them and

will continue to do so, short of ambitious and successful genetic engineering. We know enough to avoid ignoring history. Ignoring prehistory is worse still, because while history flows off into the past, prehistory lives on in our bodies, our genome, our nature.

The human species is very old. Nearly every newly discovered fossil pulled from the East African soil where we evolved drives our lineage further back in time. My colleagues Jack Harris and Sileshi Semaw from the anthropology department at Rutgers University found in Ethiopia the earliest example of a human tool. It was 2.6 million years old. Our Australian prehominid ancestors were creating art well before our vaunted species was officially launched—at least 75,000 years ago and perhaps as many as 175,000.[1] Musicologist Bob Fink of Saskatchewan, Canada, analyzed a bone from Slovenia crafted as a flute; it was dated between 43,000 and 67,000 years ago. The device suggests that Neanderthals used the same seven-note musical scale central to Western music.[2] With the latest finds by archaeologists in southern France,[3] it now appears our immediate Neanderthal ancestors used fire for cave rituals at least 47,000 years ago, much earlier than anyone had thought. There is evidence of winemaking in Iran 7,000 years ago.[4] Beer appears to have been produced some 5,000 years ago.[5] Archaeologists Meave Leakey and Alan Walker have discovered that our ancestor *Australopithicus* was bipedal 4 million years in our past.[6]

The French Nobel Prize winner Jacques Monod said, "Everything that lives is also a fossil."[7] Anthropologists cruise for information about the fossil that interests us the most—ourselves, the super-antique we see in the mirror. When you next inspect that creature in the mirror, know that your human family lineage is about 4 million years old.

Throughout virtually all of this long history we survived as hunters and gatherers. We lived directly off the land in communities that seem to have ranged in size from twenty-five to two hundred souls. We were molded by a relatively intimate setting that made it essential to understand other people and engage with them well.

Our *behavior* evolved the same way as our bodies, movement, and highly expressive faces. Along the way, the sexual and social choices of thousands of generations were genetically established. The result became our human nature for the next hundred thousand years and for now. We mastered particular forms of social interdependence. We enjoyed a level of comfort with the patterns and forms of social and sexual life that served us well. We still carry these patterns with us in our DNA, our human genome. This once mysterious entity is now being explored like a familiar neighborhood meadow. It is so detailed as to specify that the hair of your head is technically different from the hair of your eyelashes. It is also so general as to unleash in every human adolescent a near-riotous cascade of major physical changes with enormous social impact.

We have an old portfolio of social needs, aptitudes, and affections. We find biologically traditional patterns of affection and bonding agreeable and easy to learn. They served us well in the past and provide pleasure in the present. We have a knack for them. Children find it easy to babble and then to learn complicated languages.

But often these venerable forms of love at the core of our nature seem difficult to find in our new environment. A reason for this is our demanding industrial system. It has dominated the world and had a greater impact on people's lives faster than any religion ever has. In many locations industrial society has almost overwhelmed physical nature. Concern about environmental degradation has also stimulated an industrial antidote to industry, the environmental movement, a new kind of immune system.

Industrialism demands a profound commitment to time and arbitrary schedules. Nearly everyone wears a watch that taps out their time like a drum. Industrialism emphasizes values of human interchangeability and impersonality. It monetarizes intimate relationships such as those between therapists and patients. It treats Earth as if it were a manageable machine. Jumbo jets, electricity, and satellites blunt the effect of distance and the physical separation of people. People walk on a street in Cincinnati while talking to Asia. Communication media between friends and between strangers—faxes, e-mail, letters, cell phones, FedEx, Minitel—have become as pervasive as water in the Mississippi delta. The pattern is encompassing. People in its midst usually conclude that the system itself is the norm, a kind of nature. If their own experience of it is negative, they may take this as a sign of personal failure.

The impact of industry on the tender elements of private life was recognized early although little was done about its effects. Industrialization imposed itself like one of the fiery hissing locomotives that symbolized it. The quintessential pastoral poet William Wordsworth wrote with haunting and remarkable prescience to his friend Charles James Fox in 1801: "It appears to me the measures that have the most calamitous effect, which has followed the measures which have lately been pursued in this country, is a rapid decay of the domestic affections among the lower orders of society. This effect the present Rulers of the Country are not conscious of, or they disregard it."[8] Today, perhaps, the present Rulers are more conscious of the matter, if for no other reason than that there are so many thriving sources of information. Nevertheless, our community seethes with the discontinuity between then, when we set down our natural roots, and now.

A core assumption of the industrial way is that people can enjoy sex and family, but only in what is defined as private life. During much of the industrial period the discontinuity was especially difficult for females. My colleague Robin Fox has described the nursing women at work in the mills of northern England during World War II. Friends or relatives passed their babies to them over the factory wall at lunch so the infants could be fed despite the imperative rhythms of the mill.

Today it is the imperative rhythms of even more complicated industrial society that demand our attention and interrupt the natural order. But now the discontinuity presents the gravest problems, largely unexpected ones, to the males.

Cupid's Shotgun

We visited the biological meaning of Christmas. Another holiday, Valentine's Day, is about romance and lovers and courtship. Cupid is its symbol, one of the most venerable. Cupid is also rather complicated. In Hellenistic and Roman myth, he was perplexingly both the son and companion of no less a star than Venus herself. He has lingered long in the story of love. His work is clear-cut: Cupid's arrow crisply defines who is vulnerable to ardor, who will be the willing partner, who will tumble impulsively into love.

But wait! There is an astonishing surprise here. Cupid is an infant! Not a therapist, a swami, a priest, an uncle—an infant! Like all the important moralities and religions we employ, the valentine ritual, among others, was established ages before there were effective contraceptives. Cupid reflects a long-standing reproductive dilemma. I think that Cupid's ancient arrow symbolizes the intent of the modern shotgun. Cupid is society's constable. He aims his arrow to say, "Look, he's the one! He did it." He carries the message to the young man: "Marry the pregnant young woman." The man's response: "Don't shoot. We'll marry."

There is good evidence (to which I'll return in detail) from documents about wedding dates and then birth dates that around the turn of the last century between 30 and 50 percent of marriages occurred during a pregnancy. But unmarried pregnancy is largely no longer men's concern. Men have become increasingly resistant to the idea that they should "do the right thing"—marry women with whom they had sexual relations and who became pregnant. "It's not my responsibility" is the common conclusion. Such a conclusion has accompanied a general public decline in society's enforcement of responsibility, along with a rise in psychological, not moral, justifications for behavior.

There is a major shift in the productive sphere, to the apparent advantage of females. In the reproductive realm, females can now control contraception and, hence, conception. The confidence that men can have about the fatherhood of offspring has been severely reduced. A brusque sign of this is that there is negligible or only minor concern by men for the contraceptive prudence of their partners. Seventy percent of men interviewed in a study of Americans asserted that women alone were responsible for contraception, not men.[9] They have evidently come to expect free, unencumbered sex, if only because that has largely been their experience. And the large number of males who replied in a complacently selfish manner is likely to be even larger in reality; pollsters know well that people often flatter themselves when they answer interviewers. Soaring levels of genital herpes among young Americans suggests relatively casual and imprudent sexual behavior.[10] Male indifference is surely a factor in the 40 percent of births that are unplanned, to say nothing of the pregnancies that end in abortion. University of California sociologist Kristin Luker found in a California study of 1970s abortion clients that only *one of ten* male partners contributed as much as half of medical costs.[11]

Here is a major change in the reproductive system. It is drastic. It is a strange kind of public revolution that is reflected in private acrimony. The shift was like day to night between the 50s and the 70s. People who grew to maturity in the 50s and before appreciate the sharpness of the change. Everyone then knew of people who "had to get married." Abortion was illegal, perilous, and costly. Comparing marriage and birth records shows that even around the turn of the century in America, from 30 to 50 percent of children were conceived before marriage. Other data suggest that over a 250-year period, before the twentieth century, "roughly a fifth . . . of all first conceptions in England may have been extramarital, that the proportion was usually much more like two-fifths . . . and could easily reach three-fifths."[12]

Wasn't this a disaster? Not necessarily. Marriage frequently follows a pregnancy. Moral strictures aside, it presumably reveals that the couple is at least functioning successfully in one of the most significant realms of married life, reproduction. The couple is at least biologically compatible, fertile, seemingly healthy. One of the inevitable uncertainties about any marriage has been clarified even before it begins. This is presumably a gain and not a loss for human choice. Annulments for unconsummated Catholic marriages are linked to fertility, just as American Puritan marriages weren't valid unless the couple was sexually mature and able to consummate. By the end of the eighteenth century, the Puritans tolerated a premarital birthrate of about 30 percent.[13] In 1995 a British clothing firm made available a successful line of wedding gowns in white and ivory for pregnant brides.[14]

Before the pill and the IUD, the condom was the major contraceptive. Contraception was consensual, wholly social, and equally apparent to both male and female, as apparent and social as the shotgun. Secrets are often surprisingly influential. But when the man is cut out of the reproductive agreement, it is difficult to overestimate the impact of hidden contraception. That is why there is such a strong association between sexual autonomy, based on female-controlled contraception, and an unexpected array of large-gauge social and economic consequences.

Cupid is often thought to be the muse of independent romance, of lovers conjoining in the steamy dark, away from aunts and uncles and earnest commentators. But the arrow the infant aims actually reflects the interests of the wider community in the private behavior of the couple. Cupid's arrow is a sexual subpoena. The independent acts of individuals are folded into the texture and requirements of society.

We have to consider the dramatic effect on men of their contraceptive ignorance. It is overwhelmingly clear in nearly every sexual encounter that, unless they have been vasectomized, when men ejaculate in their partner, they have participated in a possible pregnancy. But if only the woman has the facts about her fertility, if only she knows the possible outcomes of the episode, what happens to a man's sense of power, to his sense of function, to his sense of responsibility?

If knowledge is power, what is uncertainty? What is ignorance?

It is impossible to overestimate the impact of the contraceptive pill on human arrangements. The most striking display of this is the baffling historical fact that *after* the pill became available in the mid-1960s, the pressure for liberal abortion intensified worldwide. This is remarkably, even profoundly, counterintuitive. It is also an implacable historical reality. Only *after* women could control their reproduction excellently did they need more and more safe abortions. The likely reason is crude but simple: If men were not certain the pregnancy was theirs because they couldn't know, then they abandoned the relationship and the unexpected pregnancy. It appears that women (and presumably their parents, friends, and some of their partners) then exerted political pressure to change the laws to make safe abortions available to them. And this pressure succeeded even in improbable countries such as Italy and Spain.

It is enough to say here that the widespread pattern of marriage during pregnancy broke down when Cupid was no longer confident concerning the recipient of his arrow. Or if he was, he did not know what to do when the target ignored the threat. The result is millions of men in the picture but not in the neighborhood, that is, not committed to fatherhood.

The body itself is elaborately implicated. The pill is effective because it mimics pregnancy. Chemically, the user is like a pregnant woman. In the economy of nature, it is very plausible that pregnant females are less attractive to men and less attracted by them than ones who are fertile. How this could happen I will explain later, but an incontestably probable result of such contraception seems to be that the sexual dynamic between male and female is affected if not significantly buffered. The biological outcome of sexual relations has been preempted through chemistry. It has even been brilliantly suggested that one reason for the possible decline in male sperm counts in industrial countries is that the pregnant status of large numbers of otherwise attractive and sexually vivacious women depresses sperm production.[15] After all, different social states of female partners affect male sperm production. For example, men having sex with tall women produce more spermatozoa than they do with shorter partners.[16] How? Does this help explain why the women who model clothes successfully are unusually tall? And men produce more sperm with women from whom they have been apart for a while. Why? And wouldn't the existence of a large group of women prepared for sexual encounters but chemically pregnant have an effect on men's efficacy and élan?

A host of issues flows from new scientific knowledge of human sexuality and emotion, for example about what once seemed simple but is astonishingly intricate—the activity of spermatozoa.[17] Once upon a time sexuality itself was thought to be relatively simple.[18] It could be adequately comprehended and managed by moralists. But evidently it can't be. An ancient pattern encounters contentious and eventful new settings, and the results are unexpected.

Take the Pill.
Don't Call Me in the Morning

Today we have industrialized our society down to the level of our bodies, in the way we control our reproduction—through the pill, the IUD, vasectomy, sterilization, and drugs for fertility and potency. Though by no means all women or even the majority have used it, the pill has had a remarkable, defining, and underestimated impact on the communities in which it was introduced in the 1960s. It was not just another drug to correct a temporary physical illness; instead it was a powerful preparation given to *healthy people on a daily basis*. It did not repair a disability but promoted robust social life. It has affected sex between men and women, the core relationship that has guided human evolution and continues to preoccupy people more than half their lives.

This change in the fundamental connection between the sexes provoked many questions: How does chemical contraception affect social behavior, not only of females but of males? Would males be as eager to copulate with females made chemically pregnant by contraception as with those who might produce offspring? Was chemical pregnancy a turnoff?[19] Metaphorically, would Mother Nature show a preference for traditional reproductive connections over those that were recreational in effect?

To try to gain some comparative perspective, a study of the impact of chemical contraception on monkeys seemed worthwhile. After all, they are our contemporaries in the long play of evolutionary time; they are our exact geological age. And so in 1972 with colleagues from Rutgers University and its medical school, we established a colony of stumptail macaque monkeys to learn about the possible link between chemicals and behavior. The experiment raised some arresting questions about the behavior of human beings, to say nothing of what we learned about monkeys.

The monkeys lived alone on a small island the distance of five minutes of rowing off the coast of Bermuda. The hilly, rocky territory was lent to our research team by the Outerbridges, the family responsible for Bermudian hot sauces. First, we observed the sex lives of macaques and established a baseline for natural unmedicated behavior. We had established the group in an environment compatible with the one in which they customarily lived in West Africa. In their home environment these monkeys are organized around a leader male and a group of adult females. The male usually monopolizes sexual access to the fertile females, though both the less dominant males and often the females seek sexual contacts when they are unobserved by the leader. Our group's male leader was named Austin. There were also nine grown females and a number of rambunctious younger males and immature females. After three months Austin had established affectionate links with three favorite females with whom he had regular sexual episodes.

Once the pattern was clear, the experiment began. On a random basis we medicated five of the females with a three-month dose of Depo-Provera injected under the skin. Depo-Provera was not then legal for contraceptive use in the United States, but it now is. It was, however, widely distributed for use in other countries by, among other groups, the Rockefeller Brothers Fund.

In the first group of five medicated females, two had been among Austin's favorites. He continued to approach them, inspect their genitalia, and groom them in the ways they had enjoyed. But none of the once-lively relationships resulted in sexual intercourse. Instead, Austin chose two other adult females as his new consorts.

After three months the drug was no longer effective. We medicated the remaining four female monkeys, which included one former favorite of Austin's and two newer ones. He continued to approach, groom, and court these females, but again something was missing and he stopped short of sexual intercourse. He resumed his sexual link with two of his original favorites who were now off the medication, and added a third.

(Three sexual companions seemed to be Austin's idea of agreeable domestic life.)

After the second three-month dose lapsed, we medicated all the adult females. Austin began to attempt rape, masturbate, and behave in a turbulent and confused manner. He approached females, inserted his fingers in their genitalia, stroked and sniffed them, hovered anxiously. But no matter what he did, there was never the usual episode of intercourse.

After another three months the medication dissipated again, and the group was drug-free. It was back to nature and to true love. Faithful Austin returned to his original three companions.

Why did all this happen?

The pill works because it contains hormones that cause the body to mimic pregnancy. While a woman is taking the pill, she is chemically pregnant; therefore, she cannot become pregnant again. My hunch was that since nature is economical, this would have some consequence for female behavior, particularly on their sexuality and beyond their freedom to have sex relatively freely.

Sexuality is about relationships. It's plausible, if not likely, that chemical pregnancy has an effect on males, too. There is commonsense evidence that this is so. Even in a highly eroticized culture such as America, pregnant women do not usually provoke the intense responses commonly associated with sex appeal. As Anna Quindlen recalled her pregnancy, "I glance at men, they glance at me. Then I watch as their eyes slide down the exaggerated pear of my midsection. In that slide I become invisible. I am clearly, hugely pregnant, and so I have been desexualized. It feels as if I've been zapped with a ray gun."[20] The very occasional cases when pregnant women are sexually arresting are the often controversial exceptions, as was the nude portrait of the near-delivery actress Demi Moore on the cover of Vanity Fair. In the pornographic trades, depiction of sex with pregnant women fills a very narrow niche. From the biologist's point of view it is a reproductive waste of time for a male and a pregnant female to go through the strenuous courtship process leading to intercourse. Its most basic purpose, pregnancy, has already been achieved. This appeared to be the practical result for the male and female monkeys—or so their behavior suggested. But why? The team of scientists involved in the study could not cite the cause definitively.

What had so decisively disrupted those sexual links normally so desirable to monkeys? The most likely cause was pheromones. Pheromones are hormones that affect social behavior *between* individuals, not within bodies as hormones usually do. These mysterious substances are rather like smells—subtle and difficult to capture and measure.[21] Chemistry, Vibes, It, Love at first sight, Buzz, the Magic—humans use various words to describe the surprise of intense intimate physical attraction. Austin, too, had his romantic favorites. In many species primate males respond to female receptivity in part by smelling and tasting female genitalia. For primate couples, sex and the perfumes of the body are inextricably linked.[22] But chemical pregnancy decisively interrupted their flow among stumptail macaques who are otherwise vigorously sexual.

There is remarkably little good information on the subject of pheromones in humans. The inventory is improving, if slowly.[23] This is strange, given how many people are affected on a daily basis. It appears to have been somehow assumed that contraceptive drugs are merely chemical equivalents of mechanical barriers. This was the prevailing social viewpoint in 1975 when Barbara Seaman published her innovative study of the pill, which was first vilified but has since been vindicated and reissued.[24] Seaman had prudently suggested that the impact of the drug could be more deleterious and influential than the medical establishment was prepared to consider, especially with the high estrogen dosages that then prevailed and that turned out to be excessive.

It is difficult to think of a substance provided daily to healthy people that affects such a fundamental element of human life. It is altogether plausible that even the limited condition produced by the pill has an effect not only on the behavior of individual women and men but also on their community at large. When we contacted the pharmaceutical company Upjohn, which produced Depo-Provera, they offered no reassuring inventory of research results to suggest that they or anyone else had sought to assess the larger social implications of chemical contraception. One researcher I asked about the effects of the pill on female behavior confidently advised me that "they get used to it."

It is obviously a high jump from macaques to humans, yet we share many other mechanisms of sexuality with the primates. We do know that for humans there are clear links between hormones and status among men, and between hormones, neurotransmitters, and the cycling of female sexuality.[25] For example, men who lose their jobs lose most of their testosterone, too. Supporters of a winning team secrete more testosterone than the fans of the losers. When men enter the U.S. Marine Academy, their testosterone practically disappears, but by the time they graduate four years later they are bursting with it. A study of sexual behavior among lesbian couples indicated that even though reproduction was presumably not an issue in lovemaking, nevertheless there was discernibly increased sexual activity during the fertile middle phase of the female cycle.[26] It is clear that castration among humans and other animals produces docility, reduced sex drive, and, when animals are butchered for meat, fatter, more tender meat.[27] A 1996 study found two seemingly contradictory patterns among ovulating women: They are especially reluctant to choose sexual partners in whom they have no confidence and thus threaten sexual risks. At the same time consensual sex increases in mid-cycle.[28] Another unexpected result in the study is that women are less likely to be raped during the mid-portion of the menstrual cycle than at other times. However, none of these effects applied to women taking birth control pills, another indication of possible interference by the pill of vital biosocial processes at the core of reproductive life.

And then there is the matter of the brain, thinking, and ideas. In a presentation to a 1980 symposium of the New York Academy of Sciences, neurophysiologist Sandra Witelson of McMaster University announced that "the brain is the principal sex organ." As I wrote about the pill and human sexuality in 1983, "The most important mechanism . . . is presumably the cognitive one. Thought being a sexual behavior, too, it is worth asking whether . . . a relatively low . . . level of interference among stumptails consequent on pill use may be magnified in the human case because of the effect of thought and cognition in extending and enhancing the meaning and expression of inner states. Does a human female using contraceptive agents change her sexual behavior in a more marked way because she understands the implication of her decision better than do other primates?"[29] Precisely because people are so conscious of their behavior, the deliberate choices they make will influence what they do. As far as macaque males are concerned, there is little information they can have about a female's sexual state apart from the changes in genital coloration and size associated with estrus and fertility. Humans have no such obvious forms of sexual indicator. Subtler, more interior, and more symbolic ones presumably loom larger.

But wait. The pill is a drug, and as with all drugs, there is no free high, low, or exit. Because the pill makes women chemically pregnant, I have suggested that there is some form of reduced attraction felt by men and perhaps reduced female interest even while there is an obvious increase in their sexual freedom. The message is complex. Its seemingly contradictory elements may not cancel each other out. They may produce quite different effects. But there are provocative indications that something is going on. Martha McClintock, then of the University of Pennsylvania, discovered during a pioneering study in 1970 that women who live together in dormitories and other close settings find that their menstrual cycles become synchronized over time, for reasons that presumably are pheromonal.[30] *Contraceptive pill-takers do not.* Since they are artificially pregnant, their cycles are controlled not by the social setting but by human will.

Women on contraceptive medication do not respond to other women the way non-contracepted women do. This is very suggestive. The pill affects how women relate to other women in a visceral way. It follows that it also affects how they relate to men. The German researcher Claus Wedekind suggested this in a 1995 report of differ-ences in responses to men of women on and off the pill.[31] Women ranked the desirability of an anonymous array of smells taken from male clothing. Remarkably, they preferred the scents of men socially regarded as desirable potential mates. If remarkable, this is also understandable. These desirable potential mates had It, the Buzz, appeal. However, women using oral contraceptives *reversed* their preferences and chose inappropriate partners. In a sense there was no point for them to select promising progenitors because they were already pregnant. The subtle system of selection had shut down. New rules prevailed.

In 1998, McClintock made another extraordinary discovery, now with colleagues at the University of Chicago. She found that women release a bouquet of pheromones during the monthly cycle that are sufficiently tangible to other women encountering them to cause the shortening or lengthening of their own cycles—in over two-thirds of women by anywhere from one to fourteen days.[32]

Why women should respond to the sexual cycles of other women is intriguing in its own right, but in reproduction how women respond to men is clearly more central than how women respond to women. This is a rich clue, both logical and biological, to what else may be going on below the level of conscious choice and verbal articulation. Sexual reproduction is the heart of the relationship between men and women when these relationships are in their most intense stage, and even when they are merely flirtatious. The ready availability of pheromonal attraction is presumably one reason for a million human rules and customs that exist to prevent, restrict, socialize, or influence sexual choices.

Even the absence of sexual congress can produce sharp effects. Imagine a social system in which 50 percent of all women between eighteen and forty-five are obliged to be celibate. In communities that must remain celibate there are usually significantly rewarding arrangements associated with it, such as religious vows (which for Catholic women means symbolic marriage to Christ and the wearing of a gold band), special clothing, lifetime employment and housing, even lustrous promises about the afterlife. How would non-celibate men respond in an ordinary community in which 50 percent of potential partners were nuns? Or non-celibate women to a male population half of priests or committed male homosexuals? There would surely be a conscious adjustment to a challenging situation. After all, the very nature of sexual selection depends on a group of available candidates within which choices must occur.

What if the group of candidates is sharply reduced in number?

Didn't the pill also produce an adjustment? Since 1960 women in industrial countries have been able to control their fertility on their own terms without anyone else knowing. Control was exercised firmly, privately, within their bodies, either with chemicals or largely hidden devices such as the IUD. There was no letter on a woman's forehead, scarlet or otherwise. Her secrecy could also be a weapon against men. Ignorance may fuel bliss, but it also produces vulnerability.

Before that time, contraception was obvious. Men would have to assume their partners were fertile if they did not use a diaphragm, which is relatively obvious. Condoms, the most widely used contraceptives, also advertised a man's unwillingness to father a child. Before the pill there was no ambiguity. Pregnancy was always a risk in the absence of an obvious initiative to the contrary. After the pill, the situation was overturned. Men assumed women were contracepted unless they were told otherwise. If they were not contracepted, that was women's choice, and so were any consequences. Nothing less changed than all the central mechanisms of sexual selection, which produced the sexual system that prompted people to engage in it all.

Sex, Drugs, and Rocking the Boat

The impact has been significant, not only at the intimate level but in public interaction. If hormonal attraction is changed and diminished by the pill, perhaps chemically pregnant females have to employ more vigorous external signals than before to feel vivacious and sexy themselves, and to attract the attention of men if that is their interest. In fact, there were such striking developments largely following the introduction of the pill in the 1960s. They were bound to affect the broad group of females interested in courtship, including those on—as well as not on—the pill.

Before the pill, women appeared to accept norms of moderation in clothes and behavior. In the 1960s women were subject to new forms of fashion and demeanor. They escalated the sex game. Rather suddenly there emerged a stunning array of candidly erotic and voluptuous novelties such as the abandonment of bras, the shortening of skirts, the popularity of tight jeans, and even the astonishing topless fashion at various resorts.

Of course there isn't a direct one-to-one connection between medication and fashion; nevertheless, fashion by definition is an intricate, highly social process. It is involved with sexual appeal and the personal negotiations surrounding it. Skirt lengths rise and fall, usually in a general public pattern. But then each woman has to choose *her* length. She has to balance her boldness with her modesty. She has to adjust the erotic impact of her appearance with the norms of her social group. She has to balance receiving attention with maintaining social poise and position. And there is almost certainly a trade-off between the responsiveness of males and being too assertive or provocative to retain the good opinion of females, especially friends.

The sexual revolution did not involve the overthrow of governments, the reallocation of the ownership of stocks and bonds, or the emergence of new forms of local government. It was intimate. It changed the sexual expectations and practices of men and women. Sex before marriage? The question is largely moot. The new question is: Sex on the first date or the second? What, no sex on the third date? In many circles this is a neon sign of a problematic relationship.

The changes were in their way amazing. The celebrants of the new bodily freedom announced it in their popular culture and private behavior. If clothing was newly brazen, so were disco dances, love-ins, clubs for earnest orgiasts, rock musicians, and their performances and sexual athletics. The Woodstock Generation and the Polaroid Swinger marked a new plateau of emotional and erotic candor.

After the pill began to be used widely in the 1970s, the most lively and intrepid women led the way in sexual assertiveness. They were first spied on Kings Road in London, then on rue Sainte-Honore in Paris, via Montepoleone in Milan, and Lower Broadway in New York. Main Street followed in its own way. Perhaps few women could be as bold as runway models or starlets or thriving rock stars or their flamboyant companions. Nevertheless, nearly all could take aesthetic and erotic initiatives appropriate to their age, sexual status, and the changing norms of their communities.

Clothes maketh the man and the woman, but not equally. Though men command more wealth and are physically larger, they spend less for their clothing. In 1995 in the United States, men spent $40 billion to adorn themselves, women $73 billion. Some changes are under way, but they are still at the margins. Even among the rural collective settlers on the kibbutzim of Israel where clothing allowances are distributed by the community, females receive larger allowances than males. When we asked why, we were told, "Women need dresses. And they need new dresses."[33]

Fashion is where sexual selection and personal status meet. There is a delicate interaction about sexual status between couturiers of imperial cities and shopgirls of provincial towns. That is what the industry of fashion is all about. Designers, models, the president's wife, the actress of the year, the magazines—all define this moment's rules of acceptable and assertive bodily display.

Who led the new parade? The sexual style-setters were the most sexually liberated women in history. They had at once both knowledge of reproduction and the ability to control it. Not for them the moody decadence of Weimar or even the gilded hysteria of flappers. No, they were direct and naive, flexible and avid. All you need is love, they sang and felt and often demonstrated in the flesh.

At the same time they were increasingly physically healthy, especially among the Beatles/Mary Quant generation in the United Kingdom, where the postwar Labour government introduced good pre- and post-natal care for the first time for working class families.[34] They were part of the influential baby boom group that pressed its consumer wishes and educational needs on the wider community. Their zest and numbers appeared to overwhelm their hardworking, often intimidated parents. Burgeoning facilities for travel (jumbo jets, youth fares) and communication (television, films, videos) created a boisterous and confident community of international dimension. Nudity appeared routinely in legitimate theater, and public sexuality burgeoned as a social fact and commercial opportunity. Rules of censorship were relaxed. Unprecedented candor defined public discussion of sex and its varieties. Fundamentalist efforts to counteract this, such as in some Islamic communities and among Fundamentalist Christians, simply underlined the graphic situation then and now. And one of the most striking and still controversial changes to follow this vigorous generational development was the controversy throughout the industrial world surrounding legal abortion.

"I Find I Do a Lot of Losers"

One day recently as I dined alone in one of those Greenwich Village restaurants with good food and relatively low prices but with tables jammed together, I could not help hearing much of the conversation at the next table. Two women in their late twenties were talking about men. In a firm manner they evaluated the various individuals with whom they were involved and the husbands or companions of their friends. They sketched how strategically they considered having sex or not with particular men as a way of maintaining or improving their relationships. With what appeared to be a sense of resignation about the quality of the candidates in her circle, one woman said, "I find I do a lot of losers." Evidently she did not approve of the sexual concessions she made to unworthy males, though she made them. The women agreed they found themselves in a poor environment.[35]

Apart from the careful connections they drew between sex and the failure of "losers" to offer the prospect of commitment and resources, I was struck by the crass, if common, formulation "I do." Here it carried a meaning precisely opposite to the traditional vow of marriage "I do." It suggested a curiously managerial sense of sexuality. In my experience, men are rarely offered access to such discussions among women. The candor was arresting. So was the sense of control, almost mastery, of the sexual episode, though not of the larger stage on which it was played.

Alienated from the Means
of Reproduction

Perhaps my nearby dinner companions were less than exuberant about their sex lives. If they were born elsewhere, like more than half of New Yorkers, and came to the city both to do new exciting work and perhaps embrace whatever customary forms of family life they learned at home, it's clear why they might be disappointed at the unexpected mixture of professional accomplishment and emotional confusion.[36] As the gate-keepers of the next generation, they had reason to question what they defined as limited options. Nonetheless, they have some opportunity to choose; they can at least choose whether or not to have a baby, but the men to whom they referred cannot. With brusque effectiveness these men were alienated from the means of reproduction. Whether they knew it or not, or cared at all, the rules have changed. The Polish government, which replaced the Communists in 1989, subsidized contra-ception, but declines of 20 percent in marriages and 30 percent in births by 1998 prompted the government to reduce such subsidies.[37] The consequences will be profound and will appear soon.

We have already seen that as many as half of all marriages followed pregnancy in centuries before ours, but there was a major change in the second half of this century. Women began to control contraception, but men didn't necessarily know what they were doing. They lost a decisive measure of "paternity certainty." We've seen that one result was that men were reluctant to marry women who became premaritally pregnant. Another result of this was the burgeoning of liberal laws about abortion in Europe and the United States. If Cupid's arrow was insufficient protection for the reproductive rights of women and the family needs of the community, then the law had to step in—and it did, in countries as religiously disparate as France, the United States, and even Italy, the headquarters of Roman Catholicism.

It is clear that this is a chronic problem for males. A male cannot be sure of his place in the march of generations. Yes, he had an episode of sex, but then what? Was he the only partner? What happened before last night? Had there been love in the afternoon? The man with sharp questions to which only fuzzy answers are given may be expected nonetheless to care for the child for a whole generation.

In the world's systems of kinship, paternity is a recurrent theme. For example, in her study of traditional rural Iranian family life, Paula Ardeheli tells how even an inadvertent and innocent touch in a public place, such as on a sidewalk in a village, by a man of a woman who is not his wife can lead to sharp recriminations between their families and even the payment of financial restitution. However, Ardeheli observed and herself experienced that men who are acquaintances or total strangers will approach a pregnant woman and place their palms approvingly on her full belly.[38] Now she is pregnant. Now there is no question of paternity. The reproduction of life may be celebrated. Nearly every time I have told this story to women in our society, they tell me that it happened to them. Dour actuaries in the next office suddenly palpate the bellies of women with whom they've barely talked before. The curves and changes of their bodies are the subject of a friendly ongoing seminar. Before pregnancy, mere mention that she had a body could cause a woman to reach for a litigation manual and call a grievance officer about sexual violations.

One major result of newly heightened paternity uncertainty seems clear: Men are less willing than ever in history to marry single women who become pregnant. One reason is that social values have changed sharply, and the shotgun is rarely celebrated or tolerated as the tool of choice of matrimony. And men may believe, or convince themselves, that the child may not be theirs. Rather suddenly there are newly available genetic tests for paternity that are quick and easy, though costly—in the $500 to $800 range.[39] These tests will have serious impact once their existence is broadly known. The embarrassment and trepidation their results may bring are compensated for by male self-interest. Numerous studies suggest that 10 percent of married men's children are genetically not their own. Who wants to know? The real question is, Who doesn't want to know? Will science reintroduce a new kind of male control of female sexuality, the way the double standard was designed to do?

This uncertainty of paternity has been a crucial if unexpected reason for an unprecedented dual convulsion. The first was that relatively liberal laws were passed about abortion. Abortion, along with contraception, permitted women to have sex without babies. The second was an explosion of single-mother births throughout the industrial world, whereby women had babies without husbands. Even prominent women who might have in the past found single motherhood a professional liability now were celebrated for their innovative behavior.[40] It is difficult to imagine more important changes in human life than these.

Let it not be thought that these concerns preoccupy only citizens of relatively freewheeling modern societies. Sex is old. The classical Romans felt besieged by the inappropriate reproductive carryings-on of their fellow citizens. Livy lamented "the decline in discipline and moral standards, the collapse and disintegration of morality down to the present day."[41] As part of an urgent program of moral renovation, he advised that "Modesty was to be recalled from the distant past, and Virtue was to emerge from neglect. All possible steps were to be taken to ensure that men between twenty-five and sixty should be married men, and women between twenty and fifty should be married women."[42] James Davidson has also offered a rollicking account of the cavalcade of sexual and related pleasures assiduously pursued by the otherwise putatively sober democrats of the legendary Athenians, whose influence on the world's politics has been so extensive.[43] And this was before lusty television, films theoretically restricted only to adults, tight jeans, and *Playboy* magazine.

In the 1960s postwar period, other factors accelerated sexual liberalization. In North America, because of the GI Bill and a sharp expansion of higher education, countless young men and women left home to attend college. They found themselves in intimate settings with numerous potential partners. There was easy and comfortable sexual access both day and night. This was augmented when from the 70s onward many college residences became coed.[44] The traditional one-foot-on-the-floor or keep-the-door-open rules, which were often supposed to prevail in dormitories, became ancient history. Educators largely abandoned their role *in loco parentis* and even took legal action to prevent women who objected to cohabitation on religious grounds from moving off campus.[45] (But even without adult rules, students evidently create norms to deal with the provocativeness of the situation. For example, my colleague Michael Moffatt in his study of dormitory life at Rutgers University found that students made clear efforts to discipline sexual relations between people sharing residential quarters. It appears almost as if incest were the issue.)[46]

Countless members of the large baby boom generation left home to find work and to live in cities without the networks of social control that might apply in more familiar small communities. Their independence was associated with the rise of a lively internationally defined youth culture. It sealed off young people even further from the influence of adults.

Hi, Al. My Mom's at the Singles Bar. I'll Tell Her You Called.

The drama is outlined by flashing lights. Female contraception is known to be widely available and a personal female choice. There is much premarital sex—often with contraception, often without. Only a woman knows for sure about her possible fertility. This is nature's "concealed ovulation" among humans carried a step further. Technology exaggerates biology. Sharply reduced paternity certainty has become a complicated cognitive matter. Marriages resulting from unprotected premarital intercourse are no longer frequently considered or arranged. The results are astonishing. Between 1960 and 1992, births to unmarried mothers leapt from 25 to 59 percent of the total in Iceland, 11 to 53 percent in Sweden, 9 to 49 percent in Denmark, 7 to 35 percent in France, 5 to 32 percent in Britain, 7 to 30 percent in the United States, 5 to 29 percent in Canada, 2 to 12 percent in Holland, and 3 to 9 percent in Italy.[47]

Men walked.

There were three major consequences: The first was that abortion became legal. The second was that many of the women who did not have abortions kept their babies. The third was that many of the women who kept their babies had no husbands.

Japan is the exception among industrial communities. In 1994 only 1.1 percent of births were to unmarried women.[48] In part this is because there remain very firm social sanctions against single motherhood. Single Japanese mothers are reluctant to make use of the public assistance available to them, and abortions are readily available. It also appears that Japanese teenagers are less active sexually than their American counterparts.[49] This may be because they have less living space and room to maneuver.

However, these exceptional Japanese data vividly support the assertions here about contraception. Until the end of 1996 the contraceptive pill was illegal, difficult to acquire, and used very rarely in Japan. Though now legal on paper, in 1998 it remained highly restricted in use. The government had claimed it was inappropriate for Japanese physiology, presumably for the same reason that American beef cannot be digested by Japanese guts and foreign skis fail to glide properly over Japanese snow. Protective tariffs may matter somewhat. It has also been alleged that the medical profession appreciates the revenue afforded by abortion, which is legal and common. Both the pill and abortion are designed to accomplish the same goal, but the impact of the pill is felt subtly and over the long term while abortion occurs more episodically and often with some drama. The end result may be the same in both modes, but how it is achieved is sharply different.

Far more salient must be the government's preoccupation with population. This is either static or declining in Japan—one reason for Japanese mastery in the production of labor-replacing industrial robots. In mid-1998 the birthrate was 1.39 children per female and the percentage of unmarried women in their late twenties has virtually tripled since 1970, to barely under 50 percent. Some 70 percent of unmarried women in their thirties live with their parents. The prevailing birthrate is well below the rate needed to maintain the current population, especially given the minuscule immigration permitted into Japan.[50] Effective contraception will have a direct impact on sexuality, whatever other particular national influences come into play. Should the pill become fully available in Japan, as the government has promised despite considerable impediments, it will be interesting to track its effect on the sexual lives of Japanese people.

In the United States in the 90s, about 40 percent of female teenagers became pregnant at least once, four-fifths of the time without intent.[51] In 1955, 6 percent of white teenagers became pregnant out of marriage, 41 percent of blacks. By 1985 the numbers were 42 percent for light-skinned and 90 percent for dark.[52] Seventy-six percent of teenage mothers were not married in 1997, compared with 15 percent in 1960[53]—before the pill, of course.

Beginning in the 1970s, abortion was legalized in jurisdiction after jurisdiction. Even Italy, the home of its most powerful opponent, the Roman Catholic Church, legalized abortion in 1978. This followed the fact that a large new class of otherwise responsible young women found themselves pregnant and unmarried. These were women with brothers, fathers, mothers, sisters, lovers, uncles, and aunts—voters all. Even President George Bush, who opposed abortion at considerable political cost, when asked in 1992 what he would do if an unmarried granddaughter come to him pregnant, is said to have said: "I'd put my arm around her, help her out, and tell her to get back in the game." The meaning of "help her out" is clear.

Seemingly strict laws changed with surprising speed to permit these women a relatively safe, legitimate, and quick exit from a situation that would otherwise take decades to resolve itself. Unwanted pregnancies of unmarried women seemed unlikely to provide optimum or even acceptable conditions for the child. At the very least, the responsibilities of motherhood could deprive a woman of the opportunity to acquire and then use the occupational skills women now need, especially given the frailty of arrangements for public child care.

Their bodies may be reproductively different, but nearly all women are productively like nearly all men: They have to work. They have to support themselves. They may also have to support children, just as nearly all men have had to work in the past to support themselves and their families. The burgeoning availability of abortion was not only the result of a change in moral and sexual norms, but it also reflected stringent economic obligations.

Both men and women must first meet the demands of the productive system, and abortion is one means by which they are able to accomplish this in circumstances that may make childbearing difficult. For example, in 1991 over 30 percent of unmarried Americans between twenty-five and twenty-nine lived with their parents, often for economic reasons. Some 50 percent of twenty-nine-year-old Italian men—called *mammoni*, mama's boys—live at home.[54] There is no point leaving just to leave. Young adults must first get a reliable job, then a promising partner. Only then can they turn to reproduction, which has to take a backseat.

The Bitterest Sexual Politics

The availability of decent and legitimate abortion remains deeply controversial. Few people on either side of the shouting match are complacent about the moral and psychological costs of abortion. Whatever they may think about the procedure legally and medically, no one finds it amusing or desirable. Everyone is aware of the consequences one way or the other for individual women and their futures if abortion becomes inaccessible. Few people fail to consider the possible impact of the procedure on the psychological, physical, and economic conditions of everyone involved.

To repeat: The issue is biological, not logical.

The drama of abortion arises from ancient reproductive strategies gone awry amid new technology and the novel conditions posed by an economic society founded on individuals, not families.

Women may be condemned by social standards for seeking abortions, but they are actually trying to accomplish what has always gone right for our species naturally—to bear robust viable babies. The fact is that most women who seek abortions are thoughtfully responsible. They do not want to engage in an imperfect reproductive exercise. Hawaii had the first nonrestrictive abortion laws in the United States. An early study there showed that more than half of the respondents wanted an abortion because either they were not married or could not afford to raise a child.[55] They are prepared to acknowledge reproductive defeat, accept its many costs without still incurring more, and "get back in the game."

In her innovative study of female mate selection, my student Heather Remoff found what seemed to be counterintuitive: The women who most regretted having abortions were those with loving husbands or companions! They had lost a tenable reproductive opportunity. Women wholly alone or unsure of who the father was had far less or no disappointment about the interrupted pregnancy.[56]

Even where abortion is illegal, as in all of South America except for Cuba, as many as one in three pregnancies may end in abortion, as in Chile.[57] In contraceptively backward communities such as the former Soviet Union, abortion serves a different function because it is often the only alternative to unwanted pregnancy. Any reverie women there may have sustained about the relationship between reproduction and having an agreeable life was sharply broken by social and economic reality.[58] "In 1990 the USSR had 98.4 abortions per 1,000 women aged 15–49," compared with 5.3 in Germany and 8.7 in the United States. In 1993, because of massive social disruption and rising poverty, the World Bank estimated that the Russian abortion rate reached two out of three conceptions. The overall public health situation is equally parlous.[59]

Note that the American rate is less than one-tenth the Russian. Yet Americans still regard it as a substantial social and medical problem.[60] The absolute numbers are, of course, important, but abortion at any level appears to remain relatively provocative.

The underlying reasons for having an abortion are often overlooked by those very people with power to affect conditions helpfully. However, one compassionate legal response that also accords with biological theory (though not directly affected by it) was from the U.S. Supreme Court in the case of *Casey v. Planned Parenthood*. In an opinion written by Justice Anthony Kennedy, it was decided that a woman was not obligated to tell her husband or receive his consent if she had an abortion. This establishes her right as a separate legal and medical entity.

It allows her to terminate a pregnancy that may not have involved her husband. The decision actually boosts family solidarity, for those situations in which an extramarital affair leading to pregnancy could threaten marital durability. The opinion reflects unusual awareness of the underlying human forces in family structures.[61]

Otherwise, biological sophistication is limited. For example, biological ignorance supports the legal, political, and census fiction that race is an absolute category based in biology while sex is not.[62] Sex is a real biological factor, however, even though in the law, in much of social science, and in the culture more broadly it is treated mainly as the result of a kind of coercive stereotyping and social engineering, even exploitation, rather than an expression of underlying forces within the species.

New female-controlled contraception has had enormous consequences for the central social relationship of our species. Women have gained control. Men have lost it. Female mammals are urged by natural forces to bear and attend their young. Male mammals seeking pleasure are also animated (not consciously, as far as we know) by genetic interests to fertilize females. They also try to ensure that the young they care for are their own. Zoologists Jonathan Wright and Peter Cotton of Oxford University have shown experimentally, if also surprisingly, that male starlings are more helpful to their own genetic offspring than to those of other males.[63] In a more destructive mode, University of California primatologist Sarah Hrdy has described how males assuming dominance in a langur monkey community actually kill the suckling infants of the male they drove out so that their mothers will cease lactating, begin ovulating, and become fertile.[64] Anthropologists Steven Gaulin and Alice Schlegel analyzed 186 preindustrial societies, concluding that "cultural patterns leading to heavy male investment in a wife's children make it likely that such investment benefits bearers of the male's genes."[65]

The issue is not solely the presence or absence of congenial affection. We are in a danger zone. Stepparents and especially stepfathers are one hundred times more likely to abuse children and eleven times more likely to murder them.[66] Perhaps like the langur males they want the interloper children out of their lives. Controlling paternity—perhaps partly to avoid just this kind of hazard—has long been at the heart of family systems and other male efforts to control women and their sexuality. Whether through property laws, religion, custom, force, or fear, males have tried to hold at bay their own fear of betrayal. And men have a more tenuous approach to parenthood to begin with. Margaret Mead in her 1949 classic, *Male and Female*, defined fatherhood as a "human invention."[67] This was in anticipation of later biological work on paternity certainty.[68] When she reviewed my *Men in Groups* in *Redbook* in 1969, she complained that I had failed to provide a physiological correlate of male bonding. That was why the rituals of male bonding had to be so intense. As sociologist David Popenoe of Rutgers University has commented, "Men are not biologically as attuned to being committed fathers as women are to being committed mothers. Left culturally unregulated, men's sexual behavior can be promiscuous, their paternity casual, their commitment to families weak."[69]

The industrial world has changed mightily from the good old days. Prevailing social expectations and patterns have partly compensated for male failings of commitment and persistence. There are strict rules both formal and implicit to make up for wobble and evasiveness. But the evident changes have not begun to solve the social problem that Popenoe identifies.

Frontlash

The situation is, in fact, far worse. Men and women increasingly share the same career models of individual work and responsibility. They are more equally independent than ever in recent history and maybe all history. The economic subordination of women is decreasing. Even in the legendary English spy service of James Bond, M15, one-half of the active spy agents were female by 1998.[70]

How have men responded? With a stunning reversal. To judge from their behavior they care less and less or hardly at all. They are abandoning women. In the past they may have deserted their partners for new ones. That continues. It supplies much of the 50 percent divorce rate. But now there is a new, substantial reason that men leave their sex partners: Their partner has a new mate—not another man, but a baby, for whom the men may not feel and do not assume paternal responsibility. Perhaps this helps explain the single-mother rate of over 30 percent of births across the industrial world.

A recent technological development is a DNA test for paternity that is relatively cheap and simple. In the United States to date less than a quarter of a million have been performed, but eventually the test may become common and acceptable—whatever its effect on the muse of romance. Males will be able to enjoy the certainty that the double standard was once upon a time supposed to offer. They will also have to endure the responsibility of paternity when they don't want it and had no idea it would emerge. Then the story we are telling here will change its course and may have a very different ending. But all the leading characters will have been affected by the events so far.

Male behavior prior to the existence of a simple DNA paternity test suggests how confounding to them is reproductive uncertainty. Parenthood without certainty appears to be too much for them to handle, or they have decided these changes are not their affair, not in their interest to contemplate. The large category of men who slip away from the two decades of support that paternity may involve contains many separate men. Each of them pointedly affects at least two other people—the mother and their child. The economic, psychological, and political impacts of this kind of individual choice are vast and ramified, on a scale only a belligerently reckless Cassandra would have dared describe barely a quarter of century ago. They involve nothing less than a Bewildered New World.

Many boys and girls grow up without a sturdy connection to or even knowledge of one partner of the pair who brought them into the world. They lack a relationship—strenuous, provident, informative, or even very difficult—with a man whose link to their lives was broad, fixed, and represents natural human sexuality.[71] In early life they will be disinherited from an irreplaceable asset in a world which requires that men and women learn how to connect with men and women. And in the U.S., some 800,000 out-of-wedlock children live with their father alone.[72] Parenthetically, one redolent and striking indication of the relative ineffectiveness of single fathers compared with single mothers is that, in the United States between 1969 and 1996, the income of households headed by single mothers increased by 10 percent, while that of households headed by single fathers declined by 8 percent.[73] Is this a measure of biosocial competence?

I have suggested that the single, most decisive new factor in the situation is modern contraception. It has more influence, in my opinion, than changes in moral structure, religious enthusiasm, the vaunted "family values"—though obviously such forces make their mark. Whether or not it is even used, contraception has changed the biological rules of the game and its outcome. It has been the catalyst and basis for a kind of independence between men and women in sex that has generated and now accompanies a comparable independence about money.

Astonishingly, Sterilized by Choice

One stark and final mystery about contraception. More American women—about ten million—choose sterilization than any other form of birth control including the pill.[74] If you add the 12 percent of men who have been vasectomized, this results in a huge number of women who engage in sex confident that they will not bear a child.[75] Of course, people tend to seek sterilization when they are older and have already had children. Nonetheless, the implications are formidable. One is the mixture of prudence and nihilism the choice reveals. Another is what happens when one sterilized person is with someone who is not. That makes two sterilized people. How does that affect the relationship? With a divorce rate as high as it is, inevitably some people will enter a new relationship and then want a child with the new mate. A student of mine who was appalled by the men she encountered after her divorce got sterilized only to marry a man who wanted to share a baby with her. There are controversies over this in Canada, where there is publically supported medical care. Governments favor sterilization since it is cheap and reduces the future load on the system, but they are wary of requests for reversals of sterilization that may not work and that are nearly ten times more costly.

While speaking at a medical convention I described doctors who do sterilizations as sophisticated equivalents of the owners of tattoo parlors. The public and private consequences of widespread sterilization are, in my opinion, inadequately understood. Sterilization is a profound choice about the body, the self, and the future. It is especially dramatic because there are other effective, temporary ways to accomplish the same goal. But this may reveal an unprecedented and not-so-hidden nihilism about reproduction.

There is a paradox here. The current situation of many males—those losers—reveals only vulnerability, reckless hopelessness, and economic incompetence. Yet an influential public perception of males persists as oppressive, potentially harassing, self-interested patriarchs. Nearly two generations of female-controlled contraception have been accompanied by a powerful redefinition of sexual values largely by female and feminist leaders. Inequities founded in the arrangements of the past, now ebbing away, have led to legal, policy, and social initiatives by male and female officials to bolster the jobs and lives of women, even seemingly to the direct disadvantage of men. How have men responded? To judge from their behavior—as mates, as voters, as fathers—repeated denigration of their moral worth has generated among men resentment, irritation, demoralization, and confusion.

That's what we turn to now.

CHAPTER THREE

The First World
(Sex) War

W E HAVE JUST CONSIDERED what happens when an industrial technique of contraception is introduced into the ancient natural pattern of reproduction. Among monkeys the effect was quick and decisive. Among humans there is far more to think about. Nevertheless, the monkey experiment showed that enormous change can result from seemingly peripheral innovations. The statistics about the change in unmarried motherhood before and after the pill cannot be ignored, either. They suggest nothing less than that the essence of the parental link between men and women was affected by the shift in reproductive control to women. If Margaret Mead was correct in describing fatherhood as a human invention, successful fulfillment depends on personal choices and explicit social controls. It follows then, given males' already tenuous confidence of paternity, that something which heightens their uncertainty can have a disproportionate impact on behavior.

Our biological endowment provides a broad if diffuse basis for our behavior. Some may say I overestimate the influence of biology. The problem, however, is not that biology is overemphasized but that it is not coercive enough. We are not like ants who can recreate a perfect ant state wherever they set up shop or like domesticated dogs who confidently scratch the pavement to cover up their feces with nonexistent soil.

The new technology of contraception accomplished two main goals: controlling pregnancy and enhancing sexual pleasure for its own sake. It has had other consequences, too, not the least is in the realm of ideas and how ideas may be formulated into law. At first the impact on men seemed less drastic than on women. Perhaps it was simply less clear. What is certainly clear, however, is the magnitude of the changes under way and the turbulence of the new psychosexual environment. In fact, the relationship between men and women in the realm of public discourse is a kind of war, one that involves and absorbs men and women in many situations and communities. It also reflects quite basic differences, if not conflicts, in reproductive strategy.

There are no territorial battle lines, camouflaged missile launchers, or official uniforms. Like the cold war, the gender war is an encounter without the defining physical bloodiness of traditional war, yet it compels countless legions to join its operation, whether or not they volunteer to play a role. There is hardly any age limit to the conscripts to the battle. Even infants are enlisted in the campaign by the kinds of toys and clothes they are given. A well-known feminist told me at a party in 1996 that the moment a baby arrived at the maternity ward, its psychosexual destiny was in decisive danger from the potentially polluting color decor of its environment—blue or pink. To her, evolution was a whim in the face of the color of blankets and booties.

Five-year-olds are prosecuted for sexual harassment in grade school. The four-year-old daughter of a friend of mine invited a little girl in her nursery school for a sleepover. The daughter's friend wandered into the bathroom where the naked father was shaving. The father had to phone the girl's parents that morning to describe his household's casual demeanor about clothes. He was wary of the consequences if he didn't call. He is a lawyer.

The burgeoning gender war shares with old-fashioned world conflict its grip on the private and public lives of countless people in seemingly unconnected societies. Immigration judges in Ontario rule on the barbarism of clitoridectomy in a foreign country and offer Sudanese and Nigerian girls an escape route from physical violation. A neurophysiologist in Cambridge publishes a report on how boys and girls learn to read so that educators in Rio de Janeiro have to reconsider their curricula. A Kenyan anthropologist discovers an isolated community in which the women work hard and the men laze around. Right away the industry of sex role studies around the world adjusts to this shift in perceived gender roles.

From organizations such as the United Nations to reproductive biologists to detectives, different groups hold complex colloquies about the rights and needs of women and the legal and emotional changes necessary to ensure them. It is so widespread and pervasive that its newness and meaning are evident only to very few of the countless people subject to its pressure.

The entire issue has been politicized with unprecedented scope and intensity. Kate Millett's 1970 book, *Sexual Politics*, was prescient in identifying a newly turbulent feature of the battle of the sexes: that sexual intercourse, though usually private, was a symptom of general public struggle.[1] What had been thought to be exclusively intimate matters reflecting the urgencies of the heart were now perceived as political choices as public as choosing political parties to vote for. Susan Brownmiller's 1975 *Against Our Will* made a link between rape and sex, and pressed the point that much of what had once been considered seduction, consensual sex, or lovemaking was actually rape in disguise. Andrea Dworkin subsequently pushed the assertion still further, announcing flatly that all heterosexual intercourse was rape,[2] a viewpoint broadly affirmed by Phyllis Chesler.[3] Poet Adrienne Rich wrote that "motherhood is the key role, the keystone of the patriarchal arch."

The reproductive, economic, and social evidence suggests the move-ment is inexorable and consistent, despite a fair amount of genuine disagreement among female commentators on the issues. The trend lines run with few detours or cul-de-sacs. Their most immediate and accessible symptom is words, and there has been an avalanche of words.

Ladies

The respected American novelist Marilyn French was celebrated for her novel *The Women's Room*. The book's jacket featured a door, presum-ably to a lavatory, with the word LADIES' crossed out and WOMEN'S inscribed instead. Her book described a group of women who shed their conventional familial and female roles to assert new feminist goals. Her words were equally to the point and meaningful in an interview she gave to *The New York Times* in July 1995 when she discussed relations between men and women: "I think men would be much happier if they behaved like women. I think they would get much more out of life and would have much more easier selves if they were like women, if they behaved like women."[4] While her assertion seems complacently simple-minded as well as insulting to men, it reflects a position widely held by many women and some men.[5] What outrage would have greeted French had she said, "Blacks would be much happier if they behaved like whites" or if she had said, "The French would be happier if they behaved like Germans." It is acceptable, however, to disparage male experience. Just compare it with life calibrated by females. Maureen Dowd in a *New York Times* column mocked men for being concerned about falling sperm counts and purchasing transdermal patches to replace declining testos-terone levels, without a thought that this may reflect genuine anguish, to say nothing of the fact that illegal steroid abuse is actually a widespread problem among young men. Steroid abuse, which may reveal their sexual insecurity, may also stunt their growth and paradoxically inhibit their fertility.[6] Indeed, the mere mention of the word "testosterone" is often enough to make females smirk. Of course, men often mock women on sexual issues, too. The new equality in this cheerless contest suggests its severity.

Self-righteous attacks on males are omnipresent in the educational world. The anti-male initiative is reflected in preferential employment and fellowship opportunities for females as well as the renovation of curricula and other teaching forms to better reflect female and feminist agendas. One columnist in the student paper at my university lamented about women's studies courses he had taken: "What has been my experience . . . is that modern feminist ideology is binary. Simply, you are either a feminist, or you are nothing. There is no room for a 'maybe' within the feminist infrastructure . . . or a plausible provision that a traditionally Caucasian man might have some redeeming societal value other than 'oppressor of 50 percent of the world's population.' "[7] Young men pass through educational institutions that confidently and as a matter of operational policy denigrate their sex. One of their first college experiences is a film and seminar on date rape. Young women learn that their communities are as likely as not to restrict and degrade them because of their sex. Nihilistically sexist insults such as Gloria Steinem's "A woman without a man is like a fish without a bicycle" become T-shirt slogans.

There is a clear-cut virtue, indeed a necessity, in many of the new policies and attitudes even if they are often expressed with rancor or exaggeration. Economic practices must adjust to the realities of female careers. Extensive inequities remain, especially in careers in which longevity is a feature of seniority. Women have to prepare themselves for self-supporting employment. The employment has to be available. So must the educational opportunity to qualify for it.

The same principle applies to what were once men-only clubs and associations. Perhaps they are social and merely convivial in their intent and conduct, but they are frequently associated with professional and financial achievement. Contemporary men routinely assert successfully in divorce court that their professionally qualified spouses do not require alimony. Men cannot at the same time prohibit women from country clubs that provide access—subtle but nevertheless tangible—to personal networks. Some prestigious American golf clubs continue to have prohibitions against female members paying full fees in an effort to keep them from using courses on the same bases as men.

Rich feminist contributions on the subject of these social changes have been made to teaching and scholarship about female experience and nature.[8] This feminist literature seems self-contradictory, however; it often excoriates men and strongly objects to any notion that differences between men and women are natural and recurrent.[9] At the same time, though, it asserts, as Marilyn French did, that men and women *are* different and that women are somehow naturally superior. Or it asserts that it is natural for people to learn their sexuality almost exclusively from their communities, at the same time claiming there is a potent and pervasive worldwide patriarchy, the existence of which would appear to imply a force of nature.

It is often difficult for those outside the academic community to appreciate the stringency and extent of controversies about sex. For example, in the context of the hoary argument about nature versus culture, there has been extensive dialogue about how and why sex roles take the form they do. Some claim men and women are what they are because there is a natural and functional difference between them that flows from biology. Others attribute any differences to an overpowering array of legal, psychological, and economic patterns imposed by men. Still others seek a synthetic approach. In North American universities and in such departments as women's studies and literature, whatever the positions people take, they assert and defend them with pointed vigor. Controversies about sex and Darwin have replaced those about money and Marx as the most pervasive subjects of university dialogue.

Nearly everyone agrees that it is important and just for the particular experiences of women to be expressed in the educational scheme. There is a wealth of material here.[10] It comprises virtually every possible point of view, from the explicitly misogynistic to the imperial lesbian, from those who link sex wholly to genes, to those who believe the tabula rasa is the only piece of sexual equipment that finally matters. And there are those who share with novelist and essayist Anne Roiphe the caveat that "biology will not be banished by epigram. It still takes its toll"—if a toll is what it takes.[11]

A vast new subject matter has enlarged the body academic. Inevitably this has also diminished the status and impact of traditional disciplines. So be it. The world of knowledge reflects the world.

Male Original Sin Is Especially Bad

Vigorous as all this is, there is also a deeper, darker cast to it, naively reflected in Marilyn French's sanctimonious interview: that males suffer from a special kind of original sin. The Eden story was metaphorically backward. Not Eve but Adam was responsible for eviction from Eden. Adam dragged us down, and he continues to do so.

Once upon a time, and for long centuries, there was an obvious double standard in Euro-American societies. It was tied to morality, controlling reproduction and ensuring parenting for children. It also hindered and even prevented the public lives of women—in voting, owning property, serving the community, at work, sexually, and in myriad other ways. By the standards of public economic life, women were certainly the second sex. But the social patterns of agrarian and feudal society decomposed under pressure from the industrial way of life and from the accompanying emergence of the individual as the central component of economic activity. Legal and social restrictions began to disappear. Informal and attitudinal barriers surely linger, but in many ways the shoe is increasingly on the other foot. As I have said, in mature industrial capitalism, the ascent of women and the descent of men is under way. In February 1996 the U.S. Department of Labor announced that since 1979 the median wages of men had fallen almost 9 percent while women earned 7.6 percent more.[12] The percentage of working men with a job had dropped from about 80 percent in 1960 to 70 percent in 1995, while the percentage of women with a job had risen from 35 to 55 percent.[13] In 1996 *half* of all births in New York City were to single mothers. It may be assumed that these women did not have a firm association with the fathers of their children, and hence these fathers, in the cold eye of reproductive success, are emotionally and paternally unemployed.

There is no sign that this pattern will soon change. It is a trend in public economics. It is repeated in other industrial countries, too, as we have seen. The shift reflects practical changes in personal expectations as well as economic and sexual forces. It also expresses an important moral change: a redefinition of the relative value attached to public life and private life, in favor of the public.[14] The stigma attached to the status "housewife" reveals moral preference for money in the commercial economy over social and emotional experience in the private sphere.[15] In its "Value of a Mum Survey," the Legal and General Insurance Company of England even calculated that the average real cost of parental care and household management was £313, or about $500 per week.[16]

The shift is most broadly reflected in the emphasis in industrial countries on the value of work over mothering. Work is redemptive, while private experience is ordinary and neutral, even negative. Paid work enjoys high moral and social status even if it involves a woman's taking care of someone else's child for money and even if she has to pay yet another person to care for hers. A mother caring for another's child for money adds to the gross national product. A mother caring for her own child does not. A 1996 poll by *The New York Times* asked respondents: Which do you think is more important—providing child care services so that women with young children can work or paying the mother so she can stay at home and care for her children herself? Seven percent had no opinion. Seventeen percent saw the virtue of providing funds for women to raise their own children, but a remarkable 76 percent favored a commitment to the money economy, clearly a central value of the society overall.[17]

In part, the commitment to paid work expresses a distaste for welfare, the expansion of which burgeoned after the use of the pill in the

United States (but that is another discussion). Welfare is thought to lead too often to pathological loss of independence and efficacy of its recipients. Nevertheless, the moral value also joins a vast shift in industrial societies from doing things oneself—parenting, cooking, mending, changing oil, counseling—to hiring paid specialists for it. It is part of an underlying bureaucratization of intimacy, of life itself. One consequence is that the income of both people doing each other's laundry goes up, though their laundry expenses do, too. Only the government benefits, with little obvious political cost. It can tax money transactions but not affectionate ones. Every time I do your laundry and you do mine, and we pay each other, we are supposed to remit sales and income tax. This is a tax increase on people and an increase in government revenue even though the net result is still the same bag of clean laundry. In the United States during the mid-nineties, for the first time more money was spent on food consumed or cooked outside the home, which is taxable unlike supplies acquired in markets. This is another vast addition to the tax base, an unlegislated tax increase for which no elected officials are directly responsible. Small wonder that governments get bigger. Small wonder that "small government, please" emerges as a twenty-first century cry.[18]

Is the Personal Really Political?

There is a larger issue here. In the prickly contest between men and women, it is a sign of exploitation if family life involves apparent service to a male. The association was first, fairly, and most prominently noted by Betty Friedan in The Feminine Mystique.[19] The patriarch is in charge and must be responsible for what is clearly unfair and wrong. All men benefit from the indentured work of women, usually ratified in marriage. As Susan Brownmiller claimed, all men share in the sexual coercion of all women. All benefit from unwanted sexual access. Hence all men share the guilt of the harsh patriarchal legacy.

The consensus is that when men exclude women from their precincts it is discriminatory—as it has certainly often been. But it is regarded as appropriate for all-male schools such as The Citadel to be forced by the federal government to admit women, while all-female schools are exempt. U.S. Supreme Court Justice Ruth Bader Ginsburg's contorted opinion in a decision denying single-sex status to publicly supported male schools protects female schools on the broad ground of historical remedy.[20] In practice, such elite all-female institutions as Smith College and Wellesley also receive federal funds, albeit indirectly as scholarships, tax-deductible gifts, research grants, and the like. Despite their traditional privilege and segregation, these schools are assumed to reflect a higher purpose and are hence defensible. Government actions suggest a broad social consensus: all-male endeavors are primordial and crude while all-female endeavors are socially worthwhile. It is justifiable to exclude men from women's institutions both in historical reparation and to bolster female self-esteem and confidence.[21] The rules differ. Preferential treatment of women is justified by historical inequity. Legal contests about this remain, such as in England where in 1994 the European Community court decided that women could not receive favored treatment in the labor force.[22] This was then reversed. In the United States the issue of affirmative action remains exceptionally controversial in law and public discourse.[23]

The matter of historical remedy raises obvious questions about the link between past unfairness and contemporary people, and about practical effectiveness, too. The original impulse for affirmative action was to make practical and moral amends for slavery. The group principally intended to benefit from it was Americans who had originated in Africa. The legislation originally proposed race as the target constituency, but sex was added at the last minute by a representative from the South who thought the entire effort so ludicrous that it had no hope of passage. Of course race and sex involve wholly different categories of reality, but the lawyers prevailed. One result has been that the principal beneficiaries have been white women, many already middle class, a matter not unnoticed by politicians of African origin as well as males of any origin. For example, two prominent members of a communications company acknowledged as equally qualified were considered for a promotion; it went to the female whose grandfather had been a president of the United States rather than the male whose grandfather had escaped from Kazakh ethnic cleansers in Russia.

Remedies may produce more trouble than they're worth. One case in point is still unsettled: single-sex schooling. If we want to regard all life as a contest, there is reason to believe that single-sex schools benefit women more than men. The customary explanation is that men disproportionately dominate airtime in class. Perhaps that it is one factor, but the underlying one which is almost invariably ignored is that classes are organized by age. Male developmental slowness retards class progress overall and, hence, female accomplishments. On their own, girls can progress faster. Even female fetuses move their mouths more than males, a possible precursor of earlier competence in speech by girls.[24] In addition, particularly in high school, females often seem unwilling to challenge males in public contests and discourse.[25] This may be due in part to strategic avoidance of challenge to potential male partners. Perhaps it also reflects simple courtesy—kindness over the real and perceived male deficit. After all, females consistently outperform males in primary and junior high schools.

Given the reality of their consistently better performance, females should conclude that they are educationally superior. But perhaps their enthusiasm and knack for leadership are inhibited by aggressively competitive males.[26] Importantly, the crucial years of educational achievement involve the same period of life in which turbulent sexuality and courtship are at peak intensity. Just as girls mature more quickly than boys emotionally and intellectually, so do they sexually. As a twelve-year-old girl entering a controversial new all-female school in New York City said in 1996, "You feel uncomfortable sometimes around boys. . . . You feel more insecure about yourself. You feel like you have to look nice for them. I don't want to go to school to be a model. I want to go to school to learn."[27] An English study published in 1997 suggested that both boys and girls performed better on exams for university when they attended single-sex schools.[28]

Coeducational behavior cannot be segregated from the underlying forces of emergent sexuality. It cannot be set apart from the influence of biology. For example, in our 1973 study of three generations of women in the kibbutz movement of Israel, of the employment histories, family patterns, political activities, and social attitudes, Joseph Shepher and I found that the females who were academically superior to males until adolescence no longer were thereafter. It is unlikely they became dumber. Something else was going on. This case is particularly interesting because of the way kibbutz children of that period were raised—by professional caregivers in collective houses, not in families. In addition, economic needs were handled in a wholly different way from elsewhere: Neither males nor females had to earn a living on their own, and both men and women received identical allowances. Membership in the commune assured women and men equal support, dignity, security, and employment throughout their lives.[29] Neither money nor independence nor self-esteem was an issue.

In fundamentally different social and economic conditions in North American society, a similar educational result occurred. Perhaps gender was the common factor. Needless to say, few prominent feminists concerned with explanations of sex differences, such as Carol Gilligan, Susan Faludi, and Carol Tavris, seriously confronted this evidence about a major long-lived human experiment by thoughtful idealists. It was easier to ignore the entire matter.

Boys Will Be

The noisy raucous behavior of adolescent human males is comparable to displays by males in the animal kingdom, from other primates to peacocks. They serve to impress and intimidate other males when jockeying for status. The immediate goal appears to be enjoyment of power and prestige, but it has more to do with reproductive strategy. Females may believe these irritating theatricals have little or nothing to do with them. They may avoid them out of a mixture of apprehension and contempt. The point of the exercise, however, is to establish a hierarchical order. Males develop reputations for effectiveness in whatever arena of male competition they choose or in which they find themselves.[30] From this group females select their mates, in important measure because they are the quarterback of the football team or some local equivalent.[31] The legendary ninety-seven-pound weakling who had sand kicked in his face on the beach bulks up his muscles and turns on his tormentor. Pow! Then he exits with the popular girl. An extreme example of this process can be found among the Yanomamo Indians of Amazonas. Forty-four percent of men over twenty-five have taken part in one of the revenge killings that occur frequently in this community. Those who have killed acquire more wives and produce more offspring than men who have not killed.[32] Far from earning the censure and punishment of the community for this behavior "boys are encouraged to be valiant and are rewarded for showing aggressive tendencies."[33] While this is an extreme case, the Yanomamo experience is consistent with the experience of other communities in which wartime violence against an enemy is converted to heroic stature among the folks back home.[34]

Male competition for the attention of females is often dramatic and clear-cut. Nonetheless, there has been a widespread failure to understand biosocial factors in both male and female behavior—behavior that is echoed in other species. A systematic and long-standing bias has caused observers to overestimate male-male competition and underestimate the female variety.[35] It neglects the role of females in establishing and sustaining hierarchies of their own and then choosing partners in that context. And then what sociologists call assortative mating takes place. Individuals tend to select partners at roughly the same level within their respective male and female hierarchies. The prom queen dates the quarterback.

It becomes easy to censure males for their boisterous behavior because it is clearly very different from that of females. For example, American sociologist Michael Kimmel in his 1996 book on maleness laments what he sees as unnecessarily assertive male behavior. Like

Marilyn French, he essentially rephrases the question posed by Henry Higgins in *My Fair Lady:* "Why can't a man be more like a woman?"[36] One answer may be that women prefer men who are not like women. And perhaps because the sentimental naïveté at the heart of Kimmel's assertion is yet another unappealing and uninvigorating example of a wan and fuzzy response of commentators on modern sexuality who fail to comprehend both its evolutionary roots and their contemporary expression.

The bellicosity of males, particularly young ones, is a burden to many communities. From adolescence on, males are overwhelmingly responsible for one of the most predictable and chronic social problems—violent crimes.[37] In some areas, as many as 25 percent of the young men are either in prison, on parole, or in some other severe relationship to the criminal justice system, *and* they are unlikely to retain nourishing links to civilian society. One heartbreaking indication of this is that while imprisoned "fewer than 5 percent of all inmates in [New York] state are ever visited by anyone."[38] Young males, especially African Americans, are also increasingly likely to be successful suicides.[39] And in arenas where it is acceptable to use force, such as in the military or police, males are decisively predominant. They are far more likely than females to be recruited or volunteer, perhaps because they are more willing and able to learn the use of force in social life, although this may be changing somewhat.

Males remain the sex most likely to engage in genocide, rape, gang warfare, plunder, terrorism, prisoner abuse, and an extensive array of other violations of military and civil decency. One female commentator noted the gross disproportion between male and female criminality and how much criminality cost the community. She suggested that all males be taxed collectively to provide reparations to the broader society for the chronic transgressions of their gendermates—another version of the Susan Brownmiller argument that all men are responsible for any rape.[40]

It is plain that men in groups can turn dangerous, reckless, and antisocial. I wrote my first book, *Men in Groups,* in part because of my alarm about this male behavior. Even well-intentioned, relatively privileged college students in fraternities may subject incoming members to hazing initiations. These have been fatal in some cases, and the source of traumatic physical and psychological damage in others. In an initiation ceremony at the heretofore all-male Citadel in South Carolina, a youngster was required to hang by his fingers from a rod with a sword held under his testicles while senior men excoriated his manhood. Another typical ritual involves extensive drinking sometimes ending in death. By contrast, sorority initiations rarely involve physical abuse but may challenge self-images and sexual integrity of young women. Pledges to one Rutgers sorority are required to strip to their underwear and parade in front of senior women who circle excess body fat with a marking pen. In another, initiation consists of describing one's first sexual intercourse. Males appear concerned with pain and stoicism, females with issues of sexuality and the body.

There is an extensive catalogue of competitive male dramas: the vision quests of Native Americans, the dueling bouts of nineteenth-century Prussian men, a young man's obligation to return with a scalp in head-hunting communities, the bungee cord initiation leaps and the public scarification of males in New Guinea, the adolescent circumcision of Xhosa males that Nelson Mandela described in his autobiography, the drug and drinking binges of urban warriors, the too-fast automobile driving of Euro-American males. These are all versions of a biologically ancient system of sorting males.[41] It is not pathological, it is the reproductive wiring underlying male adolescent truculence and bravado.

Knowing the origin of the impulse doesn't make life easier for parents, teachers, friends, law enforcers, and others who confront it when it erupts with unwanted vigor. It was not always thus. The boisterousness of young males was at the core of human male interaction when we lived in the communities that formed our nature. The ability to hunt and fight was not a contemptible sign of brute insensitivity and primitiveness. It demonstrated social contribution and potential leadership. Young men had to impress other men with their skill, dependability, and resourcefulness before they could consider attracting a mate. It was the paleolithic equivalent of holding down a good enough job to afford the diamond ring costing at least two months of income. Extensive anthropological evidence from even contemporary hunting and gathering communities shows that successful hunters are highly esteemed. They appropriate more than their share of resources and opportunities for mating. And we will return later to the enduring relationship among men, women, and resources—a direct reflection of the forces we are considering here.

Those aggressive males were our ancestors. We are legatees of the genetic system that emerged from their and their mates' collective experiences over countless generations. Their successful behavior fed our roots. Perhaps they were "demonic males," as described by Harvard's Richard Wrangham and Dale Peterson.[42] Aggression in service of the community was presumably always as highly esteemed as it is today. Self-sacrificing figures killed on the domestic front lines—police and firefighters who suffer fatality are overwhelmingly still male—are awarded prominent public honor.[43] The war hero, until now also virtually always male, earns public approval for aggressive behavior in the interest of group survival. The same behavior in peacetime could well be criminal if not pathological. What is often defined by influential commentators as a macho display of questionable practical and moral value has been the behavioral bedrock on which a great deal of male contribution to public welfare has depended. Even Islamic martyrs who strap bombs and timers onto their bodies are promised eternal heaven and their families given relatively lavish benefits.[44]

As we will see in the next chapter, males are relatively vulnerable where they start out, in the womb. But they are most at risk by where they end up—the modern world where their evolutionary preparation is no longer useful. It's a world indifferent and even hostile to many of the aggressive aptitudes and hands-on predatory enthusiasms helpful and essential to males in the past.[45] In her study of the impact of computers on work, psychologist Shoshana Zuboff of the Harvard Business School describes the modern workplace in which males may not thrive: "One's job had vanished into a two-dimensional space of abstractions, where digital symbols replace a concrete reality. . . . one operator described . . .

the new computer system. 'The difficulty . . . is not being able to touch things.'"[46] Traditional "can-do" physical practicality yields to symbolic management.

There is a durable American tradition of smoothing out the rough edges of the rugged frontiersman, for example by the school system with its female teachers or by the "refined" elements of social culture more widely.[47] In contrast to other cultures such as Native American or Papuan, in which young males are socialized into the certainly rambunctious and often bellicose community of adult males, North American boys must succeed in an educational society largely led by females and that overall appears to reward females more generously. Meanwhile, perhaps as an antidotal symbol, the Marlboro Man is the most effective advertising fantasy of North American and increasingly international consumers. He is a romantically independent cowboy. He is the paragon virile manager of animals and nature. But the Marlboro Man is just an illusion. In real life one of the longtime Marlboro Man models developed lung disease from smoking. In real life men who may admire the romantic image press buttons or deliver mail or book hotel rooms for people over the telephone or do other dreary jobs. The world of work has changed. It no longer readily rewards physical strength and endurance, which had been assets that the majority of males could exploit. This affects men without higher education most directly; they fall ever further behind in an economic contest, and their ability to provide support for children and wives declines as well.

Nevertheless, people continue to seek out those primordial experiences that formed our history. Hunting and fishing remain among the most popular of active sports enjoyed by urban and rural people; the U.S. Fish and Wildlife Service estimated that 40 percent of Americans fished, hunted, and watched wildlife in 1996.[48] When an American shop closes for the holidays, the sign often reads "Gone Fishin'." On the street floor of New York's Chelsea Hotel, which has long enjoyed an international reputation as a countercultural haven, a shop selling fishing tackle doubled its selling space in 1995 and increased it again in 1998. Even Eastern European communist potentates, claiming to be the vanguard of industrial socialist progress, maintained lavish estates where they could stalk paleolithic beasts such as wild boar. Why? The caloric and food value return is ludicrous for the extravagant expenditure of time and money. Hunting and fishing often require people to endure a level of discomfort and inconvenience far beyond anything else they encounter in ordinary lives. High-status individuals who otherwise deplore the slightest interruption of their exquisitely planned schedules will pass hours waiting to outsmart a prehistoric fish or for a skittish mammal, a deer, to come within gun-sight range. People—again predominantly males though there are many females who hunt—appear to enjoy such behavior.[49] Even if unable to take part in the life of fauna in nature, they may be willing to watch television programs on fishing, which seem wholly stupefying and improbable to nonaficionados. In mid-1998 the best-selling computer game in America—more than a half million were sold in six months—was called Deer Hunter, essentially an opportunity for an individual to mimic hunting in his or her living room.[50] Their behavior echoes urbanites who try to recapture the flora of our paleolithic roots by surrounding themselves with houseplants and gardens for reasons difficult to identify by logic alone.

But this is recreation for nearly all who do it. Nothing dire compels it. It is no longer possible for men to hunt for their daily bread and bacon in literal terms. Man the Hunter is profoundly unemployable at the job he did well for hundreds of thousands of years. His principal place of business began to close down several thousand years ago. By the time of Jesus Christ half the world's people were no longer hunters and gatherers.

That economic style was replaced first by agriculture and animal husbandry and then by industry. A minuscule number of the world's people still pursue this way of life for their main meal ticket. Guns, rods, boots, giant four-wheel-drive vehicles able to traverse deserts, and safari suits may provide frail recreational echoes of the real thing. Certainly they suggest its surprising and stubborn psychological importance, but they have little to do with real life in the communities of today.

The same is true of fighting. Fighting is almost invariably a strategy of last resort now. Prizefighters and a few athletes may be celebrated for successful violence when constrained by formal rules, but aggressive physical force is an unacceptable way to achieve social goals in the industrial world.[51]

In a typical skirmish in the gender war, boys are more likely than girls to be diagnosed as suffering from attention deficit disorder (ADD). This may simply mean they enjoy large-muscle movements and assertive actions, just as males in the other primate species predominantly do. Boys as a group appear to prefer relatively boisterous and mobile activities to the sedate and physically restricted behavior that school systems reward and to which girls seem to be more inclined. In 1998 some Atlanta schools abolished recess, claiming that no learning occurred during it. It is not unduly imaginative to see this as an anti-male choice. Psychologist Diane McGuinness found that among preschoolers, boys more than girls prefer activities that are not organized by teachers and prefer play involving construction and manipulation of objects.[52] One result is that at least three to four times as many boys than girls are essentially defined as ill because their preferred patterns of play don't fit easily into the structure of the school. Well-meaning psycho-managers then prescribe tranquilizing drugs for ADD, such as Ritalin. Countless boys are given to believe that drugs solve problems. The situation is scandalous. The use of drugs so disproportionately among boys betrays the failure of school authorities to understand sex differences in youthful behavior or even the nature of young people altogether. The only disease these boys may have is being male. They are simply trying to survive human schooling, which, unique to the primates, expects youngsters to sit still for hours at a time.

In the mainstream of industrial communities—particularly in North America where women strongly influence opinion as writers, educators, and politicians—hunting and fighting are disparaged both in practice and symbolically. The intrinsic maleness that animates this kind of forceful behavior is discouraged, even mocked. The range of moods, emotions, and attitudes associated with bellicose and predatory behavior is ridiculed with complacent confidence. The "macho man" has become a silly antiquated figure. In fact, the assertive aggression principally displayed by males has even been compared to a disease. Natalie Angier described this position with somewhat disturbing enthusiasm when she wrote a piece entitled "The Debilitating Malady Called Boyhood: Is There a Cure?"[53]

In the 1970s there was a bizarre endeavor by a respected psychologist to develop a test—the Bem Androgyny scale, named for its creator, Sandra Bem—that would reveal whether a person displayed a set of characteristics neither sharply male nor female. High scorers would be the most androgynous. They would be most desirable in a unisex world, an ideal if strange prospect for many commentators and also possibly the inevitable future in North American society.[54]

But there is no unisex. There may be un-sex or bi-sex, in themselves sexual choices. There are some few obviously anomalous individuals with both male and female forms, but these are physical abnormalities. There are two sexes and a tiny number of anomalous exceptions. The androgyny initiative was more a sign of sentimental sexual politics than of legitimate science.

Another illustration of the values of the 1970s was the gruesome case of a newborn boy whose penis was accidentally removed during surgery. A decision was made in accord with a broad belief that sex roles were culturally arbitrary: His genitalia were surgically reconstructed in female form, and he was raised as female. The case was reported by John Money of Johns Hopkins University, who was associated with that university's sex-reassignment clinic. For a time this facility was celebrated for its program of coupling psychiatric counseling with surgical and hormonal intervention to produce men of women and vice versa. The process was controversial and was eventually discontinued. As one physician said shortly before he joined the university to chair a department, "They're cutting guys' cocks off down there." At the time, Money's confident evaluation was that "the operation was a success." He pronounced the child a content and effective girl, and concluded therefore that sex roles were extraordinarily manipulable. In 1997, Milton Diamond of the University of Hawaii and Keith Sigmundson of the Ministry of Health in British Columbia tracked down the boy. They learned that he had had a dispiriting childhood, and only after an equally turbulent early adolescence did his parents finally tell him his own story. At fourteen he renounced his femaleness, later married a woman with children, and is no longer a billboard for sexual flexibility.[55] The operation was not a success, nor was the fatuous theory that it helped support.[56] It was not even minimally professional and competent to define his sexuality before the adolescent period when reproductive sexuality comes into its own. The patient was more content as a mutilated male than a confected female. Sex is real, not a fashioned statement.

Half the Sexes Are Below Average

A broad assertion made by feminists and many social scientists in the 1970s was that traditional maleness is faintly or even fully absurd and that the female way is the correct way. Such thinking has created a paradoxical perception: Sex differences are essentially nonexistent or unimportant, yet females are superior. These feminist thinkers do not believe in the biology of behavior or sexuality, yet they describe a gender gap between men and women that rests on assumptions about a biology-style hierarchy of human values. Therefore, even if sexuality is a social construction, males are nevertheless vaguely but rather elementally inferior. Why not have your cake and eat it, too?

Carol Gilligan of the Harvard Graduate School of Education produced *In a Different Voice* in 1982, an influential book that analyzed how girls came to moral judgments. She concluded that they did this not only differently from boys but more fairly, with more caring and accommodation.[57] In this tradition of thought, the reason boys and girls come to moral judgments differently lies in their different upbringings. Even though the difference is more or less universal, it is not at all connected to the human genotype. In any event, Gilligan became disproportionately celebrated for this hypothesis, for yet more Christian Science about human behavior. She was appointed to the first chair of Gender Studies at Harvard in 1997. While her research has been capably conducted, its theoretical context has more to do with transcendentalism than biology, presumably a flaw in an investigation of a biological category, sex. Nevertheless, the hypothesis of female superiority in moral negotiation remains, although it is also disputed by some other feminists such as Katha Pollitt who regard Gilligan's position and those similar to it as yet another set of gratuitous stereotypes about maternalesque femininity.[58]

Gilligan may well be correct in her culturally satisfying conclusion that females are better at negotiation than males. They may negotiate better with females than males do with males. But this embraces a moral value that accommodation is better than assertion. It implies that a network of sensitive conversation is preferable to a hierarchy of clear authority, which may well be correct, certainly for females and possibly for communities at large. But it is a preference, not a fact. The attack on hierarchical structure has been extended into business and government communities and even into the military. Countless seminars are supported by the attendance at considerable cost of organizations attracted by the prospect of reducing their hierarchies. If females operate differently from men in organizations, then it is plausible that as more women gain seniority and power in ongoing systems, they will leave a new mark on organizational character, often in the context of programs advocating "diversity," especially in the United States where the population is unusually heterogeneous to begin with.[59] Perhaps they will help provide a more convenient and prudent way to get along with people in a world with many people, many powerful weapons, and effective ways to mass-communicate hatred. For example, Francis Fukuyama has noted that "developed democracies . . . tend to be more feminized than authoritarian states . . . [and he wonders if] the historically unprecedented shift in the sexual basis of politics should lead to a change in international relations."[60]

Are women willing and able to create and sustain the large-scale cooperative systems which are the basis for both peaceful and bellicose communities? Is there evidence that they have done so in the past? Are they interested in doing so? It remains to be seen. It is not clear that it is possible to evaluate empirically the styles of work that suit human organizations better. Fashions in management theory are famously evanescent, and antipathy to hierarchy happens to accord with current political piety. It is also, if nothing else, ironic that in the very period of industrial history in which more feminine assumptions of cooperative group behavior are introduced in some organizations, countless other people are losing their jobs in the name of implacable international competition. While more sensibility and feelings may circulate within organizations, at the same time there is a worldwide process of consolidating and reshaping businesses, a process almost exclusively driven by predatory male executives and owners.

There is an additional trend as well: Female-owned small businesses are unusually important in economic growth and have been responsible for much vitality in the American economy.[61] In 1996 women established one-third of new businesses and up to 45 percent of service business in the United Kingdom.[62] Thirty-seven percent of all businesses in the New York City area are women-owned, a 68 percent increase in ten years.[63] In a study in New Jersey, Marilyn Frazier Pollack has outlined the characteristic strategies of successful female entrepreneurs and how they differ from those pursued by comparable male entrepreneurs.[64] For example, Pollack found that females are much less inclined to take perilous financial risks, whereas a male may gamble with loans from a number of sources. Women were less likely than males to fail, even if they were also less likely to expand their businesses dramatically. In addition, they tailored their businesses to their personal lives. A woman who established a dance studio borrowed to open another but rejected her banker's offer of capital for a third. The extra travel would have made it impossible for her to deliver and collect her children from their schooling and other activities.

University of Montreal psychologist Ethel Roskies questioned 1,123 senior professional women and found that those who were married with children scored highest in personal psychological satisfaction; married professionals scored next highest, and unmarried childless women the lowest.[65] There may be an instructive lesson here about the links between private and public life.

Socio-Sex-Change

What are men and women led to think of each other as a result of the collective notions of their society? How does this affect what they do and how they feel? What is good behavior and bad behavior, male behavior and female? For hundreds of years specifically male virtues—heroism, athleticism, stoicism, clearheadedness, forcefullness, nonemotionality, and the like—were supported and celebrated. Females were supposed to be pettily irrational, sentimental, loyal, swept by tides of personal emotion but not by obligations of public effort. A woman's place was in the home, with the children. She was to be seen, decoratively if possible, and if heard, charmingly, without contention.

Whatever people do and think in private life, public perceptions have turned such notions into risible antiques. There has been a role reversal. Not only are there more women than ever serving as heads of households, but more females than ever in industrial history have mastered the intricacies of occupational life. American women own some eight million businesses and employ one out of four American workers.[66] Nearly all women participate in the labor force. Nearly all want to do so or have little choice about the matter, though the largest rise in wives who work is at the higher end of the income pyramid. While in 1940 in 66.7 percent of families only husbands worked, by 1996 it was only 16.7 percent.[67] Marilyn Pollock found that among the most successful women entrepreneurs she studied, a disproportionate number were married to men who supplied an economic and social base from which they prospered and then became independent—a hardly surprising revisit of the theme "They that have, get." We have also seen that they were more cautious than their male counterparts and made good use of whatever opportunities they faced.

These women are also better informed than ever. Along with the occasionally aggressive regulatory agencies of government, the news media demystify much of what goes on behind the scenes among the powerful elite. This was once defined as beyond the comprehension of women, but now more women are able to see for themselves what is going on. What happens in the boardroom is reported regularly. Journalists, both male and female, describe to a new audience and in a new context the process of businesses and governments and the social lives of their managers. There are countless hours of business news on television. Many women are themselves equal players in the boardrooms and favored guests in executive dining rooms. They are also increasingly in governmental cabinets (a third of cabinet ministers in Scandinavia are women), gaining representation in national and especially regional governments, in stock and commodities markets, and in the potent government and private agencies that supervise economic forces.[68] Even what happens in the men's locker room, so important in male mythology, have been revealed to women. Female journalists gained access to professional locker rooms in the United States when the courts supported the claim that otherwise women could not compete with men in sports journalism.[69] At the Kellogg School of Management at Northwestern University female students take golf lessons in preparation for the business benefits of social interaction in that privileged realm.[70] Overall, what was once a kind of informal but coherent male secret society, called the power elite, has been lit and ventilated.

Nevertheless, there remains in public discourse a formalized disdain among women for men. Women who hazard support for male values, such as Camille Paglia, are widely disdained by feminist writers. The antipathy is fascinating. Why does it persist? What does it signify? Does it mean more than fashionable and acceptable social criticism? Is there a more consequential underlying angst or sense of grievance? Is it a collective response to private experience? Are women disappointed with the men around them? Do they find full-time jobs enervating, inadequately paid, and uninteresting? Is the world still too male for their tastes? Are there too many women competing in a newly integrated arena? Is there simply neither time nor energy to arrange lives both emotionally full and professionally successful?

Whatever its origin there remains an intricate barrier of opinion and feeling between men and women. It has been widely articulated for nearly forty years. Now it is part of the symbolic environment that the majority of the population inhabits. It constitutes one of the modern points of departure in any relationship between men and women. It is central to politics and the intimacies of private lives.

There have always been sexual conflicts in which the males have largely been favored, certainly in the heyday of industrial manufacturing, but now the negotiation is close to equal. The movement of advantage is to the female side.

Reproductive Bedrock

The new rules of engagement in the contest between men and women reveal primordial sexual differences of striking significance. Something emerges rather like the often noisy hostile duets between males and females of other species. For centuries these bedrock differences were obscured and mitigated. They were forcefully controlled by the power of traditional systems of law and kinship. They were usually buttressed by the dominance exercised by religious leaders over people kept unaware of competing secular theories. It was also absolutely vital since human sexual relations were poorly contracepted, that they be nearly always under the scrutiny of those with well-defined interests in the reproductive lives of their children. The Montagues and Capulets tried to do what was necessary to control their youngsters, who had few places to hide—no co-ed dorms, no Pontiac backseats, no interstate motels.

Now men and women are on their own. They have unprecedented sexual freedom and liberty from family ties. More people live alone, outside the parental home. For example, in the United Kingdom during one decade the age of marriage for men increased from 26 to 28.9 years and for women from 23.8 to 26.8 years. The average age of bridegrooms was 33.1, and of brides 30.7. These are historically unprecedented numbers. People in industrial societies have fewer children, more sexual partners, and fewer obligations. They can do more of what they want to do more of the time. They have been emancipated—but, ironically, less from human nature than from many of the rigorous social systems developed to subdue that nature. What is decried by some as a decline of family values is much more fundamental and elaborate than that; nothing less than Wordsworth's "domestic affections of the Lower Orders" are involved. The situation is not the result of simple moral incompetence and irresponsibility. It grows out of economic arrangements that depend on independent contractors, not groups of people in families. People on their own may have little choice but to pursue solitary agendas. They have neither the restraints nor the protections of traditional family arrangements.

Unexpectedly, this has permitted a classical biological conflict between males and females, who have different reproductive strategies to start with, to boil to the surface in a new and disturbing way. Natural forces come to the fore in the absence of mediating social groups. The bedrock matter, reproduction, has to be negotiated by individuals facing each other perched on their own limb. Much of the conversation between the leading man and leading woman reveals consternation and hostility.

If Food Be the Music of Love . . . Dinner for One

One indication of the decline in cooperation and dependence between men and women revolves around a simple and elemental matter: sharing food. Exchange between people reveals the extent of their interest in each other and their solidarity. One of the most obvious but central items of exchange is food. As mammals we are committed to giving, consuming, and sharing food. Among the primates, humans are exceptional in that we share the acquiring and eating of nearly everything we eat; the other primates by and large fetch their own. And we boast a remarkable interest in the varieties of food and skill in preparing it. We also enjoy providing food to others, even to animals. Just glance at the aisles of pet food in supermarkets; they are almost as extensive as biscuits for people.

There is a historical pattern to the division of labor by sex surrounding food. Broadly, males hunted animals, while females gathered fruits and vegetables and later probably innovated their cultivation. Obviously there was frequent and considerable overlap, but nonetheless a profile of division of food labor can be found consistently through the human species, though decreasingly so in industrial communities.

The significant factor is that differences between males and female were turned into interdependence. Food rituals have supported the basic flow of human survival, often in families—a man and a woman and a child or two. This is still the smallest effective group found in a considerable array of modern hunter-gatherers. An adult male and female Eskimo, for example, comprised a complete survival unit able to create, find, store, cook, and construct whatever they needed. It is small wonder, therefore, that a contemporary sign of prosperity is the quiet romantic dinner in front of the fireplace or in a dim restaurant, suggesting a cave, with generous flowers and perhaps birds singing outside on a terrace. The more luxurious the meal, the more expensive and the longer it takes. The most indulgent meals are often enjoyed by the same people who otherwise are pressed for time and irritated by its passage.

There are social connections we seem to require. The principal social setting for good emotional nutrition has traditionally been the intimate family, certainly with a partner. We inhale companionship like air, and companionship is also especially idealized in gathering and consuming food.

Now for the first time in American history half of all meals are purchased in the town with money, not provided at home for love or at least obligation. American couples in the 1990s spend less time and eat fewer meals together than ever before. The ideal food preparation time has been reckoned at only fifteen minutes; 75 percent of Americans do not have dinner plans at 4 P.M, and only 16 percent of meals taken at home are actually cooked there.[71] One-quarter of dual-income couples work on different shifts.[72] Of course love is likely to be the principal component for courting couples twining fingers over tables set with romantic dinner candles. Familial warmth fuels the satisfaction of the child who is presented a chocolate sundae after dinner. Visiting cousins are taken with pride and a wad of cash to the current, most famous provider of *cassoulet*. But in the public place each diner makes a precise and special request. He receives a separate portion, as if generated by a private bank account. He protects it with knife and fork, and a sense that it is his alone. If shared at all, it is accompanied by some clumsy negotiation and a lingering sense of the violation of manners and embarrassment as tastes of meals cross the table. Only a few restaurants serve family style, and they have to inform their diners first.

Eating out is a very specialized and rather exotic system. It is a step along the way to the decisively individualist modern style. It indicates a new brand of privacy within the family group. Moreover, there has been additional sharpening of lines of the different preferences among diners, even within the same family. Individual, not family, food choices have been made possible by newly available facilities such as microwaves, frozen foods, and whole prepared meals. A family may share a family meal but not family food. It has become increasingly acceptable in North America to announce food allergies, taboos, and sharp preferences such as vegetarianism, high fiber, no garlic, low salt, and the like. People invited to dinner feel free to produce their list of forbidden foods. Their hosts must calibrate the dangers and produce a meal that will be immune from their guests' political criticisms on the way home. In the United States, food is often defined in nutritional, not pleasurable terms. It is a form of medicine when benign but a form of poison when it contains cholesterol, sugar, or fat. Consumers await the latest nutritional verity they must follow as if they were pilgrims to Delphi. The menu is a source of tension, not enjoyment. By contrast, in the more easygoing and companionable food culture of Italy, children and adults alike are expected to eat what they enjoy, and there are always ample choices on the table. Natural preferences can be expressed with generosity, not strain.[73]

So even when North American family members eat together, they may eat different foods. They may eat at different times because of the demands of work and personal agendas. The connections among affection, food, and interdependence diminish. It becomes a discrete occasion for special holidays and personal celebrations. A quotidian matter to the food-sharing primate becomes an exceptional outing, underlined on the daily entry of the little black book.

Tectonic Sexes

The male and female sexes in industrial societies are slowly but inexorably moving apart. They share different ideas about their own sex and the opposite one. They prepare and share food together less often. Therefore, they are less interdependent. They share less time around an emotionally rich and basic process. People now are actors writing their own lines in their own script, in a play directed by forces larger than they can master. The shift is only subtly apparent to participants who do not see the larger picture because they are too busy adjusting their lives to the new conditions they now face.

They are like threatened trees relentlessly besieged by a new ecology of the forest that they do not perceive or understand.

CHAPTER FOUR

Guys and the Theory
of Relatives

E INSTEIN'S THEORY of relativity showed a startling and unexpected relationship among energy, physical mass, and the speed of light. Old realities acquired a new meaning and proportion. Nature became at once more complicated and more understandable. A cavalcade of scientific findings and their consequences followed, including those about atomic power.

The biological sciences have produced nothing so crisp, decisive, and literally explosive, but important theories have begun to reveal unexpected regularities in the relationships between individuals. The outlines begin to emerge of an unexpected social order based on family affiliation in what may seem on the surface rather disorganized social activity among mammals. For example, it turns out that bats through some mysterious mechanism know who their genetic brothers and sisters are amid the milling crowd of the lightless cave. On some equally obscure basis, tadpoles distinguish between relatives and non-kin. Scientists who observe primate behavior over several generations now know how the lives of youngsters are affected by the lineage and behavior of their mothers. They perceive that there is a fine balance between an individual monkey or ape's assertiveness and its acceptability to the group. Animals once thought of as incapable of complex and positive social behavior sustain genealogies as elaborate as royal families. Studies of creatures in their native habitats indicate that though we don't know how they know to do it, animals favor relatives over nonrelatives when there are choices to be made. Also, they usually do so as if they know the levels of genetic relatedness that the scientists have discovered. Patterns of animal life become clear that had been as unapparent to social science as the details of atomic fission were before modern physics. And these patterns are sufficiently similar to basic notions of human kinship that the term "the theory of relatives" is accurate. Animal social nature reveals an elaborate balance between kinship links and the demands of the environment. Animals clearly display a kind of morality insofar as their selfish behavior is consistently modified by their obligations to their families and even extended kin.[1]

But the order of nature is not only benign. While there is obvious cooperation between partners and relatives, there is also unexpectedly intricate and implacable conflict in their natures. The remarkable research of Robin Baker and Mark Bellis of the University of Manchester found that men produce not only sperm that seek to impregnate a woman but also "warrior spermatozoa" that chemically attack any spermatozoa from other men that may linger in a woman's body and potentially impregnate her. Would anyone have predicted sperm wars and a division of sperm labor? Harvard's David Haig has described how a fetus may endanger or discomfit a mother by favoring its own health at her expense.[2] Thus morning sickness and nausea are the fetus's way of protecting itself from potentially perturbing or harmful food during the weeks when its basic skeletal formation is under way. And during mate selection it is clear that females may assess the reliability and health of males as potential partners with far greater severity than males can ever know or match in their own courtships. For example, the plain-Jane peahen assesses a potential mate's health and sturdiness by the luxury of his peacock fan. One result is that males in various species, evidently including our own, are impelled to strenuous and often perilous competition for a place in the reproductive sun. They know not why they do what they do, but they do it nonetheless.

Each sex has its own agenda whether or not it knows what it is. Creatures such as birds, bees, and buffalo conduct their reproductive activities efficiently, as if they knew contemporary genetics.[3] Among humans, Baker and Bellis have found that women with regular partners had sex rather evenly over the menstrual cycle, but when they sought additional partners, they were especially vigorous when they were most fertile.[4] Presumably this extends their portfolio of reproductive and genetic options. The women may well be unaware of the underlying reason they do what they do, but their actions would make astute or at least comprehensible genetic sense to a biologist observer.

Here we are in the realm of what Freud described as the "unconscious." "Unconsciously" is how fundamental encoded biology impacts our ongoing behavior. Freud forged a link between the inventory of feelings and behavior that humans inherit through evolution and our daily behavior in the here and now. Call it the id or the unconscious. Call it human nature. It is our legacy whether or not we want it, just as our bodies are echoed in the prehominid bones uncovered in Ethiopia and East Africa. And since we are social animals, the behavioral equivalent of bones is in our history, too.

In the search for our most important roots—the roots of behavior— something new has developed. The battle of the sexes has always provoked dramatists, malcontents, comedians, theologians, and sofa philosophers. Now it is also the territory of scientists exploring unexpected sexual regularities, and they have discovered that *there really is a battle of the sexes!* The next scientific decades will witness the emergence of a new view of sexuality as an intricately charged encounter, more raucous and demanding than imagined, more dramatic than

Samson and Delilah's negotiation, more discordant than Adam and Eve's morbid and peculiar rhapsody.

It begins early, this unannounced contest between boys and girls. From the moment of conception onward, males are the more fragile and vulnerable of the two sexes. Male fetuses die more readily than female. So do male newborns. So do male infants. So do male adolescents. So do male adults. So do old men.[5] A Royal Commission in 1996 found that the Indian women of Canada lived 7.1 years longer than their men. Forceps and other medical developments, such as the simple notion of cleanliness, have eliminated the greatest natural peril that women faced—childbirth, evolution's bottleneck. In poor environments they perish still, but there is an expansion of the norms of obstetric health. One result is the growing productive and reproductive robustness of women in the industrial part of the planet.[6]

There could not be a more basic reason for the long-run difference in mortality in non-smoking men and women than women's reproductive robustness. The story of Genesis had its sexual priority the wrong way around. Adam should have been grafted from Eve's body because the master model of our species is female. Females are more robust because, as in many mammals, the core physiological system is female. The male is a kind of add-on. Maleness is an extra ingredient to the underlying mammalian process. Creating a male places special demands on pregnant females. It requires that a pregnant woman produce decisively more male hormone than usual, at precisely the right time. She has to undergo a form of temporary endocrinological sex change.

Things can go wrong and do. Pediatric history is replete with the evidence of what can go right and go wrong in the intricate cookery of pregnancy. We know that alcohol, nicotine, and other drugs—to say nothing of toxic environments—affect the fetus, both male and female. Pregnant females who use legally prescribed sedatives while carrying males produce less testosterone when it is needed most. This has been shown for monkeys, mice, and rabbits. Using among other data the excellent pharmacological records of Denmark, June Rheinisch and Stephanie Sanders of the Kinsey Institute revealed that the finding also applies to humans. The sons of women using barbiturates are much more likely to be "feminized," to display bodies and behavior more typically female than male.[7] Millions of American mothers of boys, an estimated eleven million in the 1950s and 60s, used barbiturates, and millions still do. A compelling thought is that this may have something to do with the evident increase in the number, or at least prominence, of male homosexuals. Myriad factors determine a person's sexual orientation, of course, but it is provocative that just as nicotine, illegal drugs, and alcohol have known effects on growth in general, medicinal sedative drugs may have an effect, too, such as on a pregnant woman's ability to produce testosterone in her body, which affects male offspring. There is a grim precedent for this specificity on a particular sex: Of the children whose mothers used DES medication to facilitate pregnancy, only female offspring were significantly affected.

The Science of Inner Affection

Now we explore the underlying social biology of sex and reproduction.

Isaac Newton defined vertical gravity in physical life. He showed how objects were attracted to each other. The largest object, the Earth, attracted all the other things. So they fell down.

Charles Darwin discovered the horizontal gravity between living creatures in social life. He identified forces that drew creatures to one another and explained why they loved, fought, competed, rested, and groomed. The two main processes were sexual selection and natural selection. The first explained how and why animals choose mates. The second explained how these choices end up forming species, including our own.

Darwin discovered horizontal gravity. It is the basis of the theory of relatives, which essentially demonstrates that while animals, including us, act in their own interest, they do so to support, protect, and help prosper genetic kin. With often mute stubbornness they contrive to have their familial genes survive. Darwin revealed how and why reproduction is central to sentient life. Zoos in which the tenants reproduce are held in high regard by other zookeepers, who appreciate the challenge of recreating natural environments. If the conditions in which the animals live are benign and resemble native habitats, they are likely to breed. Now let's ask: Where are the benign human zoos? What conditions echo the environments in which our species prospered for millennia? What modern conditions enhance or inhibit the horizontal gravity between men and women, fathers and mothers, parents and children?

People readily have sex. It is phenomenally pleasurable and absorbing. On occasion people may engage in sex specifically to have children, but mostly they have it just to have it, as often as they can.

Bringing the lead players together is easy. Keeping them apart is usually the challenge. It is another matter to induce partners to stay together, with each other and with their children.

A planetary snapshot of the contemporary human zoo would reveal a growing number of children maturing in relatively small groups. These groups often lack an adult male participant. In the United States, two out of every five children do not live with their biological fathers. One of the primary reasons for this is the high divorce rate. In the United States the rate has grown from 5 percent of all marriages in 1867 to more than 50 percent in the early 1990s.[8] The trend has apparently peaked in the United States and is now lower, at about 43 percent, but it continues to climb in other countries.[9] Even in relatively conservative Japan, where the rate remains in single digits, current trends suggest a 20 percent divorce rate is in the cards, and the legalization of the pill may accelerate the rise. The divorce rate in China doubled between 1982 and 1992.[10] In Catholic France there is a divorce rate of about 50 percent in Paris and 20 percent elsewhere in the country—overall about 33 percent.[11] Fewer French people are marrying than at any time this century, and the average age of first marriage continues to rise, to twenty-seven for women and twenty-nine for men. Furthermore, among those who do marry, "the deliberate rejection of parenthood did not become a visible alternative until the early 1970s," which of course has had its own impact on birthrates.[12]

If we humans have to depend on a social invention for social stability, then a clear and quite desperate problem stares us in the face. Our biology is sufficiently hard-wired to propel people into love affairs but is far less effective at keeping them there. Maintaining a relationship is far less dramatic and exciting than the tournament of courtship, and it requires deliberate and thoughtful decisions. Social choices become all the more important.

Naturally Familiar

The family in industrial communities has changed its form. Scientific understanding of its evolution has changed as well. Stable principles about the nature of our social nature have emerged from what was once thought to be a "buzzing blooming confusion," as William James called it. Hobbes asserted that every man's hand is raised against others, that nature's principal weapons are teeth and claws, both red with blood. This is not true as far as kinship is concerned. I've noted that tadpoles can distinguish their siblings from the crowd of strangers and that bats can separate those in the cave into kin and non-kin. Birth creates a web of interaction that explains how and why the world is not just a random place, why people have certain affections and disaffections, and why some behavior is easy to embrace and others difficult.

The broad question, as Robin Fox put it, is "the question of social order. And the response is that of Aristotle rather than Hobbes: that the nature of order is part of the order of nature. It is not that man is as culture does, but that culture does as man is. Thus perhaps we can return, by the biosocial route, to . . . the question . . . what is man?"[13]

One answer to the question is informed by the theory of relatives, which will probably be as important for social science as Einstein's theory of relativity was for physics. It has helped scientists uncover a regularity in the social world unknown before.

This is not reductionist or an oversimplification. It is the opposite. It complicates the picture. It adds elegance and depth to it. The theory of relatives is now essential to understanding human affections. It casts a new light on seemingly unrelated and puzzling features of families and love, and not only love but also antipathies. Yes, there is often trouble in paradise—family trouble—but now it is better understood why parents and offspring can find themselves in conflict. *It makes good genetic sense.* The theory of relatives uncovers constructive sources of common human antagonisms. For example, "sibling rivalry" is an old banality, but there are new ways to understand its functions.

These may be positive and troubling at once. When three downy white egret chicks are hatched in the nest, the two eldest frequently attack and kill the youngest. Mother and father stand by idly. Why? The elder chicks receive a larger dose of testosterone from the parents, which helps them survive to maturity. Egret environments usually provide fare for two chicks but not three. There is an order to survival and even in the disorder of struggle. In both, the invisible hand is finally revealed of the economy of nature and of genetic persistence.[14]

There are other surprises. Uncles and aunts may be celibate but genetically fruitful in their own fashion through their nieces and nephews. A provocative and responsible case, especially from Deborah Blum, has been made for the genetic value of homosexuality.[15] There are even new ideas about the broad impact of incest. Hard, good answers to age-old questions.

The underlying reality is that human beings boast a general profile of social behavior. We learned from Noam Chomsky and others that while a host of different languages exists, there is only one basic structure of language.[16] Since it is too complicated for children to learn, the inevitable conclusion is that much of it is in our wiring to begin with. There are firm biological bases to a program for learning. As Mark Flinn of the University of Missouri has asserted in a persuasive essay, "Human learning mechanisms are products of natural selection, and hence process information in ways that reflect evolutionary design. . . . *The central nervous system and its learning capabilities are unlikely to acquire . . . cultural traits randomly with respect to natural selection.*"[17] There is an evolutionary design for language. There is an evolutionary design for learning languages. And there is an evolutionary design for learning different languages. But language is a relatively recent human acquisition.

There is also an older evolutionary design for more fundamental kinds of behavior that are linked to survival and prosperity; that design has established what is easy to learn and what an individual wants to learn.[18]

There is generic verbal communication, and there are dialects. The same pattern holds true for behavior. There will be differences in social patterns from community to community, just as there are in languages, but there is basic human language and basic human behavior—what Robin Fox and I called the "behavioral biogrammar."[19] It is not rewarding to pay too much attention to wildly different languages, such as Chinese and French, without being aware of what two such different codes share. Otherwise we would never have gained any insight into human linguistics. Robin Fox warns us against "ethnographic dazzle," which may blind us to general human similarities and hence restrict our capacity to identify and understand human nature.[20]

Social changes may occur, of course, but familiar patterns often reemerge. For example, people used to remarry mainly after widowhood. Now they do so overwhelmingly after divorce: About two-thirds of divorced women remarry, and three-quarters of men.[21] Extended connec-tions in modern families are created, often in patterns still only barely understood. In southern California, where divorce is common, children refer to "steps" and "biologicals" as if they were describing the flavor of adults. Single parents offer one set of kinship relations. The children of homosexual couples must confront yet another array of category prob-lems and social obligations. Do we know the effect of all this on children? Where do grandparents sit at the table of this new family at Sunday lunch? What about legal responsibility and obligations? Can children divorce their parents? Can the product of fetal development be sold by contract and by law?

Alimony, palimony, patrimony, matrimony, parsimony—these are words in a newly tumultuous story. It involves people—us—with an old hominid life cycle, emigrants from another era of human history. We still have habits from "the old country." Consider breathing. No one will deny that breathing is biological, vital, one of those taken-for-granted matters. But breathing what? Air? Just air? What about polluted air? Is that the same as fresh? No. We discovered a major issue about the relationship between industrial air and healthy breathing. Between nature and human nature.

Is there also a comparable issue in the relationship between industrial social systems and parents and children? It took decades before scientists demonstrated that smelly air was not only unpleasant but unhealthy. It took more decades before political action was taken to protect our huge inventory of air.

We have to ask: Is there behavioral pollution, too?

Our own cognitive evolution equipped humans to deal with ever more complicated projects, many of which we brilliantly created our-selves. But it appears that competence for the simpler tasks of life has hardly been enhanced. Rocket scientists cannot please their spouses. Captains of global industry cannot make it to the school play of their only child. Leaders of potent states jeopardize the imperium in the warm beds of inappropriate partners. Has our species been orphaned by Mother Nature?

The Inheritance of Orphans

Our species inheritance confers social skills and emotional enthusiasms for family and love life. My effort here is to identify these and then consider how people, and men in particular, have adapted to the new conditions. We can gain perspective even from physical space. The buildings and houses we choose to construct and the form in which we do so may make affectionate communities difficult to accomplish and enjoy. Common sense often tells us why. It is obvious why a species that evolved to live in rural environments finds urban parks more peaceable than cement. We know that people's blood pressure reduces in natural settings. Patients in hospital rooms overlooking meadows recover faster than those peering at brick.[22] People like to live next to parks or make their own private parks, called gardens. Gardening, now a popular

American recreation, is a broad social movement to recapture sensual elements of our Paleolithic past. Paper-white lilies smell better than burning rubber tires. There is no perfume called "The Subway at Rush Hour."[23]

Hundreds of thousands of years of evolution conferred on us a spectacular bag of tricks. We were able to learn how to deal with virtually every known climate and environment from the Amazon to the Arctic to the backyard garden we create for ourselves. We interact skillfully with most of flora and fauna. We understand them instinctively, as we do people in life, and intricately with the help of exquisite science. We can communicate, contend, and conjoin with ever larger, ever more complex human groups. We're at the top of the food and wine chain.

But what is the order of that chain? What are the links? Obviously, human social behavior is not random. It is not subject only to the rules of chaos. The new social patterns we assume as we nestle into our economic system are only decades old. The emotions surrounding the process— guilt, love, loyalty, rebellion, and so on—still come to the fore. They are Paleolithic moods probably at least a million years old.[24] Psychiatrists Michael McGuire and Alfonso Troisi provide a thorough exploration of the origins of moods and their contemporary expression in their work *Darwinian Psychiatry*.[25]

Sociologists talk about "cultural lag" when one social pattern changes more quickly than another. Here we have to consider a more serious lag between the biological nature we inherited and the social community we created. An important symptom of it is the discontinuity between the passions that surround family experience and the difficulty of establishing acceptable rules about it. Helen Fisher has described foxes as an example of a reproductive system operating according to a rather clear plan.[26] Laid down genetically, it is supported by social and political pressures among foxes. Foxes court and pair off. They reproduce and raise their pups. Males and females cooperate. The alliance lasts for an annual season. Then the pups go off on their own to begin another episode of the same play. There appear to be no fox-priests, fox-psychiatrists, or fox—talk show hosts inviting other foxes to describe their unhappy families or the abuse they suffered in preschool or in the sandbox or in hailstorms. Even if foxes could read, it's unlikely there would be a Benjamin Spock manual of procedure on baby fox care to which they could turn when youngsters woke in the lair and vocalized irritatingly. They wouldn't need that well-worn paperback about raising baby foxes. Foxes' family work gets done. Their lives flow. There is a clear nature to their social forms. It enables them to adapt to their social and economic environments when these change. They have something strong going for them. In significant measure it is the result of what went well for them in the past. Their genes are a literal inheritance, in the positive way people use the word when they think of inheriting money or land. The genes locate, abet, and define the life cycle and social life. And new information about these genes is endlessly forthcoming. For example, in the *New York Times* of September 29, 1998, Nicholas Wade reports an utterly stunning finding in rodents by English geneticists who have located a specific gene—the Mest gene, as it is called—provided by fathers, which imprints on the mothers of their offspring to turn on their maternal instincts. Males lacking the gene will impregnate females who will not perform even rudimentary mothering. The gene is also carried by humans who share many traits in this context, and the finding has potentially dazzling implications for the overall role of males in family life beyond the act of fertilization.

Human beings boast remarkable skill and resources but appear to have a far harder time than foxes in accomplishing the same objectives: get born, love parents, play, grow up, find a partner, enjoy fertility, raise young, grow old gracefully, pop off. Most people are able to do so, but sufficient numbers cannot—or do so with difficulty and anguish. It is therefore prudent to ask: Have we too many Paleolithic emotional legacies? Are we equipped with such a vast inventory of capacities that we are self-flummoxed? Do we have too many enthusiasms and too few usable tools to pursue them decently? Are we driven by emotions but without a map? Is our genetic inheritance inadequate to acquire affection and commitment?

Mechanisms of Affection

Infants and children are the most vulnerable members of the human group, but they enter the world with a tool kit. Anthropologist Phyllis Dolhinow of Berkeley has shown how effectively primate youngsters wield "the tactics of immaturity" to secure what they need from adults.[27] Human infants and children use techniques ranging from tears to smiles to tantrums to kisses in order to guide and charm adults to perform the services and provide the setting within which healthy growth can occur. Moreover, now we know these strategems can be physiological as well as social. For example, the new mother is suffused with hormonal stimuli for affectionate caretaking and breast-feeding. These are real, tangible, measurable bodily substances, such as vasopressin and oxytocin. They demonstrate the underlying genetic readiness for parenthood and family life encoded in the body itself.[28] More of such physiological bases of psychological and social experience will almost certainly be found.

Except through personal experience and commonsense observation, this was unknown not long ago. In an unexpected and rather striking way, the social setting of family life stimulates internal secretions programmed by nature. When an individual is in a frightening, dangerous, or tense situation, adrenaline flows—a chemical boost that helps survival. When a baby or a lover requires affection, other substances support its provision.

Destiny becomes anatomy. The mind-body divide is bridged by social behavior. Culture creates nature. Physiology requires appropriate social experience and settings in order to emerge.[29] The skin is not just a container but a means of transmission.

What mind-body problem?

The hard-wiring is in the body, but it needs the software—the appropriate behavior and situations—to animate the program. Here is total connection between social life and internal physiology. It also raises the question: Do factors in the social cultural world prevent the emergence of substances so that we cannot do what otherwise comes naturally?

The findings go still further. People who become parents are physiologically changed by the experience and by the inner physiological adjustments that accompany it. Perhaps it is analogous to the loss of virginity. Is one hormonal result of parenthood an increased tolerance of and affection for children? Is this why Martin Daly and Margo Wilson's study of family crime in Canada and the United States revealed that stepchildren are one hundred times more likely to be abused and eleven times more likely to be murdered by stepparents than biological parents?[30] Or does stepparenthood stimulate oxytocin and vasopressin, too? Are stepparents who are also parents less likely to abuse children simply because they have themselves been changed at the level of the cell? Studies of systematic infanticide among other animals, such as langur monkeys, wild horses, and rodents, suggest that stepchildhood may well be a broadly hazardous status, overwhelmingly when the stepparent is a male.[31] Suddenly the dark side of the theory of relatives becomes all too real.

While it can't be mapped with certainty, there is clearly a relationship between inner and outer experience. Parenthood is a substantial social role. It is difficult to find parents who have not experienced a personal sea change as a result of it. This is hardly surprising given the intense physicality of childbearing and rearing. When traditional anthropologists visited remote communities, one of the first categories in their checklist of information about grown women was whether they were *parrus* or *nulliparrus*—whether or not they had borne a child.

The question haunts the mind. Is there a different politics and a different tone in a community in which an increasing proportion of people have never been parents? Does this affect attitudes about such matters as school taxes or taxes in general? How are political pressures for tax cuts related to fertility? Are communities with low birth rates in some tangible, physical way different from more fertile ones? Do low birthrates in industrial countries dispose them to reduce taxes because there is less of a feeling of interdependence among their members? Is one reason for strong pressure for reduced government spending the unusually low birthrates of industrial communities? As one congressman from Wisconsin has asserted, "Single people and couples without children should not bear the brunt of the cost of children."[32] Do employers unfairly penalize childless workers when they provide flexible arrangements for parents and require less inconvenient business travel from them than for non-parents whose lives seem relatively free and clear?[33]

The children themselves play a part and are not merely onlookers. Do they secrete something comparable to oxytocin that induces them to be generally cooperative and dependent for a period of life? Perhaps kids secrete a "for heaven's sake smile sweetly at your parent" hormone. There may be a "dependency hormone," just as we know that increased estrogen levels of pregnant women positively affect their sociability. If anyone were performing basic family planning from the beginning, it would seem sensible or at least prudent to provide children with some inner magnetism that draws adults to them—similar to the one that drew their parents to each other in the first place.

The Rapid Decay of Domestic Affections

Difficult family life is not a recent invention, as can be ascertained from the earliest literature such as the Greek myths with their remarkably turbulent kinship dramas and the ancient religions with their bristling behavioral admonitions.[34] But the emergence of the industrial way of life was one of the most dramatic catalysts for the perturbations we have been considering here. It involved a real shift, a major jolt, an unexpected array of demands on human adaptive skill. I have already referred to the stark prescience of William Wordsworth, who in 1801 wrote of the Industrial Revolution and its "rapid decay of the domestic affections among the lower orders of society."[35]

Not for nothing did Marx and other rebels rage against the epochal movements of people and resources that dragooned increasing numbers of an essentially rural species—now nearly all of us—into an urban zoo.[36] But the living arrangements of those unplanned game preserves were far less sensibly attuned to human nature than contemporary aquariums or monkey hills or herpetoriums. Biologists studied animals in their natural habitats and then thoughtfully adjusted modern zoos to the evolved realities of their tenants. Even then, cages and bars are necessary. Without them the tenants will flee.

We have become, in effect, both practically and symbolically, an urban species. Our communal life story is being filmed not on the savannah or down on the farm but in Gay Paree. There, and in its sister cities around the world, there is effective contraception. There is declining arranged marriage. There is relatively easy divorce. There is relatively easy sexual access in an intricate gavotte from partner to partner that offers at least the rumor of possible reproduction and some nostalgia for a future family. There is much opportunity to engage in what biologists call the "proximate mechanism"—the courtship, flirting, self-enhancement, and management of allure. Every party, every dinner, every visit to a museum or bowling alley or bar offers an opportunity to mobilize anew the seductive skills of an absorbingly sexy species.

Exercising the "proximate mechanism" becomes an urban industry of its own. The rumor of possible courtship is a salable product. People select countless strategies to participate in the prereproductive duet whether or not they want to or ever will become parents. To position themselves they subject themselves to dating services, and to decorate themselves convincingly they may even choose such devices as body piercing and the attachment of pieces of metal to body parts. A colorful pageant of behavioral fashions becomes associated with love, sex, and the assertion of sexiness or potential fertility. There is much advertisement but little product—what the biologists call the "ultimate mechanism," namely reproduction itself. The proximate process may be colorful, invigorating, and absorbing, but its end point may never be reached. No baby.

A clear sign of the decay of the domestic affections of the poor is no domesticity. One practical result we have already discussed is the relatively low birthrates in industrial communities and the residential patterns of cities. In Manhattan, for example, nearly half of the people who rent apartments live alone, and in central Oslo some 70 percent of inhabitants. The family becomes ever less significant to the lives of people and decreasingly important to the conduct of communities as a whole. The family has become so specialized in its role and impact that chronically contentious discussions of "family values" and associated matters become possible *because* the family is so distinct or so isolated from the overall sweep of the forces of society. The family effectively becomes almost a subset of society rather than the central system of society itself.

It is rather like some cult, large but with its own rules and enthusiasms. Once upon a time kinship relations were fully defined in religious terms. These were inescapable to all members of the community, from Renaissance Venice to colonial Brazil to the obviously rich moralistic history of Euro-American civil society.[37] Perhaps this was not fully embraced by our ancestors; a cult can become a prison, too. Nevertheless, the obligations of individuals were clearly identified. They were supported by threats of religious disaster, such as compulsory residence in hell. There was an identity of purpose and, indeed, of personnel between members of families and members of societies. But this was before the domestic affections of the poor—and the rich, too— began suffering the undermining impact of the clamorous new industrial way of life, which, to repeat, has conquered the world more rapidly and more fully than any evangelical church or political creed or military force.

Farmer John Moves to Town

The forces of evolution have continued to operate in our social worlds, but they emerged in a setting very different from the one in which we now live. Primordial forces were undoubtedly only partly adequate as frames and guidelines for behavior during our time as hunters and gatherers, but at least they operated in the kind of community in which humans generally evolved. And there was some relatively robust connection between the ways in which people fed, housed, and entertained themselves and the family systems that linked individual reproductive activities with generally acceptable norms of public social behavior in the modest-sized communities in which people lived.

Presumably they fitted considerably less neatly into agricultural and pastoral communities. This is a story in itself. The shift to agriculture and pastoralism stimulated the moral creeds that emerged during that period of trial and uncertainty. Those moral systems just recently celebrated at services last Friday, Saturday, and Sunday mornings were necessary because our evolutionary information was not specific and coercive enough to ensure harmony and fertility during our migration to and in the new-style human colony. The religions and moralities—Judeo-Christian, Buddhist, and Islamic, among others—were the work of shepherds. They were efforts to fill in the blanks and sharpen the fuzzy maps.[38]

In the industrial world the disjunction is far greater between our inheritance and how we can use it. Nonetheless, the legacy continues to provide direction. It suffuses us with emotional tendencies. It biases our behavior. We continue to be subject to an array of psychological mechanisms derived from evolution. These have been comprehensively and recently described, and they continue to operate even in seemingly inappropriate, irrelevant, or hopeless circumstances.[39] In *Darwinian Psychiatry*, Michael McGuire and Alfonso Troisi describe comprehensively both the human evolutionary legacy and medical intervention in the context of a major inventory of scientific knowledge. A common human suite of enthusiasms, passions, vulnerabilities, and apparent verities such as greed and generosity persists. It permits humans everywhere to understand one another through the means of communication and particularly the gifts of artists. But more babel and noise than ever surround it and make it difficult to discern and to enjoy and to follow.

And the evidence is mounting that of the two sexes, the male has found the least secure and rewarding link between nature and nurture. At least women can bear children, to have and to hold. If present trends continue, by 2004 nearly half of all Americans born will be to single mothers. But the male cannot pursue his nature because the environmental nature that produced it no longer exists. He is ill-equipped to provide nurture directly and poor at securing it. He finds it difficult to live up to his part of the bargain reflected in the theory of relatives. The male is baffled, if silent, about his plight. The male is becoming so much trouble for everyone that in the future, in societies willing and able to control such matters, he will be lucky even to be born.

No Men Need Apply

Are there better and worse ways of raising capable children? Is there a form of natural law to which communities can refer when they evaluate their living arrangements? What is the special impact of the industrial way on a human primate evolved to live in communities far smaller than now and in families much larger than now? We have seen that even simple variables such as taking sedatives during pregnancy can have an impact on a child. More complex social ones such as single parenthood have major effects. For example, 70 percent of incarcerated juveniles in the United States were reared in single-parent households, overwhelmingly by mothers. The relationship between families and maleness obviously has an important impact on social and economic trends.

Truant and criminal behavior are largely male specialties. Modern communities face no greater social domestic problem than in offering young males play, work, social relations, and growth to adult roles. What socially acceptable activity will reward the individual young men and contribute to their communities? Surely not the prisons, whose populations overwhelmingly of males mount inexorably. In American inner cities and increasingly in European ones, and soon in North Africa and elsewhere, we can see the crisis most dramatically. We know how restricted the job opportunities are for relatively unskilled people in industrial communities.[40] The statistics portray the ongoing generality of people's lives as we learn that the broad contribution of males to the overall economic pie is declining. For example, in England, the number of males of working age employed fell from 91 percent in 1977 to 80 percent in 1992, while those without skills dropped from 88 percent to 67 percent.[41] In the United States about one-fourth of wives earned more than their husbands, a sharp increase—or nearly one-third, according to Gail Sheehy.[42] The trend is likely to continue as more women than men graduate from high school and college. These patterns reflect and predict profound changes in the direction of a matrilineal and possibly matriarchal form of social life. For instance, there is legal pressure in Italy to name children for their mothers, not their fathers. This is a step to matrilineality. It reflects the reality of single mother-hood, economic control, rates of divorce, and the issue of paternity certainty.[43]

The families from which come unskilled young men therefore have direct economic impact. Frequently there has been no father in the household, perhaps not even a cordial avuncular male with whom the youngster can become familiar. The young men involved are uncomfort-able with the docility often needed for entry-level jobs. Among black males those who succeed in school may be accused of "acting female," an understandably bewildering accusation to insecure young males.[44] Young men in general appear to crave more challenge, more glory, a more noisy swath in the neighborhood than a clerk cuts, so they do not clamor to become clerks. They literally frighten potential employers with their idiosyncratic gusto and ambition for some self-enhancing *action*. In poor neighborhoods they may translate their ardor for recognition, respect, and meaningful social groups into street gangs that employ violence as their club banner.[45]

Meanwhile, more women work on. Those who have been employed 80 percent of the time since their first child was born are two times more likely to be divorced than nonworking mothers.[46] Money may buy goods and services for economically capable women, but it also buys freedom.

The fathers of their children are less necessary economically—and perhaps socially as well. Perhaps these men do not or cannot work. Perhaps women find the two-career family dispensable. Why not simply go it alone? After all, low-paid or unemployed men divorce or are divorced much more readily than those with high pay.[47] Whatever the reason, the outcome is a disrupted life for the offspring.

The unexpected good news is that many single mothers are occupationally effective. The bad news is that this may mean absent or marginal fathers. No one wants this bad news, but social patterns do not simply reflect value judgments and preferences. They are based on real situations that have effects. As an example from a simpler animal with simpler needs than ours for social competence, a six-day separation of young rhesus monkeys from their mothers produced significant consequences in the infants' level of anxiety and fearfulness thirty-two weeks later.[48] Few would deny the implication of this—that early experience matters in very practical ways—though there remains an astonishing public dialogue about the relevance for early attachment to competent adult life.[49] But when the impact of contemporary family arrangements becomes obvious and irritating, a common response is to make loud moral assertions about who is at fault. But the issue may be economic. In Spain, which has the lowest birthrate in western Europe, the general unemployment rate is also the highest, 22 percent; among people under twenty-five it is 40 percent.[50] Surely there is a connection between love and money.

More confusion is created between blame and causation. This may satisfy the already comfortable. It will certainly sustain the employment of the concernocrats whose careers are intertwined with these problems. But such bulletins appear to yield little or no practical effect. Not all react with aplomb and competence to their family situations. They may become the domestic equivalent of *deracine*—without real roots, shaken from their social soil. David Popenoe has provided a careful account of research on the consequences of divorce on children. There seems little question that the effects are clear, long-lasting, even if subtle.[51] The tripling of the divorce rate and the number of children in single-parent families in thirty years and the quadrupling of out-of-wedlock births in the same period suggests the starkness of some of the core changes.[52] Barbara Whitehead has also sketched a picture of the broadly dolorous impact of divorce on the lives of children.[53] We can see the trend lines in heavy ink—in heavy red ink, sketching a decisive social deficit.

Casualties of Domestic War

Hard realities emerge from the conditions of modern love and modern families. Children beaten when young are more likely than usual to become beaters if they have children. Try as they might, the poverty-stricken young men and women of Victorian working-class London had few opportunities to enjoy the psychic—to say nothing of the material—pleasures of the ideal Victorian family system even though it set the tone for the entire society, and in a way still does.[54] Ill-favored contemporary children have to be more flexible and austere in their lives than children privileged by domestic order and some material comfort.

Writers on these issues perceive a trend and offer little reason to expect it to change, even if they warmly wish it would. The available numbers confirm important elements of their predictions, with the exception that the increase in divorce rates has leveled off or slowed markedly in North America, while it continues to rise in Europe.

There have always been non-intact families. But in less medically sophisticated days, death was the principal cause of change in family state. Often the mother died in childbirth, to be replaced by the "wicked stepmother." The legendary effect in folklore of these new women on a household suggests the significance of what surrounded them. By 1974 death was replaced by divorce as the principal cause of such change. The long-range work on divorce of Sandra Blakeslee and Judith Wallerstein suggests that youngsters of hitherto effective families who function very capably and ordinarily right after their parents' crisis begin later to show signs of their differences from other children. For example, they experience more depression, more hazard in schoolwork, and more sociosexual difficulty even ten or fifteen years later when they are exploring their own adult relationships.[55] Not only that, but in what may be a form of not-so-subtle revenge, children of divorce have less contact with and provide less care for their aged parents than children of intact families.[56] The fact that 80 percent of caregivers to aged parents are women suggests that males may be especially resentful of domestic upset even when they are fully adult.

Faulty or absent behavior affects social behavior, too. It appears to be quite ludicrous to even question that the dreadful treatment endured by Romanian orphans will have a substantial effect on their behavior, even after they have moved to caring and thoughtful adopted homes.[57]

All human arrangements and all human lives are experimental. Human societies have no choice but to carry on, but we cannot simply cancel the adventure. People will love, marry, have sexual relations, and become pregnant. Some babies will not be born because of abortion, some will miscarry, and a very few will suffer infanticide. But there will be children, wanted and unwanted. There will need to be resources and adults for some years of their lives. They need at least a spare bed tucked away in some corner of the inn.

The norms of behavioral nutrition have risen along with those of food. Standards for psychological health have risen, as have those for healthy water and air. But the demands of contemporary economies appear to condemn marginally skilled people to abrasive marginal lives. Community, parents, and children aspire for more from a family system that struggles to accomplish less and less. Is there a guidebook to a better day?

Back to Nature for Family Values?

Is it possible to develop a set of values about family life derived from natural science? If we are careful not to confuse the "is" of nature and the "ought" of cultures, it may be helpful.

Begin at the beginning. Human infants crave touch and interaction, and prosper with them. Brains develop better when their owners are cuddled—just what you'd expect from a needy complex mammal. Touch is like fertilizer. Cuddling infants is both an "is" and an "ought."

In a sexually reproducing species, a growing individual benefits from as much contact with both sexes as possible—having a balanced behavioral diet while learning how to conduct various kinds of relationships. This is a human right that other animals who are well cared for also have: to know the behavior of all elements in one's own species.[58] This is especially pressing among humans. People have to learn to respond to social flexibility. A person has to learn what to be flexible about. Children should learn about the other sex as well as their own from direct interaction with adults of both sexes. The problems of single-parent families in raising children are plain, especially for boys.

The modern nuclear family needn't be the only vehicle for learning about social behavior. The theory of relatives shows how and why. An extended kinship system provides uncles, aunts, cousins, and other relatives with whom children can have constant and challenging interaction. They are unlikely to be isolated in a single-family dwelling remote from relatives. For example, in a West African family in which marriage is arranged, the children become the collective responsibility of the two kin groups involved. Even if the parental couple ends up despising each other or divorcing for whatever reason, the two broader families involved in the marriage in the first place retain their interest in the child or children. This is sharply different from the American pattern in which grandparents have gone to court to establish that they have rights to see and enjoy their grandchildren even though their son or daughter was divorced.

Disarranged Marriage

It is impossible to contemplate arranged marriage in the industrial world, but what about disarranged marriages—pairs that split relatively easily, readily, and without encumbrance? Easy divorces and their effect on children and the broader community are an issue. Foxes do not appear to practice divorce. They separate when the parental job is done. Is this a guide to what humans should do? Is easy and rapid divorce an unnatural outcome of a system of independent contractors sustained by a sense of selfish entitlement to agreeable psychological experience, to happiness?[59]

In the Euro-American tradition it is still the custom to read the banns, the public announcement of a wedding in a church, some weeks before the ceremony itself. As English journalist Janet Daley has commented about the original purpose of the banns, "Marriage had an inner dimension of domestic and sexual life, and an outer dimension which involved a role in the community; it testified to one's faith in continuity . . . and the role of law in private life. That is why breaking up a marriage was a kind of crime."[60]

In those firm old days, anyone with a dispute about the acceptability of the marriage could raise a public objection or else "forever hold their peace." A community's interest in a contemporary marriage is almost always a formality in practice. Nonetheless, it reveals an expectation of public connection even to this most private of agreements, a marriage.

No one reads banns for a divorce. There is no legitimate right of concerned people to interfere formally with the dissolution of a marriage, though the State of Connecticut requires counseling before divorce by parents.

It is almost always easier to sever the most fundamental of human connections than to install a Coke sign in a landmark part of town.

With divorce, only the courts count. What is known about public opinion on the matter suggests this is in dispute especially when the divorcing couple are also parents. A 1984 Canadian study found that fully 65 percent of women approved of divorce for childless couples.[63] Between one-third and one-half of respondents to a survey in Britain, Ireland, the United States, and Germany thought that divorce should be easy for couples *without* children, but only 18 percent were as liberal about those with children.

Nevertheless, that old sanction is gone.[62] Postmarital connection withers—countless fathers pay no child support. Only 17 percent of women receive alimony. Even a quarter of a century ago the public resistance to divorce was disappearing. It was replaced by the vision of divorce as a private psychological preference of the conflicting couple, a kind of psycho-right, not a violation of a social obligation.[63] It was a station on the way to psychological self-expression. Even princes and princesses now do it if they are sufficiently irritated. The archetypically perfect symbolism of royal weddings is no antidote to personal surliness, the avoidance of obligation, erotic curiosity, pique, and anger.

The situation is interesting from another point of view. Notwithstanding its relative legal ease, people who divorce often find the process excruciating, demoralizing, and costly in a host of ways. It may be the worst event in life, aside from the death of parents or children. Yet in many places half of marriages result in divorce. I once commented that if one-half of 1 percent of taxi rides ended in broken elbows, taxis as they are known would be banned. Yet the major traffic accident of divorce receives hardly any advance attention.

Contrast the difference between the attention paid to tiny trace elements of pollutants in the environment and the attention paid to the major intimate as well as public convulsion of divorce. The body clearly takes precedence over the spirit when the authorities decide when and where to butt in. The body is treated seriously in a medical sense, but less so in a behavioral sense.

The quality of this behavior is governed by the social setting within which the child grows. The two-parent family is obviously not the ideal or the only setting for successful socialization. Cooper, Steinem, Friedan, and Howard, among others, have questioned the psychological and political outcomes of that traditional pattern.[65] There is also a long tradition that predates them of criticism of the family as the source of bourgeois repression and social rigidity, but the question remains: Are there better or worse ways of raising children and providing parents with a sense of zest, competence, and fulfillment in what they do?

I have described the emerging *statistical* "normality" of the single-mother family pattern. It may be practical, but it is hardly an ideal response to new contraceptive and employment patterns. Nonetheless, as I will assert in a later chapter, it is a much more robust social form than many moralists claim. It reflects much more sagacity and effectiveness of mothers than they are credited with; they are making do with their lot in life, which is often just a little. However, this new normality has reduced the intensity and scope of male commitment to both the productive and reproductive sectors of life. It generates severe social issues, particularly among those hectic, unfulfilled young men—many of whom become yet another generation of the absent males in the wider adult culture.

What Is Our Freedom of Maneuver?

Mother Nature together with Father Nature are the founding principles and principals of our human system. But both may not attend the wedding party. We've considered families with one parent. What about families with two fathers or two mothers or perhaps even more of each flavor? Are these environments biosocially less desirable than those where the individuals who created the physical child also create its social world? If not the biological parents, isn't the optimum hothouse for children one that reflects the normal way of producing children, namely with men and women who like and respect each other? Who are prepared to cooperate in the banal but essential activities of daily life?

Such symmetrical units as one male and one female parent are neither always available nor chosen by people. For example, what of homosexual couples raising children? In the United States, estimates range from six to fourteen million children being raised by homosexual parents in four million households or more. These households are often successors to heterosexual unions in which one parent subsequently became actively homosexual.[66] Or a child may be the result of non-marital or anonymous artificial insemination. Or adoptions may occur in novel familial settings. Or communes may raise children.

Such variety has generated controversy about appropriate family behavior and desirable sex roles, particularly in North America but also elsewhere. In England, for example a schoolteacher refused to take her charges to see Shakespeare's *Romeo and Juliet* on the ground that it reflected heterosexual partisanship. In my city, New York, school authorities were convulsed for months over a proposed curriculum that would include among other readings *Heather Has Two Mommies*, a depiction of a family led by homosexual women. Much acrimony about such issues focuses on phenomena such as books, curricula, and other symbolic factors.

These are always salient in our especially cerebral species, but what may be far more important is that countless homosexual couples without megaphones are quietly, affectionately, and responsibly raising children and providing them with love and stability. The majority of homosexual parents do not openly reveal their sexuality. A bitterly important distinction must be drawn between publicly advocating a particular flavor of sexuality and privately going about one's business. Styles of privacy do not need publicists. Some preliminary research results suggest that unconventional but discreet family units may produce children as resilient and conventional as other children.[67]

Nevertheless, it is plain that even well-meaning studies of controversial issues may yield precarious conclusions. So may social experiments. For example, segregated schools for homosexual children—there's at least one in New York City—raise provocative issues. The long-term effect of the human situation we are considering makes the long-term view mandatory.

The contemporary situation may or may not be ideal or even desirable. It may offend religious people who calibrate behavior according to a revealed perfection. But the lives of children will surely be made worse, not better, by hectoring the people trying to raise them. Moralists may righteously attack the texture of intimate experience with the savage knife of absolute conviction, but there are children involved who need whatever parental attention they can get.

Human communities have been endlessly concerned with the sources of rectitude and guilt. The first universities that ultimately became temples of science were initially founded by religious institutions. The contest between "is" and "ought," between nature and culture, has been continuous ever since. It remains substantially difficult to settle on what may be an ideal balance between these pressures.

When universities were established hundreds of years ago, there were far fewer people in the world. The major religions associated with the major universities made stern claims about behavior when there was minimal awareness of the immense variety of ways in which people lived. But then vast populations and countless exotic cases of human variety were discovered by various explorers. Questions about human moral and familial freedom were more difficult to answer.

Industrial production has complicated the issue of reproduction still more. In no area are the sounds of confusion louder than in the family room, particularly about what many citizens see as heterosexuality undermined and familial traditions scorned. And special dilemmas are beginning to surround males who have had apparent freedom of action and hegemony for centuries.

There are at least two saving graces. One is that science offers a way to study not only what is different from society to society but also what is common and hence what we "take for granted." And the second is that with the exception of sociopaths, who are actually very rare, most people want to do what they consider the right thing in their lives and for the lives of others, especially children. Thus, science and sympathy underlay the vital new challenge of exploring the possible pollution of behavior.

Meanwhile, new conditions have generated new familial and sexual patterns, new erotic directions, new styles of commitment and disengagement. Food advertisers confidently print "all natural!" on food containers, but what is "all natural" about behavior?

CHAPTER FIVE

Can These Savings
Be Married?

D URING A LULL in one of the final matches in the 1996 Wimbledon tournament, a male voice called out to Steffi Graf, "Steffi, will you marry me?" Graf was startled for an instant, then called back, "How much money do you have?"[1]

Graf was then one of the finest athletes in the world and has earned at least $25 million during her relatively brief career. Yet in view of a worldwide audience she responded, albeit mockingly, with some elemen‑ tal truth to a traditional question. What were the suitor's prospects? She echoed the woman in Katie Webster's blues song, "No Bread? No Meat," who candidly established the connection between bread and meat, between money and sex, and presumably between commitment and affection. As Alan Feingold of Yale University has found, the largest differences between men and women asked to define their preferences in mates is that "men focus more than women do on physical attractiveness whereas women accord more weight than men to nonphysical factors (e.g., socioeconomic status)."[2] Both Katie Webster and Steffi Graf emphasized a central factor in courtship: money. Contemporary sentiment and ideology urge economic independence of both men and women, yet a stubborn theme persists, if often only sentimentally: Is the male likely to have income adequate to support his wife and children? She may decide to work, either because his income is too modest to support the family or because she enjoys the activity, but heretofore the expectation of society had been that while she may have a choice, he has none. Of course for many women there is no choice. We also know that through their working career women supply 40 percent fewer hours to the labor force than men. Only recently has there begun a decline in male contribution, too. Nonetheless, in general, males are assumed to be willing and able to work throughout their adult lives. Even among managers, the New York survey group Catalyst found that 36 percent of women expected to work part time at some point in their careers, compared with 11 percent of men.[3]

Diamonds Are a Girl's Best Clue

Countless human societies have expected men to "have good prospects," to be "good providers." This may be expressed in an explicitly calculated "bride price," as among the Masai in the form of cattle or other goods. Whatever the source of wealth in their particular society, from playing drums to retailing debentures to teaching geography, young men are expected to display resources enough to marry. Presumably the difficulty in satisfying this obligation is one reason for the increasing age of first marriage in industrial societies. In the past, a woman (and perhaps her family) considering marriage had to make perhaps the most serious credit check of her life. Many do still, and may even turn to commercial rating agencies such as Dun and Bradstreet if they are playing in that monied world.

The wedding feast itself may be part of the process of seeking some assurance of economic and hence reproductive promise for the couple. Of course both families will with equal avidity spray the new couple with real or paper rice or some other symbol of fertility. Patterns of sharing the costs vary, but the point is the same. The bride's family may pay for the wedding feast. The groom's may help supply a ring, especially if it is unusually expensive, more than the customary two months' salary. Both families guest lists will generate wedding gifts that are usually assumed to be the property of the bride, though in France gifts are shared by the couple. The bride's family must supply the wedding party, with no explicit economic benefit to her beyond what the groom also receives. In this respect the wedding is a form of dowry in the old-fashioned sense, though it is not commonly identified as such. There are many local variations on a general theme. The broad pattern is that young marrieds are provided some material platform on which to perform their family duties—even down to the practice of offering wedding guests an explicit list of household objects such as glasses or fish forks, from which they can delicately select their contribution.

The problem of merging, in a limited way, two separate familial economies through marriage has to be faced. Several societies have embraced an almost hilarious solution. Look at the third finger, left hand, of many engaged or married women. The diamond industry provides a succinct if costly answer. It has managed to convince many young people, particularly in North America and postwar Japan, that a diamond is an appropriate sign of earnest commitment. Three-quarters of American grooms provide a diamond engagement ring, as do 80 percent of Japanese courtiers. It is supposed to cost at least two months' salary. The industry has advertised heavily to establish this as the minimum standard. The more expensive the jewel, the better.

This is prodigiously wasteful. The diamond engagement ring is essentially useless, an arbitrarily overvalued object.[4] Perhaps it is thought to be a conceptual promissory note—money in the bank against a rainy or too-dry day. Though a diamond is forever, its price tag is not. Unless it has historic significance, special antiquity, or provenance, a diamond is exchangeable for cash at rarely more than one-fifth its retail cost.[5] It is a symbol far more than a store of value. Try selling or even pawning a diamond.

Then why diamonds? Diamonds are a girl's best clue to reproductive willingness and productive competence. The rock on the ring is a remarkably objective symbol of abundance and liberality with resources. It is a public promise of a future stream of goods and services to support the forthcoming family. Even a wealthy bride virtually never gives her poorer groom a ring. The flow of gravity is in the other direction. The gem remains the female's no matter what.[6] It signals sparkling intentions when love purrs. It is a consolation prize when it fizzles. The diamond symbolizes the alloy of love, enthusiasm, and trepidation that becomes a marriage.

The diamond is an improbable but direct symbol of our prehistory. As a very durable conservative species we remain substantially the same creature as when we were hunters and gatherers in small communities. As men and women we retain many impulses we had then about the link between love and resources, so much so that one of the most financially independent of modern young women, Steffi Graf, could excavate from somewhere in her experience and being a revealing answer to a basic question.

The Long Division

Now I want to look directly at the matter of modern marriage and money in the context of the impact of the industrial way of life. We learn from the Human Relations Area Files at Yale University that societies all over the world have divided work between men and women.[7] Males make metal weapons; females weave. Males hunt large mammals; females gather an array of fruits and vegetables. The list is endless; it is also arbitrary and frequently appears to be completely senseless. Nevertheless, virtually everywhere men and women have had more or less different work in sex-typed jobs.[8] Whatever the religious or customary justification, whatever the physical or attitudinal reason, whatever the fairness or practicality, the sexual division of labor was a constant.[9]

The sexual division of labor in the mature industrial economy is now fading. Slowly, yes, but surely. Even if men and women don't do exactly the same jobs (though increasingly they do), both men and women now have at least similar kinds of jobs with the same characteristics. They need equivalent training and credentials. This is presumably why 55 percent of U.S. college students and 60 percent of Canadian are female and why the number of American female college graduates over twenty-five years of age has grown from 12.5 percent to nearly 19 percent over eighteen years.[10] The percentage of first professional degrees awarded to American women increased from under 3 percent in 1961 to just over 40 percent in 1994![11] And they will usually earn more or less the same money for their effort, or even more during teen years.[12] In 1996 American girls between ages sixteen and nineteen earned an average of $51.55 a week while boys earned $46.45.[13]

Later in life the average American woman earns 77 percent of what men earn. This statistic is widely quoted but seriously misleading.[14] It is based on whole groups of male and female adults having different characteristics. The principal one is that the average woman has been in the labor force six years less than the average man, leaving usually to bear and care for children, often for years at a time. In addition and directly linked to this, women are far more likely than men to work part-time, an option that many women choose precisely because they are then able to meet the various obligations they have. Inevitably, they accumulate less seniority. The difference between the average male and average female income would be more than eliminated by a 5 percent annual increment in salary over five years. If women did not leave the labor force even temporarily, the relatively normal development of the career would create parity or near parity between the groups.[15]

Basically, the cause of much of the income differential between men and women is obvious and coercive at once: pregnancy and child care. Even highly sophisticated workplaces are influenced by simple and primordial biology. Children affect work, often decisively. It also affects women who enter politics, which they usually do some six years later, on average, than men. Politics and work take most people from their homes, which is where at least very young children remain. Time as well as space are supposed to be subject to the needs of the productive system. Affection for children or partners or parents is not supposed to inhibit occupational or political success. Despite corporate lip service, a conflict endures between personal time and work time. Evasive and nonsensical notions such as "quality time" are no antidote to the physical reality of where a person is—with a child or partner or parent, or in an office. One result must surely be declining birthrates, less because children are no longer an economic resource than because their demands on adult time reduce adult freedom in the labor force and are therefore an even greater financial burden than the direct cost of raising them.

Work may interfere, sometimes overwhelmingly. A friend working on a partner track at a major law firm had three children within six years. She decided she could not cope responsibly with both kinds of demands on her time, energy, and enthusiasm. She abandoned a job generating $200,000 per annum. In a statement that occasioned much controversy during her speech to the 1998 graduating class at Barnard College in New York, the Metropolitan editor of *The New York Times*, Joyce Purnick, stated, "If I had left the *Times* to have children and then come back to work on a four-day week the way some women reporters on my staff do, or taken long vacations or leaves to be with my family, or left at six o'clock instead of eight or nine—forget it, I wouldn't be where I am."

It is clear that children are chronic pressures on working women that erode their peace of mind.[16] There is evidence that working mothers show consistently elevated levels of the hormone cortisol, which is associated with stress.[17] Even mothers preparing for the labor force— that is, students—now demand and receive day care for their children on some 1,700 American campuses.[18] Other women with unmanageable demands on their time may simply leave their jobs, at least for a period that may stretch for years. For example, for many female employees breast-feeding a child becomes a flurry of home visits, breast pumps, staggered work hours, and stress overall. For the 60 percent of American mothers who nurse their babies, the pressures and potential guilt were sharply enhanced in December 1997 when the American Academy of

Pediatrics doubled the recommended period of breast-feeding from six months to a full year. But women tend to return from maternity leave after twelve weeks, and only 20 percent of mothers continue breast-feeding beyond six months.[19]

Other women seek more direct solutions. For example, a significant number begin their own businesses. That way they hope to operate on their own schedule and in the context of the rhythms and affections of family life, especially if the fathers of their children are not helpful or only marginally so. A direct indication of this in the United States is that between 1987 and 1992 there has been a 43 percent increase in the number of businesses owned by women.[20] In a very different kind of community, one facing economic difficulty from scarcity, not plenty, women in former communist Germany have also turned to private businesses, some 150,000 since 1990.[21] There are indications of efforts to establish businesses owned by women in Islamic communities, which otherwise have been restrictive over female behavior.[22]

This is a pattern similar to the long-standing history of female entrepreneurship in West Africa where women are the effective and successful conductors of retail and much of the wholesale trade. It is tied to a kinship system in which the female line is the core element of social life; a woman will depend first on her own effort and resources, and then more on her brother for help with her family than her husband. He, in turn, will be responsible for his sister's children. In this system men are overall more confident about their genetic links to the children they support, especially since relations between men and women take a somewhat different form from the monogamous scheme that prevails, at least in theory, in Europe and North America. In West Africa in the early 60s the Euro-American form of nuclear family was sufficiently exotic among the mass of peasant farmers that the children of men and women married to each other were referred to as "same muddah, same fadduh."[23]

Remember: The individual, man or woman, is an independent contractor who has to come to personal terms with the overall economy. This even begins with schoolchildren assigned a number to take standardized tests graded by machine. They will continue this anonymous contest against a statistical universe well into adulthood. The sources of social value and self-esteem are increasingly fed by work and other activities in the public and economic sectors, not in the swirls of private affiliation.

The social trend is clear. The growth in jobs for women outpaces that of males. In Europe, additional jobs for females has totaled thirteen million in recent years but only 600,000 for males. The economic movement is women up, men down. MIT economist Lester Thurow has described how among American men between twenty-five and thirty-four the median wage is down 25 percent, and one-third of them earn less money than is needed to keep a family of four at or above the poverty line. If they abandon their family responsibilities, their income jumps by 73 percent.[24] But they no longer have families.

Then what happens when people decide to accentuate the affection-ate? What happens when people enter into serious emotional contracts about their lives? What happens to men in a world in which it is increasingly common for women to keep their natal names when they marry, and women are neither their legal property nor labeled as ornaments of their entourage? What happens to women when the men they marry lose jobs or can only sustain ones that are beneath the promise made on their wedding day?

We have to visit marriage first, the core unit of what we consider here. Marriage is not strictly or even principally about love, housing, and style, though it must be that, too. It is also about production, inheritance, wealth, and commercial and political power. This truth is revealed for the price of an American newspaper. A clue to the links between love and money are wedding and engagement announcements. It has become the fashion for the educational and occupational attainments not only of Romeo and Juliet to be enumerated but also the full resumes of the progenitor Montagues and Capulets. Sam is a cum laude graduate of Georgetown, now the prince of arbitrage in Bucks, Morebucks, and Partners. Sue triumphed at Princeton with a magna and now is marketing director of Random Newhouse Publishing Company. The occupational dog tags of their parents and stepparents are also given. If there is a particularly noteworthy grandparent, such as a senator or founder of an investment house or inventor of the zipper, that individual is also added to the socioeconomic catalogue.

Nowhere is it revealed that someone loves ballet, coaches field hockey, detests bean soup, supports Basque autonomy, or is devoted to Japanese films from the 50s. No favorite authors, colors, grains, principals, politics, or attitudes to censorship are listed. The sharp focus is on their place in the economic system. This is so obviously necessary it happens without comment. "The most important thing to learn about a community is what it takes for granted." The description of one of the most romantic episodes of life, marriage, resembles a collective resume of the wedding party, as if the whole group was applying for an enviable directorship or World Bank consultancy.

Strictly business. Here are arranged marriages of a sort, even if they are arranged by the marrying pair themselves. The credentials and assets of extended families seem as tacitly relevant as in a Rajasthan village or the marriage celebration of the oldest son of the Duc de Bourgogne in 1739.

Money is obviously important in people's lives. It determines and affects countless conditions of life. But there is reluctance to confront with candor its role in romance, except perhaps to be critical of it. Explicitly marrying "for money" is decisively less morally pure than marrying "for love." The fiscal motive is questionable. The gold digger has the ethical status of a strip miner. I have personally been shaken from my own sentimental naïveté when female friends have sought my help to secure introductions to male friends who were both wealthy and single.

The essence of the issue is this: For families, children are not only people to love, instruct, feed, amuse, challenge, or deplore but are also the link to the future, the next generation. Without having asked for the job they are a family's first-team players in the great game. Most families do what they can, often heroically, to help kids play the game well. A packet of money from which to draw is a crisp advantage, but so are love, attention, and helping hands on every side. Even the number of words that parents use with their small children is a surprisingly influential factor in performance at school.[25]

The affections are as intricately interwoven as the insides of a walnut. They do not easily correspond to the stern schedules and social demands of the modern independent pattern. The child will grow to a life self-chosen and self-governed. Each child is finally and fully responsible for finding his or her own money after getting whatever help the family can advance, if it believes in helping an adult child with finances (many families do not). Except for a small battalion of affluent inheritors, each child must be a worker out of necessity.

But each child has to find love as well as money. Perhaps he or she will be lucky to become a lover out of persistence, inspiration, or naked need. Parents may be unable to help. Given current psychological cant they may be advised not to try. But this is a statistical novelty in humankind. Arranged marriages are historically far more common. Many may find them oddly perplexing, as I have whenever I have encountered them as straightforward plans of otherwise "modern" people. For example, an Indian friend of mine in graduate school at the London School of Economics told me that after she returned to her upper-class Indian home, her civil servant father would choose a husband for her, as was done for Benazir Bhutto who became prime minister of Pakistan after attending Harvard and Oxford.[26] Both women had one less problem to solve than their fellow students facing "still the same old story, the fight for love and glory." In India, 99 percent of women are married by their early twenties. There is a barely 2 percent divorce rate.[27] The system seems absolute.

What do the participants think about it? That's a different matter.

Marriage Arrangements and Arranged Marriages

Let's put this in perspective. Romantic love is not a widespread basis for marriage. The overwhelming proportion of marriages in the world continue to be arranged by the parental generation. Money and fertility are very explicit concerns, although it is obviously best when people who marry ultimately care for each other. That is why traditional Indian couples who may never have seen each other before marriage were supposed to be given a copy of the Kama Sutra and up to a year after the marriage to learn its manifold sexual techniques and develop their bond—an outdated version of the much briefer contemporary honey-moon.

Commonly, two other factors are more important than personal emotion: inheriting property and social status, and ensuring descendants. The link between male and female has to be maintained long enough to support children. Recall Margaret Mead's "Fatherhood is a human invention," and it has to be supported. Forms of male dominance in marriage are a way of preserving this invention. Paradoxically, they also discipline men by imposing on them an extraordinary lifelong financial if not also emotional responsibility to spouses and children. The fact that men possess these obligations may lead them to believe they control the system for their own benefit. This can yield arch and brittle forms of male power, often ones in which females collude, such as female genital mutilation.[28] Or the more coy Euro-American form where women were supposed to "love, honor, and obey" their husbands.

But there is no more "obey."[29] What now?

Remember, we are dealing with an intelligent ape with a long life cycle and immense emotional needs. The ape has built a zoo in which it lives with feelings ranging from luxury to astonishment to imprisonment. There is a challenging problem of animal husbandry here. The old seek control of the sexuality of the young in various ways, some highly dramatic. For example, in an extraordinary and chilling finding, California anthropologist Mildred Dickemann described how traditional infan-ticide in India resulted in the killing of newborns who were mainly the females of the highest-caste Brahmins and the sons of the lowest-caste untouchables. As elsewhere, females were expected to marry males higher than they in the social and economic system. But there were no men of higher status for the elite Brahmin women, or women of lower status for the degraded untouchable men, so they were sacrificed to the requirements of the long-term economic and reproductive ends of their families.[30]

The remedy was extreme. The challenge was common. A potential matchmaking problem had to be faced at the outset, explicitly and with dispatch. There must be fulfilling and dignified lives for women of such high status; hence, they took positions as nuns in elegant environments in the Roman Catholic church or as esteemed scholars in the "seven sisters" female colleges of the American elite.[31] Even contemporary information about the sharp imbalances in the rates of male and female births where amniocentesis is available, for example in India and China, suggests that a new form of the old pattern still persists even though abortion, and not infanticide directly, is the mechanism used. A Chinese census in 1995 found 100 girls for 121 boys among one-year-olds. Both willful and casual maltreatment of girls as well as medical malpractice may be responsible.[32] In 1997 the Statistical office of South Korea projected that by 2010 there will be 123 men to 100 women, while the ratio in Taiwan will be nearly 127 men to 100 women."[33] Demographer Nicholas Eberstadt of the Harvard Center for Population and Development Studies has outlined an impending shortage of brides through East Asia, which appears to him "a seemingly irremediable problem. It is a problem already in place, ready to unfold in the next century."[34]

Another solution to the management of money and fertility is described in a detailed ethnography by the Japanese-American sociologist Matthews Hamabata.[35] He chronicled the marital goings-on in three prominent Japanese families, including one that owned a five hundred-year-old commercial firm. Effective and public business decisions are made principally by the men at work in the firms. Their wives, mothers, sisters, and daughters were in intense, unrelenting, if subtle interaction about the personal matters facing them, such as finding appropriate schooling for the children, finding potential acceptable spouses, and possible careers. Of course the personal is also the functional, and these background negotiations directly influenced the course of business.

In the family on which Hamabata focused, its eldest daughter, Reiko, reached the age of *tekireiki*, prime time for marriage. The question arose about which suitor would be appropriate for *omiai*, the exploratory preliminary for an arranged marriage. The role of the family's venerable matchmaker was pivotal. He had served it effectively in the past. No one wanted to irritate him. There was also the need to choose a young man who could plausibly fill the role of family leader. The judgment about the first serious candidate was harsh and terminal: "As proof of his lack of merit, he had just entered a third-ranked university, best known for the number of foreign sports cars on its campus, while in comparison, Reiko was finishing her degree in the elite faculty of economics of one of the nation's most prestigious private universities."[36]

Another option was to marry her to a *muko-yooshi*, an ambitious son-in-law who would be adopted by the family after he changed his name to the family's to affirm his new loyalties. He would succeed to family headship at least nominally. The broad assumption is that he would be guided by his wife. She would train him in the ways and in the interests of his new family. She would also endure some initial mockery for marrying a man—her male bride—spinelessly willing to yield his name and history for an enviable spot in the social structure.[37] (In his interesting play *Ballad of Yachiyo* about Japanese Americans living in Hawaii in the early twentieth century, Philip Kan Gotanda describes similar concerns of his grandparents about their daughter.)[38]

In Japan the matter is particularly trying when the eldest son, who should ideally inherit the leadership, is thought unequal to the task. Birth is obviously an advantage in the family business, but biological sons must demonstrate adequate competence. Often they do so by graduating well from a demanding Japanese or American university. Then they are assumed to be capable of managing successfully. As far as competent Japanese females are concerned, the situation of the crown princess is a direct reflection of the set of forces in play. Before she married her prince in 1990, Masako Owada was an elite diplomat in the Foreign Ministry. She had mastered five foreign languages, which she employed in extensive professional travel. After marriage she became virtually invis-ible apart from formal appearances. Her and her husband's overwhelming priority is evidently to produce an heir to the throne. This removed all elements of occupational independence from the princess's life.[39] Meanwhile, the best known and most accomplished Japanese female athlete, tennis player Kimiko Date, among the ten best female players in the world, confounded her country by retiring at age twenty-five. This was apparently a prelude to marriage and typical among talented professional women in Japan.[40] Some 50 percent of women are in the Japanese labor force, many part-time, and endure the burdens of home and work with increasingly limited dispensations from the wider society.[41]

The *Danshen Guizu* in Her Single Bed

In another Asian community, Taiwan, the unusually rapid industrial growth has had remarkably sudden and dramatic impact on marriage. In 1979 the age of first marriage of women was below 24; fourteen years later it was 28.2. Men marry at 30.9 years of age, compared with 27 in 1980. There is a much-talked about new group of *danshen guizu*, "single nobles"—professional women with high incomes who focus first on their careers and very secondarily on their prospects of marriage to the relatively small number of appropriate and available men.[42] One thirty-four-year-old banker commented, "Taiwanese men are still very old-fashioned . . . [and] . . . don't want to marry a woman with a higher level of education. All they care about is looks and whether a woman can have babies."

Like other states, the government of the territory evidently cares about population, too. It urges, unsuccessfully, that women marry at twenty-five and men at twenty-seven. Matchmakers continue their trade, especially among the rich families, but there is growing resistance to their work.

Whatever outsiders may think of them, the Indian, Japanese, and Taiwanese systems boast the advantage of explicitness if not the attractive mysteries of romance. People know what they are doing, why they are doing it, and what their goals are. They are able to knit together the old and the new in the lives of contemporary brides and groom. The Euro-American community has adapted somewhat more slowly, perhaps with some self-deception. Even the carefully wrought prenuptial agreement of Beverly Hills, Zurich, and Easthampton is hardly a novel historical adventure. The only new thing is its limitation to just the two principal players and not their clans.

Love and money remain closely related even though in the ideal picture they are supposed to be separate. In the romantic context of contemporary love, economic concerns may indeed persist, but they become covert, irritating, almost shameful. But individuals are largely on their own in the educational and economic systems, so why should intimate life be different?[43] Will systems such as the Japanese with five-hundred-year-old businesses and the group orientation of Shintoism and Confucianism be able to survive the individualism associated with the new industrial way of life? Or will the heartbeats of the lovers overwhelm the cold demands of funds and status, as in the allegory of Lady Chatterley and her common-born gamekeeper?[44] How do up-to-the-minute industrial people conduct the relationships that reflect our human nature?

The Missing Weak Link

If we are to judge from the differences in how men and women perform their roles as parents, we are driven to the conclusion either that men are less well adapted to modern conditions or that these conditions are inhospitable to them, or a mixture of these factors. We have seen that the social invention of fatherhood is essential for the effective continuity of the human pattern. What happens when it becomes as frail a bulwark as it appears to have become? Why do men act as they do? Is it because they are *very* "independent contractors"—emotional entrepreneurs who are not members of an organization, do not receive benefits, and are free to move in and out of particular activities? Are they distinct legal entities able to negotiate their own deal with the economy? Are they also independent contractors of the heart? Are they nature's cads?

Or do they respond with special frailty when social conditions are unsettled? If a child is from parents who have divorced—a huge and growing crowd—even the rules of basic family loyalty are indeterminate. Inexperienced youngsters are expected to navigate among relationships that their parents, who should provide an example, have failed to sustain. They may be raised with two homes, two systems of affection, and one profound uncertainty about the permanence of love. The child must become an adult able to learn a skill and earn a living without an appreciable parental boost. The young person must also find and secure a mate. Wrenching personal trials in disastrous families have become part of the formal architecture of countless childhoods. Severe experience of childhood may make it difficult to create an adult home. Given male tenuousness about reproduction, created in part by new technology, it is easy to see how and why men are the weak link in an already somewhat rickety system, and are becoming weaker.

There has been a massive migration of men from domestic responsibility, as if they boarded ships for Australia or the New World. Contraception is only one reason, though a major one, for the shift in how they use their time and resources. It has been compounded by a broad and general antimale ideology tacitly accepted by the main body of commentators on these issues. It is a pivotal weapon in the first world sex war. It is unlikely to help secure male cooperation. It is not clear if the ideology is a bitter response to the nonfamilial behavior of men or its cause. The answer is probably both. And new economic and educational initiatives by women that will change the social order lend practical force to ideological urgency.

Men and women need salable skills to carry them through life in a newly strenuous economic environment. We see the difficulty that males face when they lack preparation. Women without credentials appear to find unskilled labor more readily than men. African-American women are more likely than African-American men to receive entry-level jobs.[45]

They are also more likely to acquire credentials over time, perhaps because they are more willing than men to accept part-time work. Eighty-five percent of part-time employees in England are women, 66 percent in the United States, and 91 percent in Germany. In Britain and Australia more than 40 percent of women work part-time; in Holland more than 60 percent.[46] What appears to be an initial compromise offers a starting point for more substantial employment and a structure for further schooling. Part-time work appears to be a compromise that men are unwilling or unable to make, to their collective cost. It may also be an option that women choose because it provides them flexibility to integrate their various responsibilities. Perhaps men do not acknowledge their responsibilities or believe that the only way to meet them is to work full-time. Meanwhile, as *The Economist* reported, "the number of American men in full-time employment is falling by about 1 million a year."[47] Gary Burtless of the Brookings Institution in Washington, D.C., notes that in 1940 half of all men were still at work at age sixty-nine, but in 1997, only 47 percent of sixty-two-year-olds were still at work.[48]

The economic gap grows between educated and unskilled people all over the industrial world. The safety net under the ever-higher wire is less and less dependable. And women may be more adept than men in responding to economic opportunities. Even the language a woman speaks where there is a choice may reflect her economic judgments and aspirations. For example, in Hungarian communities that border on Germany, women may learn German so that they will be able to move away from the agricultural economy in which they remain disadvantaged if they marry the available Hungarian men who are peasant farmers. Instead, they project themselves linguistically into industrial Germany.[49]

The changes are not necessarily restricted to industrial communities either, though they emerge there first. Contrary to earlier demographic certainties about "rich countries getting richer and poor countries getting children," birth rates have begun to fall even where there is no clear industrialization.[49] Contraception for women is a root cause of change. But women in poor communities may endure the same disaffection with their potential mates as their wealthier sisters. The pressure grows on them to earn their income in the urban money economy.

Here is a critical and fundamental break from the past. It's a new world. *Both men and women must play separately by the same rules rather than together by different ones.*

The social trend is clear. The growth in jobs for women outpaces that of males—in Europe jobs for females increased by 13 million in recent years but for males only by 600,000. MIT economist Lester Thurow has described how, among American men between the ages of 25 and 34, median wages are down by 25 percent; a third of them earn less money than is necessary to keep a family of four at or above the poverty line. If they abandon their family responsibilities their income jumps by 73 percent.[50]

Let's review the historical movement here. In the beginning of the industrial revolution people moved from rural regions to cities. There was a division of labor which saw men working outside the home and women within.[51] One income was usually considered adequate for a family, though there were countless two-earner families and families without adequate income altogether. It was Karl Marx's observation that the capitalist system would have to pay industrial workers just enough to support a man and his family, not a shilling more. It is worth reemphasizing one of the most remarkable features of the situation overall: *Men who were industrial workers or managers spent their entire adult lives at work and by and large turned over all their income to their wives and families.*

Why would men do this? Why such a relatively high level of consent? As Michael Young, Peter Willmott, and Norman Dennis pointed out about English workingmen, before this social class had bank accounts they would carry the currency they earned to their wives. They would be provided an allowance for beer and occasional bets with a bookie.[52] Household finances were largely a female responsibility. Most household expenditures were decided by women.

Presumably both men and women found this an acceptable arrange-ment. The pattern achieved a kind of functional apotheosis during the 1950s when in North America and elsewhere families were raising larger families than would be seen again. They also did so in obeisance to demanding middle-class standards of consumption, comfort, and health.[53] Four, five, six children were raised with the proper dental care, education, counseling, recreation, and the like. The result was a robust and numerous generation.[54]

Not a Sheep but a Sheepskin

But a new economic order was looming. While in 1970 some 70 percent of American households were families, by 1996 only 54 percent were. Characteristically, through gifts at marriage, communities seek to provide resources to new couples. However, in the industrial countries of Europe, North America, and increasingly in Asia, education has become the most practical and ubiquitous form of dowry or bride price—not two hectares of prime vineyard or three healthy cattle or a baker's dozen of sheep, but credentials and skill carried around in the young person's skull. A sheepskin, not sheep. This is one reason for the large increase in its costs and for the dogged willingness of parents to endure privation to supply their children with this newly portable dowry.

The change is particularly dramatic for a woman. Her hope chest is now her brain. No sensible female or her parents can permit her to come to maturity without marketable skills on the assumption that she will marry and thereafter find adequate and permanent support from her husband. The adaptability of women to their new situations is reflected in their growing mastery of the system of higher education. Twenty-three percent of working women had bachelor's degrees in 1995, compared with 20 percent of men. We have seen that American women will earn 55 percent of all bachelor's degrees in years to come (60 percent in Canada).[55] This has more than doubled the number of customers and the demand for education, which again explains the continuing rise in its costs, faster than general inflation. In 1975, 18 percent of students at Harvard Law School were female, while it was 42 percent in 1997.

If nothing else, the sharp reduction of alimony and a North

American divorce rate of between 40 and 50 percent dramatizes the riskiness of the old depend-on-husband strategy. And where there is no enforcement of child support, a payment rate of under 18 percent from divorced fathers colors it red for danger—scarlet red.

We have examined profound changes in the pattern of sexual interdependence. In return for the wide array of activities usually performed by a woman to sustain families and home, a man would undertake to turn over to his domestic setting nearly all the money he earned over his lifetime. She provided fertility, he resources. In various societies that industrial people consider exotic, explicit payments provide an economic platform to marriage, such as bride prices or dowries. A man may have to supply her family with a cache of wealth before he can receive a bride. A woman may need a dowry of money or other property before a husband's family will consent to a wedding—an economic starting point for the new family unit. There is room in this system for abuse, as in India where some males receive dowries from the family of their brides and then insist on additional payments later on. In extreme cases, males who regard themselves as desirable mates will actually kill their young brides, often with little practical risk of legal sanction, and then enter into yet another marriage and acquire yet another infusion of dowry wealth. Under current India law, none of this is legal—dowries are prohibited—but the situation persists. And because of demographic changes largely associated with amniocentesis and abortion, there is an excess of potential brides over potential grooms, a situation that has sharpened male avidity for dowries.[56]

Job Wanted

The earlier pattern had been acceptable and workable for the majority of women until after World War II. This was particularly so when the baby boomers were being born, raised, and educated—often to rebel later as feminists and warriors against a family system in retreat from sentimental perfection. What changed? What set of conditions could have caused such a turnabout in the soft arrangements of private life and the firm rules of public order?

We have already explored some features of the sexual world of reproduction. Wasn't another reason for the turbulence of that period the new pattern of production that obligated women to enter the labor force as vigorously as men? While the end-of-century pattern of two-income families was not yet fully established, the emerging pattern was already formed. There was a paradox. As the community became wealthier and more secure, two paychecks seemed necessary for acceptable life. A refrigerator-freezer is more expensive than an icebox. Two suburban adults at work often require two cars, three if they have college-age children. But more was going on than an escalation of consumption. What has been broadly identified as feminism chronicled and directed many of the changes by encouraging female independence. We can learn from a classical insight in sociology. Karl Mannheim in *Ideology and Utopia* suggested that ideologies broadly follow the ineluctable basic movements of a society. Ideas follow realities. The ideology of female equity in employment followed the reality that women had to work. Communities had no choice but to support their full and active role in public life.

The situation was different in the planned societies of Eastern Europe. Women there were impelled into the monetary labor force because, notwithstanding Marx, economists could and did simply decide that individual salaries would be inadequate on their own to support families. Two salaries became necessary. Two followed. The Euro-American pattern was subtler and less organized, but it had the same result. Now many families decide that they "need" two incomes given the level of expenditure to which they have become committed.

Especially in North America since the 70s there has been widely expressed feminist anger against men. Does this reflect, among other things, resentment against the mounting obligations on women to join the money economy? Do women feel betrayed because they are compelled to seek equality in the workplace despite their unequal obligations at home? Are women bitter because when and if they have children, as most do, they are forced to choose between the wordless pleasures and flowing demands of beloved youngsters and the precise requirements of work in places owned and directed by strangers? In my experience, mothers feel this ache more sharply than fathers. Hardly any mothers leave their children; they leave their jobs instead.

Whatever the cause, women have entered the labor force, increasingly in influential roles. They take over existing slots in education, work, politics, and elsewhere. Women are increasingly more responsible than men for creating new, initially small but effective businesses and new jobs. In response, men have slowly but inexorably withdrawn from the broad traditional requirement of manhood: that they provide resources to women and children. They are divorcing more, supporting their children less, and simply earning less money overall.[57] Between 1979 and 1993 in the United States, the median income for white men dropped 10 percent and for black men 8 percent, whereas median income for white women increased by 10 percent and for black women 8 percent.[58] "Nonemployment"—being effectively out of the labor force altogether—doubled for men twenty-five to fifty-five years of age between 1970 and 1994 in the United States, while in Britain, France, and Germany it has tripled. In the relatively prosperous Tyneside area of northeast England, only 45 percent of men over fifty-five are working, whereas in the 1960s 70 percent were employed.[59] The remarkable film *The Full Monty*, about the lives of working-class men in northern England, reveals that when they are unable to find any work in traditional male jobs, they turn to what exigent women have often done—stripping their clothes off for paying customers of the opposite sex.

Men are working less and pocketing more of the smaller amount they earn. The trend lines of the graph of economic power are absolutely clear. This seems a portent of further alienation to come. The economic situation of African-American males is the earliest sign. There are also three and a half times more white families with no husband at home than in 1950. Out-of-wedlock births among white women has increased from 2 percent in 1950 to 20 percent in 1995. Political scientist Andrew Hacker of the City University of New York has said that both black and white American young men "feel their lives are not amounting to much."[60]

The significance of this *common* pattern among historically *different* white and black communities cannot be emphasized enough, given history. Now they share contemporary social forces as if they were both immersed in a slow but enormously wide river draining a large area. A new delta is forming.

"I'm Working for Two"

We began our explanatory story in the 1960s with the changes in private and public life stimulated by the pill and intrauterine devices. There was a sharp reduction in paternity certainty. Premaritally fertile couples were less likely than before to marry and more likely to secure an abortion. For such reasons, as well as new social values about the sources of female self-respect, women needed as much education as men.

Practically speaking, they may need even more. They may be obligated not only to support themselves but also the children they may bear. The result is that more women occupy the jobs to which the educational system is directed. Whereas there were once few women in law, medical, business, architectural, or other similar schools, there are many. And of course there is a direct connection between women acquiring an education and their level of participation in the labor force. Many barriers remain. Nonetheless, the situation differs sharply from two generations ago. For example, 44 percent of doctoral recipients in the United States in 1992 were women, compared with 36 percent in 1982.[61] A survey of over two hundred thousand American college students in 1993 revealed for the first time that there were more women than men who planned to secure postgraduate degrees. As I've noted, 55 percent of all undergraduate college students are women. Whereas in 1900 about 20 percent of American women were in the labor force and

80 percent of men, in 1993 the numbers were about 46 percent for women and 54 percent for men, with an increase in female employment of 2 percent a year.[62] In 1992, two-thirds of American women with children under five were in the paid labor force.[63] Of the over two million Americans who enroll in colleges after the age of thirty-five, women are two-thirds of the total, up from just over half in 1972.[64] In Sweden the pattern of male employment has scarcely changed since 1963, while virtually every new job has gone to a woman, most often in public and local government.[65] In general, participation rates in the labor force have been rising for women and falling for men. In the 1980s this was particularly rapid especially in the United States and Australia.

Women's entry into the labor force in such numbers and consistency reflects both choice and their considered judgment that they may have to be self-supporting. It suggests they enjoy their work and are confident they can do it well. And because they may have to support a child as well as themselves, they are working for two. Necessity and opportunity unite.

The cumulative impact of these seemingly inexorable changes will be great. It has only begun to be felt. There are and will be effects in psychology, patterns of consumption and the organization of work, the military, and the symbolic lives of communities. The changes are not confined to any one racial or ethnic or national group. They permeate industrial communities in general. Females as a group will expect decreasing cooperation in raising children from men as a group. The male sex partner, even the progenitor, may be a rental, not a genuine partner.

The industrial world may be in the first stages of a movement toward an economic system dominated by women.

Matriarchy at Last?

This powerful undertow of social change has taken a while to define its new direction. It is likely that there is an immensely consequential and permanent shift in how women and men interpret the possibilities of life and how they spend their time. In the United Kingdom "some time later this year [1996] . . . the first time ever in peacetime, the number of women with jobs will exceed the number of men with jobs in Britain."[67] The phenomenon is worldwide. In Europe the number of men with jobs has fallen by 1 million, while women have acquired 13 million new jobs. There are 2.1 million unemployed men in the United Kingdom but only 630,000 unemployed women.

Understandably, many women seek professional security before entering reproductive life. If they have children at all they tend to do so relatively late in life. One result is problems with both conception and healthy birth. Fertility clinics bear the brunt of what has become reproductive difficulty, particularly among women who are bountiful economic producers. Some American couples have used Ghanaian fertility icons to help them conceive.[68]

Other women were led by the ideological intensity of feminist commentators to evaluate reproduction skeptically or to avoid it altogether. At the very least it had to be embedded in satisfying and rewarding work. Prompt maternity could be a sign of political retrogression. But when the biological clock strikes the eleventh hour, ideology may yield to other imperatives. As one forty-one-year-old TV executive, a victim of this gender Leninism, told me, "I spent years trying to avoid pregnancy while I was establishing myself as a professional. Friends of my age did the same, and then suddenly we looked around and saw the women older than us we called 'video widows' who did nothing but work—day, night, and weekends. They had neither strong personal relationships nor, certainly, children. In a rush we began to have children or tried to. I've now had three in vitro fertilization trials at——Hospital and have been on the waiting list at——Hospital for a year. Now I want to adopt, but my husband's heart isn't in it; he is a father from an earlier marriage. The younger women coming up seem to have learned something. They have babies right away."

This woman and others like her are the opposite of the generation of parents that produced the baby boom. They are casualties of ideology, almost as if they had been brainwashed and then purged in the good old communist style. They are victims of a profound misjudgment about the satisfactions of reproductive life and the complex costs of productive success.

They are people for whom it was bizarre not to have sex but normal and even honorable not to have children. They now endure a private, if common, tragedy.

Public Affluence, Private Squalor

For a couple facing the demanding outside world, there is more than double complexity in confronting the stream of requirements for family and work lives. Occupational demands may not be compatible with the needs of intimate life.

Should they have a child or children or have to care for an elderly parent, the demands on the couple and their relationship grow geometrically. But the resources available to them expand arithmetically. The strenuousness of the situation is general and pervasive. Each person has a private life, and yet the requirements of the labor force continue to compress leisure hours while new forms of technology such as cell phones, home computers, e-mail, and the like render ever more porous the barrier between work and privacy.[69] A study of employees in 1992 by Boston University's Center on Work and Family found that more than half wished for more family time "always" or "most of the time."[70] There are urgent public dialogues about child care, parent care, the scheduling of work, and the like. There are roiling efforts such as flextime, shared jobs, or mommy and daddy tracks to adjust to the current state of affairs. They reflect the omnipresent cost in emotion, resources, and time of cooperative family life in a community designed for independent contractors.

In his influential 1958 essay *The Affluent Society*, economist John Kenneth Galbraith described how at the time private wealth and comfort grew while public resources and social infrastructure starved for support. Suburban homes had excellent laundry equipment, but city schools had twenty-year-old textbooks and grimy floors. Public transport was threadbare, while single individuals traveled in elegant, costly private vehicles. Billions were still spent on luxurious clothing and personal decor, but tens of millions of Americans lacked health insurance. Highways swooped in elegant profusion, while city streets sported degraded pavement and sanitation. Even the vaunted highways of the United States cannot be properly cleaned by public funds alone, and an "Adopt-A-Highway" program leaves public thoroughfares littered with signs advertising entities from funeral homes to film stars, who have each provided tax-deducted monies to clean a mile or two of the public's highways. There was public squalor and private affluence.

If we calculate emotional and social wealth and not financial, the situation is reversed. There is private emotional squalor as people struggle with their personal schedules and dilemmas. In the United States, married people fail some 40 to 50 percent of the time to tune their realities to their expectations, if the divorce rate means anything at all. Meanwhile, there is public affluence as they earn regular packets of money from a workplace that may be far more luxurious than their homes. And the workplace may provide more than money alone; it may offer adult stimulus, brilliant communication systems, social interaction, comfortable air, clear notions of social contribution, and the brisk swish of tangible action. Small wonder that in 1997 sociologist Arlie Hochschild found that Americans increasingly defined home life as problematic and abrasive, and work life as satisfying and absorbing.[71] Yet time becomes a precious commodity. In America the workweek has lengthened and commuting time increases. Both men and women of a household are held to the same level of exigent work. Chronic fatigue is a discernible problem; sleep deprivation is a subject of public discussion. "Burnout" is almost a legal disease and in Japan an acknowledged cause of death. While traffic accidents from overuse of alcohol decrease, those from fatigue and people literally falling asleep at the wheel are on the increase. A *New York Times* report of November 11, 1998, reveals that even children play less and "work" more.

John Kenneth Galbraith's essay was wrong. Private life is not altogether luxurious. Public life, for fortunate people with jobs, may be full, interesting, and colorful. This is one reason that women want to enter this public arena—it has knowable rules and clear rewards. There is a seemingly inexorable shift away from protected private experience to the demands and rewards of the public realm, most explicitly in its economic sector. Americans think it is better for poorer women to work and hire someone to take care of their children than to receive public money and care for their own children themselves.[72] There is a sculpted profile of social value here, and it's kind of cracked. People move from the public affluence of bustling relations-rich work environments to the private squalor of lonely lives or lives with family members coerced by hectic schedules and pressures. Both erode the sense of haven that domesticity has always specialized in providing.

Because there is no homemaker, there is less likely to be a home, at least in the traditional sense. In the United States in 1991, 53 percent of women with a child under one year old were in the labor force, compared with barely 20 percent the generation before, in 1965. In the past the homemaker was almost invariably a woman. Women and men may now find this socially and even ethically unacceptable. In any event, the press of economic events appears to render it largely impossible.

Changed public conditions yield changed private experience. Money may flow fulsomely into the home, but usually with diminished interaction between parents and their children—40 percent less time than thirty years ago, according to Lester Thurow.[73] This affects the complexity of emotional interaction, cognitive stimulation, and the like. At the same time the demands increase on children for various kinds of accomplishment.[74] Children who have adults to talk with, who use rich vocabulary in a caring manner, simply do better in their schooling and presumably in their lives. Parents know this. The hunt for "quality time" with children reflects parental and communal dissatisfaction with catch-as-catch-can child care largely revolving around the demands of work. However, "quality time" is a revealingly absurd import from the world of management. Small children like to spend elegantly casual time with people who love them. Doing nothing affectionately is likely to be more important than resume-building with skilled professionals. In my faculty dining room I overhead a professor describe a Manhattan neighbor who was shepherding her three-month-old child to a course in music appreciation.

Of course, there have been some societal changes in the proportion of small-child care performed by men and women. Men provide more child care than before, though there remain substantial sex distinctions so that women often do at least twice as much domestic work than male partners.[75] Whatever the division, the overriding demand still falls on women if only because the number of single mothers has risen so sharply. It is also possible that when they have the choice, women prefer to care for their small children rather than let the males, whose skills may not inspire confidence.

Efforts to bureaucratize the intimacy of parenthood in day care and other arrangements may or may not meet the perceived or tacit demands of children at the beginning of an immensely complex life cycle. Researchers at the universities of California, Colorado, California, and Yale have found that "the care provided by most American child-care centers is so poor that it threatens children's intellectual and emotional development, according to a four-state study of hundreds of such centers."[76] Meanwhile, parents navigate a turbulent sea of changing forces, a major one being the need for money earned by mothers. Graphic episodes of maltreatment by hired child care providers are symptoms of the societal problem and exaggerate its impact on bewildered parents. Sue Shellenbarger in the Wall Street Journal of October 21, 1998, describes the sharp negative impact of labor shortages on day-care providers when rapid turnover of staff—up to 50 percent at some centers, 31 percent on average—causes small children a variety of more or less significant deficits because of the lack of stability among the adults in their tiny worlds.

These changes also reflect the fact that there is no certainty of cooperation between males and females to raise children. Once upon a time there existed a sense of entitlement or expectation: A woman could rely on a man's economic support for maternity and mothering and even beyond. This was expressed by courts that awarded divorced women alimony through their lifetimes, separate from child support. However fragile this post-maternal entitlement may have been before, it has since been firmly eroded. Women used to have an entitlement to *receive* money. Now they have an entitlement to *earn* money. One consequence is reduced family size, not only in the wealthy industrial countries but in poor ones, too.

Nothing Is Certain but Life and Taxes

So far I've reviewed what happens within families, what keeps them together or apart, or precludes their existence altogether. Now I want to place them in the larger economic context of modern states where governments and families meet most directly—on the issue of taxes.

There is always war between families and governments. Governments tax families. Governments take from families money that they would presumably use as they want and bequeath as they could. The government largely uses money for non-private purposes—for public projects, defense, essential services, and police protection to the wider community. Governments may also decide to provide for individual families in the form of allowances, entitlements, public education, and health. A great deal of the tension surrounding contemporary politics has to do with whether or not the state should tax individual earnings for public uses and how much.

Finding this money has always been a challenge for governments. People keep two sets of accounts, one for the family and one the government. Whole countries have operated that way. Many still do. But because of computers, electronically coded checks, and other devices of modern communication, governments now have better methods of surveying, invading, and confiscating flows of money to families and individuals. They collect more money more easily. Hence there are cries about "big government."

And there is another quite profound, if seemingly banal, development: When once-domestic activities such as cooking and cleaning are performed for money, government taxes extract still more money from families. Every meal in a restaurant and every shirt cleaned at the dry cleaner's is a tax increase. This has immense financial implications that are largely not understood by those concerned with government control, on one hand, and family stress, on the other. But it represents a new plateau of power for the economy of money rather than of intimacy that cannot be quantified.

The connection between governments and families is at a historically high level of intimacy. Almost everywhere this remains one of the most irritating and controversial of the demands of citizenship. Governments hover or fall as a consequence of how abrasive these confiscations are. "Right" and "left" in politics are often precisely about this issue.

Among industrial communities we see how energetic the contest is. As an illustration, we can note that tax revenues, including Social Security, as a percent of gross domestic product were estimated for 1994 to range from about 38 percent in Japan and about 33 percent in the United States to nearly 50 percent in France, Germany, and Italy.[77] Mr. and Mrs. Front Porch have to contribute to the management. In Japan, where cartels, zoning regulations, and price controls are omnipresent, but elsewhere, too, household consumption is stringently assessed by tariffs, taxes, and rules that inflate consumer prices. Products made in Japan often cost far more there than in America or Europe because restrictions on trade and prices deny consumers an open market.

There is a more significant effect of taxes on modern families, on the dead. Taxes are one effort to remove the mountainous inequality that can develop from the growth of wealth across generations. There is a broad contemporary trend, toward some restriction of untrammeled inheritance of monies earned and taxed over a lifetime. In Canada the parents of baby boomers are, in actuarial terms, poised to die. They have accumulated a trillion dollars in assets. Fully half of this will be taxed before estates are passed on to their heirs.[78] What's left is then distributed roughly equally to direct family members.

Societies differ substantially in how they do this and how they treat inheritances. The French case is particularly well defined. One of the most interesting results of the French Revolution was abandonment of primogeniture in favor of broader inheritance. Bequests flow to family members in equal proportions. The estate of a person who dies leaving a spouse and two children will be obligated to turn over at least one-quarter to each of the three close family members. The only optionally disposable funds are 25 percent of the estate or the same percentage as the family members receive. That can go to friends, lovers, employees, charities, and the like. Some individuals are able to circumvent these regulations by locating their wealth in independent companies, the assets of which can transfer in various directions. But their broad obligations are very explicit.

French law is clear, coercive, and oriented to the family pattern. Children from former marriages share in the estate in the same proportion as children and the spouse in a current marriage. Divorced spouses have no claim because the legally mandated divorce agreement separates family assets into those brought to the marriage by husband and wife. Then the remainder is shared to reflect the respective contribution of the partners to the family resources. Often, if there is a family house involved, this will pass to a daughter, with compensating cash or other assets to a son to maintain a family business if there is one.

The French bias is to maintain socioeconomic continuity while satisfying some needs of future generations, securing money for government activity, and reducing inherited privilege in a less drastic manner than the revolution. Among industrial societies, Russia, with 25 percent, and the United States (where laws vary between states), with 33 percent, are unusual in not requiring that at least 50 percent of inheritance flow to members of immediate family.[79]

The links between family and government have a direct and complex impact on the intimate lives of people at home. Property, which can be accumulated within the private family, can only be transferred between the generations with sharp curtailment by what is defined as the public interest. The grim contemplation of the death of family members must be trammeled by an array of inheritance arrangements ranging from simple wills and irrevocable trusts to offshore stashes, earnest foundations, and bequests of buildings to schools.

The prime case of what can happen when there are no inheritance taxes is the English royal family. Uniquely in England the monarchy had always been exempt from inheritance and other taxes, putatively to spare it the embarrassment of disclosure of relatively intimate matters. Because of this decisive advantage over other investors, the royal family has accumulated vast holdings, even though it has done little to earn it, except perhaps its art collection, which remains a form of national wealth. But in the 1990s even Elizabeth II for political reasons elected to pay some tax, emphasizing the power of the antifamilial egalitarian agenda. For more modest families with some assets there is no choice. Death and taxes are faced at once.

Family Business

Modern political systems are broadly committed to equality—at least they claim they are. No longer is there public allegiance to a monarchy, aristocracy, or even the leadership and privilege of the current party. Income redistribution is a pervasive modern value. In the past the whole *point* of being rich was to have more money and power than the poor. As much as possible people with resources sought governments that protected this goal. They still try. But the ethos of the times sharply limits such freedom of action.

Important here is the spirit of the law as it affects modern families. At least officially, the strict communist countries or collectives such as the kibbutz movement were the most keen to deny families the opportunity to accumulate or even enjoy wealth. A large part of the world was and still is affected by this quite epic principle. In various jurisdictions, family-owned property of "the bourgeoisie" was simply expropriated. Families could not own their own housing or their farms or their places of work. Even in capitalist communities there remains a strenuous struggle between defenders of the economic rights of the untrammeled individual and the needs of society.

In the United States, family businesses produce about half of the gross national product. Nevertheless, only three in ten family businesses last into the next generation and only one in ten reaches the third generation, and much of the shortfall has to do with taxes. Another cause is the reluctance of otherwise effective people to contemplate and plan efficiently for their own demise or to separate family needs from business needs.[80] Death and taxes conspire to strip families, with equal finality.

By contrast with the tightly controlled system of French inheritance discussed earlier, it may seem that the American style favors change more firmly, almost for its own sake. Nevertheless, even in supposedly dynamic America, with its relatively low legal requirement for family inheritance, patterns are strikingly conservative. As Debra Judge and Sarah Blaffer Hrdy of the University of California at Davis found in their study of 1,538 wills filed in Sacramento, California, between 1890 and 1984, children and/or spouse received an average of 92 percent of the wealth of the decedent. Seventy-one percent of parents with two or more children saw to it that the children were treated identically. There was no evidence of a preference for one sex or the other.[81] These were private choices, not constrained by law, and in the American state often considered the most flexible, if not *deraciné*, in its social arrangements!

Governments may or may not exact tribute from families, but parents are not without power. In the old days in Europe and America, and in many places still, families were responsible for providing dowries for daughters, bride prices for sons, or some other support for the next generation.

Perhaps the most important gift now between generations is educational support and opportunity. As we have seen, the youngster's brain becomes a safety deposit box for family wealth. In practical terms, family money becomes college opportunity and fees for tuition. When a couple announces that they will marry, arrangements such as the bridal engagement shower will be set in motion. Gifts are principally directed to the female. They focus on the domestic equipment of the family. While hardly universal, the pattern persists at least in the upper middle class whereby the new couple registers their choice of dining equipment with as elegant a shop as their milieu will tolerate. Gift givers supply various elements of the complete array. This is a kind of collectively generated dowry and is one of the few ways in which families and friends can provide direct economic boosts to children.

The Japanese wedding feast is typically very elaborate. It reflects social and business ties of the parental generation as well as that of the bride and groom. In 1996 the celebration overall cost an average $83,000, including a $10,000 gift given by the groom to the family of the bride. The mountainous cost of the ceremony is thought to be one reason for the relatively low frequency of Japanese divorce. But there is a movement away from such ceremonies. Young people have increasingly turned away from such traditional practices, which is associated with a decrease in this pattern of stability.[82] Still, transfers of wealth and property bind the newlyweds' families to each other economically. There is a discernible tendency for costlier weddings to predict stabler marriages than less expensive.

Out on the Limb on the Family Tree

In this chapter we have examined the connection between the ability of independent contractors to earn money, what happens when they become dependent members of families, and when families become dependent on them. Even though modern culture inextricably links money with notions of personal dignity and value, it also harbors a reluctance to acknowledge that love and money and reproduction and resources are associated. We are willfully inexplicit about the size of the dowry or bride price that will support the next generation, and there is little general understanding, at the level of whole societies, of what flows of intergenerational wealth are all about.

Economist and philanthropist Gordon Getty has proposed—to simplify his assertion drastically—that the ambient current interest rate reflects the cost of raising the next generation. He asks why "rate of return is typically a few percent per year, rather than per second or per millennium."[83] Getty identifies an underlying principle. In natural economics, organisms seek to convert resources into future organisms. The industrial way of life boasts many ways of approaching, suspending, or avoiding this matter altogether. Nevertheless, the link remains between resources, children, and the future. Its character reveals a great deal about what is happening between men and women. Maleness and femaleness are forces within a larger system. While that system can and does have an often massive effect on how they conduct their lives, there remain relatively pure essences of reproductive sexuality which resurface in each generation, whatever the setting of their expression.

CHAPTER SIX

Mother Courage in an Abrasive World

MARRIAGE IS AN EVENT of engulfing personal importance often linked to religion and the supernatural. People commit their only life cycles to each other. "Till death do us part" is the point of departure and a bulletin about the intended ending.

A family is supposed to be the whole story, not just a chapter. Almost all betrothed couples experience a warm sense of promise. Yet many families fall apart. One simple reason is that human plans sometimes fail. Illness and other abrasive realities change the shape of people's lives and limit what they can do. But there are other early identifiable factors. The economic relationship between men and the wider community affects the love and reproductive relationship between men and women. When it comes to children, while some men are single fathers, the overwhelming impact of damaged or broken marriages and the demands of childhood are on mothers—on women. Now I want to focus on the failure of the contemporary kinship system to protect the mother-child bond from the vagaries of the male-female link. Remember, this protection of that mother-child bond is at the core of kinship systems in the first place.

Playwright Bertolt Brecht created an unforgettable character called Mother Courage in his play about a woman who must endure a cavalcade of misfortunes, cruelties, and inequities, almost always on her own. The Mother Courage of modern society has for various reasons rejected or been abandoned by a partner. Or she never had one she could call "partner" in the first place. This Mother Courage is not all women, she is not the majority, yet she is numerous. Her tribe increases each year. Her aspect looms large as people—especially women—try to define the world in which they live.

We have already explored the profound significance of the Virgin Mary of the Christians and reflected on how Christmas reflects the human life cycle as a story about mammalian bedrock, about the foundation event of human experience. Perhaps the most successful holiday in the world, it is biased in favor of human generosity, not meanness, especially toward the care of mothers and infants. Without resources, Mary bears and must care for a child. Again, she has to confront alone a central mammalian spasm and needs assistance at a crucial time. Mediated by divine intervention and the wise men, the community provides the means for life to continue.

The story of Mary captures not only the drama of birth but also the fervent dilemmas that surround fidelity, loyalty, and responsibility during the long years of parenthood. We have seen that, unlike foxes, people are not able to move coolly on after one breeding season. Brief marriages are nearly always lacerating or at least inconvenient and embarrassing. Nevertheless, people often want to move on to another partner to capture that newness. The episode may begin as adultery with the expectation that its enjoyments and passion will be extensive but its broader impact sharply limited. Then it may turn into a bitter disappointment or the beginning of a new marriage. However it begins, there appears some readiness to start a new cycle whether or not the participants have procreated in their present one. Monogamy and loyalty and fidelity may be well established in custom and in law. But with disruptive and demoralizing frequency many people begin adulterous relationships with a new person who promises sparkle, intrigue, color, a bright discovery—who promises a tempting upgrade of experience.

The incidences of adultery vary from community to community, and society's responses to it vary, ranging from frank polygamy to stoning adulterers to crafty deception.[1] But however it is handled, the elation of fresh passion and commitment has apparently to be managed by the authorities. Someone must be concerned with the community's supervision over individual affection.

An early and influential regulation was designed to deal with the matter: "Thou shalt not commit adultery." One way the community protects the mother-child bond from the often fractious male-female link is with firm restrictions such as the Islamic *sharia*, the precise codes of which govern even intimate personal action.[2] These are often puritanical and sometimes savage. Together with legal and financial impediments, the commandment may work. Even where it doesn't and married people have lovers or mistresses, obvious or covert, there have always been legal means to require payment for supporting children, for restitution to aggrieved or humiliated families, or outright punishment for violating norms of behavior. In the United States Navy, men and women who have committed adultery on board ship may receive dishonorable discharge, with all the negative financial and personal implications that predicament carries. The colonial Puritans interrogated midwives and expelled unmarried women who did not identify their babies' fathers. In an echo of the present, the men named would be required to pay child support.[3]

The anti-adultery commandment and why it is necessary are symptoms of human nature. They reveal the turbulent inner scheme of our species. By and large, if people don't want to do something, there won't be laws or rules forbidding it.

Surely no responsibility can be as serious and compelling as parenthood. Then why is there any question at all whether people will perform it adequately?

There is some indication that people do respond to a primordial schedule for child rearing. At least for a time after a baby is born couples appear to withstand or suppress the exciting attractions of new potential partners. Helen Fisher showed that the most common time for divorce is after four years of marriage. This is just about the minimum time for the human pair to bring a child to sufficient competence, assuming pregnancy occurred before marriage or the child was conceived soon after.[4]

The existence of "bureaugamy," which defines a family pattern involving a mother, a child, and a bureaucrat, indicates that at least one parent, overwhelmingly the mother, acts as the dutiful fox. These parents stay around to do the best they can even if they have to seek the colorless support of impersonal and even hostile officials and governments. Contemporary single parents can't raise young on their own without great difficulty—without a spouse, a servant, a good job and a servant, an inheritance, a government payment, or an active relative or friend. Our offspring require far more than the ministrations of one breeding season to acquire the heft and skill to live on their own, and most parents find it challenging and ennervating to go it alone. Most receive or at least crave some assistance from their specific kin group or the community at large.

The supportive bond between fathers and children is sharply unreliable compared with the bond between mothers and children. Divorce, single motherhood, bureaugamy, non-marriage—all are indications that there can be a frail link not only between mother and father but also between father and child, for a variety of reasons ranging from paternity uncertainty to welfare practices to confused notions of maleness and fatherhood to restricted economic opportunities for young men. As a result, the connection between men and children fails frequently to endure in the way it should.

What happens to women when they can't depend directly on specific men as husbands or fathers of their children? Is the situation as desperate as has been asserted by countless people concerned with family stability and social calm? Is bureaugamy the best solution?

What Does Mother Nature Think About Single Mothers?

Is there even a problem? In the eye of nature, having children is good in itself. Being poor is biologically serious only when it interferes with the gold standard of biology—raising healthy children who can go on to have children themselves. It is the most fundamental test of how effective the individuals are in a community. Contemporary industrial communities have turned this ancient measurement on its head. A common complaint about welfare is that it stimulates dependency among women, their children, and *their* children. But that complaint is wrongheaded. On the contrary, it is precisely what a healthy population should be doing—being dependent on one another. It is a signal of biological robustness even though many people consider it a political and moral failure. It works fine as a reproductive system if not as a productive one.

In fact, not having children or having a few or hardly any is the pathology. A low or zero birthrate may suit some contemporary standards about population, pollution, and the needs of the labor force, but it is the so-called welfare queen who raises her children and then helps with her grandchildren who is, in the terminology of health food stores, "all natural."

Even if the situation is not wholly natural, it approaches normality in the statistical sense. Single-parent births have become increasingly common in industrial countries and are increasing: 30.2 percent of all births in the United Kingdom, where the number of unmarried single mothers has doubled in one decade; 11 to 13 percent in Germany; and 5 to 6 percent in Greece, Spain, and Italy.[5] In France in 1990, 30 percent of all births were to unmarried parents.[6] In the African-American community the majority of births are to unmarried women: 62 percent in 1989 and up to 80 percent in especially poor areas. The white rate was at least 20 percent and climbing rapidly, to an estimated 30 percent by the turn of the century. Among fifteen- to nineteen-year-old women, the highest numbers are in Britain, where 87 percent of births in this age group are to unmarried women; the incidence in the United States is 62 percent, while Japan shows 10 percent, with an 11 percent rise in 1996.[7] Meanwhile, in the *Washington Post* of November 16, 1998, D'Vera Cohen reports that one-third of households in the Washington area are headed by women.

Canada appears to be an exception. Despite the fact that welfare benefits for single mothers are nearly twice as generous as in the United States, the birthrate of single mothers in Canada is less than half of that in the United States.[8] Among women under twenty-five the abortion rate has declined from nearly half of all pregnancies in 1981 to just over one-third in 1989. These patterns, so anomalous to the rest of North America, have been explained as the consequence of effective family-life education in public institutions.[9] If that is the principal reason, it appears to work at least for the present. Presumably other cultural factors, such as the origin and nature of immigrant communities and the lower population density, play a role as well.

In the United States in 1960—*before good birth control*—only 5 percent of all American births were outside marriage. The rate was 22 percent for black Americans. Thirty years later the national number had risen to 24 percent.[10] By 1993, Senator Patrick Moynihan's Senate Finance Committee estimated that the rate of births to unmarried women was 30 percent, an increase of 82 percent from 1980. Single women accounted for 71 percent of births in Detroit, 65 percent in Washington, D.C., and 45.2 percent in New York. One expert testified that the national average would rise to at least 40 percent by the year 2000.[11] Data from Jamaica suggest the large dimensions of the issue in a partly industrial community and in the Caribbean region as a whole. A study there of 229 first pregnancies in 1969 found that only 6.4 percent were to legally married women. Strikingly, "union instability was positively related to reproductive performance."[12] Relationships *without* durability produced more children than stable ones.

What about fathers? We've seen that the progenitor male may not be sure that he is the father of a child. Or he may well not care about the child even if he is sure. He may remain largely uninvolved or may not be part of the supply of help and resources for the child. While a general pattern is emerging, there is variation. In the United Kingdom out-of-wedlock births are 30 percent of the total. Of that number, 40 percent are registered to two parents, unmarried but living at the same address.[13] These couples are not prevented from receiving welfare benefits as they are in the United States, though there are some U.S. initiatives to begin supplying welfare for fathers living with their children and their mothers. It isn't clear how durable these English non-marital relationships are. Birth registration follows quickly, perhaps while the new baby is casting a spell. What happens later is uncertain.

There are many fathers for whom children are a low priority or not in their plans. They don't possess a commitment to the offspring remotely comparable to the mothers'. Rutgers sociologist David Popenoe found that unsecured unions in Sweden are more likely to break up than legalized ones.[14] In the past there was no sure way to attribute paternity other than by assertion, but now there are accurate genetic tests of paternity. So far these have had little general impact except in cases involving money, criminality, or substantial other legal consequences.[15] The tests are becoming cheaper to administer—between $300 and $800—and are increasingly accessible to the public. It is difficult to foresee what use of such a test will mean for courtship, mating, and family life, but it is clear that when governments can compel child support payments from genetic fathers, as some jurisdictions already have, widened use of paternity tests will have a volatile impact on what men and women do.

We have seen that countless people do not use readily available means to avoid maternity and paternity. They are equally reluctant to use technology to confirm paternity, which is more difficult to acquire, more costly, highly demanding emotionally, and has burdensome conse-quences. They have more to do with lawyers than lovers.

In many cases the father figure remains just that, a figure.[16] The original welfare legislation to supply funds to women and children was designed to aid widows with dependent children. There was literally no father. In more recent times there may be a living father, but he may be unable to find adequate work or is absent or is not actually the father or is utterly unconcerned. An adult man living in a household may restrict it from benefits. The rules fight themselves. They discourage precisely the responsible connection between men and women that the legislation is supposed to encourage. In many jurisdictions married women with husbands cannot receive assistance whereas single ones can. It may also become a de facto stimulus to "living in sin" since an unmarried partner may be less detectable than a legal spouse.

The unit of the mother with child can be taken as the core of social organization. In the past, however, and in many places today it has not been defined as "normal," normative, or acceptable. Unwed mothers were expected to experience shame, not pride. Their children were bastards and illegitimate.[17] The rules were clear.

But no longer. The stigma attached to single motherhood has rapidly declined, particularly for women who are financially able to supply their own resources to their children without tapping the public treasury. In a widely publicized case in 1993, a successful English attorney and Tory city councillor had a so-called love child with a cabinet minister in John Major's government. When her identity was finally revealed, there was considerable outrage that the minister had hidden the fact and violated his government's commitment to "family values." He then agreed to provide some support for the child. Meanwhile, the mother adopted a firm and proud public stance: "'I am quite capable of making my own decisions. I am in full-time employment, and neither I nor my daughter are a burden on the state,' she told the London *Times*. The article called her a new breed of single mother who verges on being the archetype of the modern professional woman: self-sufficient, resourceful, and well placed to bring up her five-month-old daughter, Claire-Marie, by herself. In the age of choice, Stent is viewed with something bordering on admiration."[18]

The Bureaugamous Solution

A new kind of Mother Courage? She may indeed be a model heroine to many other women confronting the intersection of fertility and practical life, but this is an unusually elegant case. Nevertheless, there is growing acceptance of teenage pregnancy among unmarried youngsters in the United States, even if they do receive public money as welfare. Many of them live with blue-collar parents who a generation ago would have provided neither shelter nor approval. About half give birth, a third abort, and the rest miscarry. About one-fifth of conceptions do not come to term. These women are far less ostracized from schools, churches, and even their families than in the past.[19] New York City high schools provide high chairs for the children of their children. Among mothers seventeen or younger, the number completing high school nearly tripled, from 19 percent in 1958 to more than half in 1986. The majority of unmarried adolescent mothers are able to complete high school. They find full employment off welfare. Two-thirds of their children complete high school. Three-quarters of their children do not become teenage parents themselves. It has been asserted by sociologists Sally MacIntyre and Sarah Cunningham-Burley that in the United Kingdom "data do not support the argument that teenage pregnancy per se results in poverty and disadvantage."[20]

These are arresting data. Deeply rooted values have changed. When public acceptance greets single-mother Conservative politicians in England, Dominican teenage mothers in New York, and fertile cheerleaders in Texas high schools, something substantial is under way. Perhaps this reflects battle fatigue among people who may disapprove but are overwhelmed by the numbers. Perhaps it reveals an appreciation of the ineluctability of human sexuality, to say nothing of the intrinsic love parents and grandmothers feel for babies.[21] Given the difficulties of parenthood in its modern version, perhaps blaming the victim seems no longer the public policy of choice, except perhaps by politicians voracious for votes or moralists skating on the thin ice of their personal certainty.

Mr. Senator and the Wicked Stepfather

Modern biology as a science has had little to do with forming social policy. There is a discontinuity between what we know about biology and how we expect people to behave. It creates chronic and vexing circumstances for men and women engaged in family life. Neither in the Bible nor in the Book of Bureaucratic Rules is there much evidence of practical thought about the reproductive biology of our species. Ideology and biology are drastically unsynchronized. It is ironic, for example, that officially Catholic Italy has one of the lowest birthrates in the industrial world, 1.3 children per woman; replacement of the population requires about 2.2 children per female.[22] The State of New Jersey contrived the bizarre innovation that, yes, a married woman can receive welfare, but only if her husband is *not* the father of her children.

Well-meaning public servants and politicians struggle to define acceptable policies. There is a welter of initiatives, experiments, bold new welfare reforms, and political squabbles alternating between restriction and support. Political conservatives avidly approved the State of New Jersey's law of 1993, which prevented women on welfare who became pregnant from receiving benefits for their additional child or children. But this had the effect of increasing the rate of abortion in the state—not a high conservative priority—which led to lawsuits alleging discrimination against innocent youngsters.[23]

Legislation that promotes policies contrary to the tendencies of human biology will enjoy the same success long-term as laws that demand that objects fall upward. If legal assumptions about human behavior are wrong, the behavior that results from these legal changes will be unstable. Federal Judge Richard Posner of the Court of Appeals based in Chicago and of the University of Chicago Law School has sharply criticized "rejection of biological and economic science, rejection of liberalism, rejection of the evidence of one's senses" as a feature of efforts to coerce social behavior by legal fiat.[24]

What do laws do about paternity uncertainty? This became a large issue for men once women were able to control contraception without male involvement or knowledge. Often, the realistic assumption is made, as in New Jersey, that the stepfather will be less likely to support a child than the biological father, so the state steps in. But this provides a benefit for a woman and her child precisely because it replaces a father who has left what should be his post. It releases that man from his obligation, especially if he is neither able to provide child support nor able to be found by authorities—though there is increasing success in finding delinquent fathers. And it may cause a child to endure a formal separation from its father. There was even an astonishingly hapless British program that required divorced fathers *to send checks to the government,* to be divided among all the offspring of all divorced spouses, not just their own. Any interest a father maintains in his own children may be sharply diminished if there is no direct connection between his money and his children's well-being. He may endure a bureaucratic trampling of whatever commitment he may feel. Such incomprehensibly bizarre blunders will fail to generate the ideal family system that lawmakers and planners presumably want. They do not know the biology they are confronting.

As if there weren't difficulties enough, many welfare plans fail to acknowledge findings such as those compiled by Martin Daly and Margo Wilson of McMaster University in Ontario to which we have already referred on the physical danger to which young children living with stepfathers are subjected. Astonishingly, such children are sixty to one hundred times more likely to be beaten and eleven times more likely to be killed than children living with their natural parents.[25]

Obviously, most stepfathers live lovingly and constructively with their new children. Sixty percent of children in the United States who have never lived with their biological fathers reside with a surrogate or a stepfather by the time they are eighteen.[26] Nevertheless, increases of child abuse have been widely reported. I believe these reflect the biologically based pattern we consider here and should be considered a serious public health issue. Prevention is surely possible. Social workers and others concerned with stepfamily formation should acquire expertise in reproductive social biology. At the present time public money is being spent with the best of intentions and the most depressing of outcomes.[27]

There are even implications for international economy and the competitiveness of whole societies. Laws affecting family and bureaugamy are redolent with implication. Quantity and quality of children matter. Family experience helps provide them with a sturdy emotional and intellectual platform on which to stand to confront the wider interdependent world. For example, in his compendious study of contemporary productivity, Harvard historian David Landes suggests that the real and psychological segregation of women in fundamentalist Islamic societies not only reduces their ability to contribute to economic activity but also inhibits the competence and freedom of initiative of their husbands and sons.[28]

One reason Japanese children appear to perform effectively and dutifully in school is that their mothers are usually home and able to provide a custom-tailored second school system for them. This advantage will ebb away as more women work, or delay or avoid marriage altogether. Traditional Japanese family patterns are becoming less attractive to Japanese women than the workforce.[29]

As to quantity, the Japanese government has been alarmed enough about its low birthrate to create a new category of welfare. The third child is greeted with a bonus of nearly $7,000. For similar reasons, the German state of Brandenburg pays parents $650 for each new child.[30] The province of Quebec has similar concerns about sustaining a large and healthy population. It now pays women a monthly stipend when they breast-feed their babies, which is believed to enhance social and intellectual performance.[31] This is in addition to a *bebe-bonus* of $1,000 for the second child and $6,000 for the third and all subsequent children.[32] Nonetheless, the birthrate in Quebec is 1.5 children per female compared with 1.75 in English Canada, which offers no special subsidy. It is also significantly below the two-plus needed to keep the population at least stable.

Both single parents and married ones have to cope with strenuous parallel demands from the private family system and the public economic one. Help is not always available. In Canada, a nation with a relatively cordial attitude toward family welfare, an estimated 60 percent of mothers of the 1,165,000 Canadian children under three are in the labor force. But in the whole country there are for all ages only 333,082 regulated day care centers.[33] There are also 1,125,000 children between three and five. Meanwhile, only 34 percent of primary care parents in Canada considered full-time work their most desirable option. Nearly one-fifth "experience severe tension on a daily basis."

But work they must. The human fox's lair must be adequately provisioned far beyond one year, even when one of the parents must work for some other foxes down the ravine. In the United States, between 1980 and 1993 there was a 16 percent increase in the number of parents of preschoolers who both work, bringing the total rate up to nearly 75 percent.[34] Not until a child is five is its community obligated to offer it supervised and constructive time away from home—in the school. Meanwhile, Mr. and Mrs. Canadian Fox are taxed overall some 44 percent of their income. In the United States and the United Kingdom, as well, married people pay more tax on their combined income than single people.[35]

Good Value from Good Welfare

We have explored the relationships that exist between marriage, money, governments, taxes, and families. We compared the needs of children with the turbulent temptations of the long human sexual cycle. We have seen that the movement to bureaugamy is caused by the failure of marital bonds—the effective cause of over two-thirds of single-parent families— or no marriage in the first place.

It is necessary now to turn to the issue of "welfare," a word that reflects public efforts to confront some of the strains in private life. Around it circulate political remedies, to keep it from being relied on. Some states limit welfare payments to two years, after which the recipient is expected to be employable. But this is almost certainly doomed to fail since children continue to need to eat even after two years whether or not a parent has work, and we have noted the increase in abortion among mothers approaching the two-year limit.

The hue and cry about welfare policies is that they create a permanent class of dependent malingerers and incompetents. But the fact is that the majority of single mothers seek to support themselves and their children on their own without government subsidies for most of the time. "Fewer than half of all single mothers are on welfare at any time in a given year," wrote Peter Marks in the *New York Times*.[36] In the United Kingdom two in five single parents work, and only 9 percent say they never want employment.[37] In the United States some 30 percent of single women and their children are recurrently on welfare. Perhaps 20 percent of this number has been hindered by the difficulty of finding suitable employment in a competitive, changing, and demanding economy in which jobs decline for relatively unskilled people.[38] During a period of available employment, women appear to leave welfare for work. Economist Jeffrey Leibman of the Kennedy School of Government found a decline in the rate of women with children on welfare, from 19.4 percent in 1991 to 10 percent in 1997.[39] While inadequate public transportation for poor people stranded in the centers of cities can be a decisive blow to the search for work, the rolls of recipients are in decline as the American economy generates more jobs and while welfare benefits are under challenge. Perhaps the American experience will prove reassuringly benign, but it is yet unclear what will happen to the children of those who have to leave welfare.

The principal focus of discussions of welfare is on single mothers. Single motherhood may be the most arduous role in the whole social system, yet many choose it. In a fascinating revisionist study, Mikhail Bernstam and Peter Swan of Stanford University demonstrated very early on that single mothers are far from reckless and nonstrategic in their reproductive lives.[40] On the contrary. In the United States single mothers bore children in response to three broad factors: (1) the level of employment of the males in the age and social group from which they might expect to secure partners, (2) the level of the minimum wage these men might earn, and (3) the level and ease of receipt of welfare benefits in particular communities. When good employment opportunities for males increase, single motherhood declines. When there are few or no jobs for males, single motherhood becomes the principal reproductive strategy. When available welfare benefit packages change significantly, the women try to move to a better welfare climate. Here is thoughtfully strategic behavior about both love and money.

Bernstam and Swan's iconoclastically informative study depends on data gathered before 1980. There have been obvious demographic, economic, and attitudinal changes since then: global competition, declining male income, and government policies in flux. Perhaps these findings do not apply as sturdily as before, though they may be even more than less, especially given fading job prospects for unskilled men.[41] But the lesson learned is very likely more relevant than ever: *Young women are strategically astute in making reproductive choices. They take the limited economic opportunities of potential mates into careful account. They assess their own economic realities. Then they respond to the economy with enlightened calculation about what will be to their reproductive advantage.*

What Are the Realistic Options?

Few of the poorer young women in the situation we are considering are given the choice of single motherhood, acquiring an MBA degree, or marrying an orthodontist who drives a Jaguar. For most, life is highly circumscribed by economic, racial, familial, and other factors that deny them easy movement from occupational success and prosperity to reproduction. They may be facing mating options among a group of feckless men who resent or are ambivalent about prosperous women. For example, the unemployment rate among potential male mates may be as high or higher than the 40 to 50 percent of young black males in United States cities.[42] Almost 7 percent of adult black men were in jail or on parole in 1994. The total number of people in prison and jail tripled since 1980.[43] These figures reflecting all minority groups of the population increased over a number of years as cities became more segregated. In addition, low-skill jobs flowed out of the United States to low-wage countries. Ill health and drug addiction are other debilitating factors. Employment that generates family-size wages increasingly demands a level of education which is extraordinarily difficult for such young men to receive. What was possible for young men of the 50s is almost a dream for many in the 90s. How many men of any race or ethnic group can confidently assume they will, like their fathers, be able to support a spouse and several children in a seemly manner on their own check?

Among black women in the United States there is evidently some widespread perception that the men in their communities are unreliable.[44] In the United Kingdom, one-quarter of black males share a family unit with a white woman, an arrangement that is 12 times more likely than a black woman sharing a family unit with a white man.[45] But the issue is not primarily one of ethnicity or of culture—there are generic changes seemingly underway. The overall income of all men in the United States and other industrial countries is declining, both absolutely and in comparison with women. In a remarkably large and rapid change, during the 1980s the number of men working full-time dropped by 9 percentage points. On the other hand, women are working more, either because they want to or because they have to in view of the declining contribution of men to women and children.[46] These changes also take political form. It seems clear that working-class men delivered an extraordinary voting rebuke to the Clinton administration in 1994—the most dramatic to a party in power since 1894.[47] Presumably this was a reflection of policies directed to female interests.[48] The majority of these votes were from white males who deserted their traditional leaders. It left a legacy of unprecedented sex differences in voting preferences, which came to fuller effect in the election of 1996 when men and women diverged more than ever. Perhaps men resented the poor reputation they felt they had among women. Perhaps their votes reflected the sense of economic frailty we see in the overall national data about income. In the face of assertions by many women and some men that men have been patriarchs, perhaps white men by their votes denied that they were the crass exploiters and privileged princes of a system they somehow managed to sustain against the interests of their own gullible mothers, daughters, and wives.[49] A growing gender gap electorally in Germany may also reflect similar forces as more women enter the labor force while male unemployment remains high.[50] It has been projected that any Israeli political party which articulates the political agendas of female voters will disproportionately succeed in election.[51]

So we can expect the same pattern that Bernstam and Swan described to become more sharply etched as a new family pattern forms. Young men will face formidable difficulties becoming employable in jobs paying enough to support families. This applies in the United States increasingly to whites, though blacks and some other minorities (but not all) have experienced the problem first. Elsewhere, almost half of Spaniards under twenty-four are unemployed, and more than 25 percent of men in Italy and France.[52] Women may well conclude their marriage prospects are marginal. They have a finite window of biological opportunity. They will take advantage of the limited but real resources available from the bureaugamic system. We can see the tough numbers already pouring in.

Poor young urban women face other constraints. They may be living with their mothers or in cramped quarters. They may have few occupational skills with which to confront an economy offering them little or no access. They are also as healthy as they will ever be, at the prime of their sexuality and able to gain from it some status, some entertainment, and the possibility of a relationship with Mr. Right. Since males are eager to join in, however temporary, the mix seems combustible. The result is often a child.

Pregnancy may allow a woman to leap over years-long waiting lists for a subsidized apartment, though some governments have curtailed that boost and require unmarried mothers to live with their own families—except in the military where single mothers are able to escape barracks into an apartment of their own, as people who marry do. Pregnancy may yield health and welfare benefits superior to those available to non-parental single people. Perhaps most elementally it may also offer a sense of adult status to young women who when they look around them perceive few other practical and indisputable ways to secure this. And, surely, the state of pregnancy itself provides intrinsic satisfactions.

Let's for a moment consider a positive evaluation of the behavior of these women. In one pleasurable act and then in the rewarding process of pregnancy, *these young women achieve both productive and reproductive success at once.* They receive money for what they have done. Now they have a child, a source of beguiling love, social place, and self-esteem. They may acquire adult housing. They must begin a campaign on behalf of their new domestic unit. We will see that they do this more effectively than heretofore thought. They can feel they have begun to solve several of the largest issues humans face. They are in the big grown-up game. From this perspective they have aced an unpromising system. They have made a real choice with direct impacts. Whatever other people may think, from their standpoint they have achieved an upgrade.

The empirical evidence about the advantage of their life choice is the increasing rate of single motherhood. In the United States the rate of teenagers having babies rose inexorably each year after 1987 and leveled off in 1996. The United Kingdom rate has doubled in a decade, as elsewhere.[53] The behavior of these women is very different from that of the wider community.

But spend time in a children's playground. Watch the children of mothers apparently on state stipend. You will derive some sense of the care with which many dress and groom their children. Despite their source of income, these women are not necessarily casual mothers. Particularly during the years when they can control many of the conditions of their children's lives, they seem as skillful and loving as mothers can be. Of course the intimate years of early childhood pass, and then there are legions of issues these mothers cannot avoid or even imagine. Intriguing careers may seem closed to them, with no opportunities to move to different neighborhoods, different cities, or even different countries. Time will be stolen by the endlessness of child care. Energy will flow from mother to child as if from a tipped bucket.

Nevertheless, they have accomplished something. They have someone. Someone has them.

I have a clear position here. I am unwilling to accept the notion on face value that having a baby is less valuable than acquiring a law degree or a small business. It is not self-evidently better to become a lawyer than a mother; it is not self-evidently worse to be a welfare mother than a math instructor. How would the world look if the value of earning money was subsidiary to the importance of parenthood? Why chastise women for having babies at public expense when we would otherwise regard them as admirable citizens if they supported the children on their own? In return for very small stipends don't they forgo opportunities for larger incomes they could earn in the private sector, at least in theory, money that they wouldn't have to share with a child or children?

Whether it is desirable to advance the purposes of productive economy and not reproductive nature is an open question. The public argument on the issue has to focus on the fundamental question: Why should a woman on welfare taking care of her own two children on a small allowance receive less public approval than the woman employed to take care of the one child of two attorneys with a huge allowance? Is the young woman who aspires to become a nanny to the child of officials in a welfare agency morally superior to her sister who rears her child with funds from that agency? Is a young mother receiving public money she hasn't earned different from the young mother receiving trust funds she didn't earn? Of course there are laws of property, but as we saw from the story of Mary and Jesus, people also retain some commitment to notions of responsibility for persons in need.

The single mother is not only at the heart of the ancient mammalian process, she is also at the center of a major conflict of the modern period. Bureaugamy has emerged as the system that mediates between two large forces, one new, one old. The new one is the demand of an economy that puts a premium on the independent contractor at work. The old one involves the ancient imperatives of a sexually eager species that tries to maintain a premium on responsible reproduction. There is a fundamental conflict between the Marxist focus on production and the Darwinian attention to reproduction. The single mother, Mother Courage, drama-tizes this underlying confrontation.

A common response to this—ironically, most often from political conservatives such as Charles Murray, who would abolish welfare for young mothers—is that Marxist production is defined as more valid morally than Darwinian reproduction. There is a contest between love and money; it is not a heartless contest because there are far-reaching and urgent questions about the impact of the bureaugamic system on the lives of children.[54] In some barely articulated but heartfelt way the emergent rules of public decency say, "Choose money! Choose money!"

Have a Baby, and a Job Follows?

Even by the limited, largely male-centered standards of economics, however, welfare mothers are astute and sensible. It seems they will end up after all with both reasonable jobs and healthy babies. They will please the Marxists and the Darwinians at once. Arline Geronimus of the School of Public Health at the University of Michigan has drawn a number of conclusions plainly heretical to the conventional view that single mothers are relatively reckless, relatively ill-advised, and certainly economically doomed. Younger is healthier. Late teen mothers (though obviously not thirteen-year-olds) produce robust children. Older women may have suffered health deficits because of poverty and associated conditions. According to Geronimus, "Within poor African-American communities the infants of mothers in their 20's or older may fare substantially worse than those of teen mothers."[55] Teenage pregnancy is relatively rare (but increasing) among advantaged sections of society; in 1994 in the United States only about 4 to 5 percent of children were born to single mothers with incomes of more than $50,000, but 75 percent were born to mothers with incomes of less than $5,000.[56] Geronimus says single motherhood "is the statistical norm in disadvantaged segments. . . . Teen childbearing is not necessarily an emblem of pathology and can be adaptive." Particularly in poor, disrupted, and violent communities "caregivers at very young ages could be profoundly influenced by their experience in many ways, including an incentive towards early childrearing."

These young mothers may be making an adjustment to their real situation to confer a health benefit on their offspring. Not only are the economic costs of teenage pregnancy to the mother discernibly less, "perhaps dramatically less than have been claimed," but, says Geronimus, "the children of teen mothers appear to do as well as, or occasionally better than, the children of older disadvantaged mothers on indicators of their cognitive and socioemotional development."[57]

Most dramatically of all, Geronimus and Korenman report that *women who have children early experience an increase in their level of motivation and skill.* Their subsequent educational experience may be as good or better than equivalent women who do not become teen mothers.

Overall, welfare mothers do better in the economy. Why should this be a surprise? Becoming a parent is a challenge. Why shouldn't the practical demand of parenting stimulate rewarding insights into how life in the adult world works, just as it has traditionally done for young "family men" who "settle down"? Why shouldn't the responsibility and focus of a child concentrate the energy and skill of a young woman so that she becomes a more eager and adept recruit to the labor force once she has completed the relatively few early years of baby care and can move more freely than before in the wider community, especially if child care is available from a relative or her employer? In a review of relevant studies in *Family Planning Perspectives* of September/October 1998, Saul Hoffman of the University of Delaware expands the analysis.

A similar gain in competence appears among well-paid female executive-mothers compared with males. In the words of a senior female lawyer at the Atlantic Richfield Company, "Many women are working . . . and I think in order to survive on a daily basis, they have to be extremely organized and productive."[58]

Suddenly we see a replacement of the logic of economic activity with the biologic of reproduction. The outcome is not the disaster often predicted. The single mothers are not the reckless women they have been caricatured to be, nor the inept disgraceful vixens that politicians love to stone. They live sturdy life cycles. The suggestion has been greeted with a hefty ration of bitter controversy. This reflects less the frailty of the evidence than the prejudices of economic determinists who insist that people, particularly poor and young ones, must make money before love.[59]

Youth Chooses Darwin?

Darwin before Marx? A new political trend?

We are witnessing here a relatively private and intense form of political radicalism. In the severity of its challenge to the status quo it is comparable to the actions of early socialists and Marxists. But the struggle is not about production. This time the challenge is about reproduction. This time the leaders and heroes are not the intellectually confident party members, manifesto makers, and orators who look like Trotsky. Nobody promises to lead the way to a stunning utopia. These are just young women with babies.

Usually most visible rebels are men, but here as elsewhere they are fading out of the picture. The activists are young women who are deciding for themselves what is significant in their lives. They act with definition and some stubbornness. They defy conventional wisdom and established practice.

This response is not news. In puritanical times sexual behavior itself was a sign of radicalism, courage, and progressiveness. This was as much the case in Greenwich Village in the 20s, in the Israeli kibbutz, in Moscow after the revolution, in American utopias of the nineteenth century, and in Weimar Germany.[60] It was also the experience of young women post-pill who suddenly had few restrictions on their sexuality, at least until sexually transmitted diseases created what American writer Katie Roiphe suggests is the medical equivalent of traditional morality.[61]

The striking innovation here is that young women have taken the process a major step forward. Their radicalism is *not just about sex, it is about reproduction itself.* They are often members of low-status groups. They are female. They are young. They are the accused, not the accusers, in the debate. They do not consider themselves politicians. Can these be political pathfinders?

Perhaps they are. Perhaps, as communist parties once claimed about their own ideology-driven efforts, these women are in the vanguard of social change that has affected the major industrial societies—change that may extend its reach to such countries as India and China as they industrialize. And the movement to "make love, not money" is not restricted primarily to members of minority groups who receive a disproportionate amount of public attention. "Between 1965 and 1973 the white and non-white illegitimacy ratios rose 61.4 percent and 59.2 percent" respectively in America alone.[62] It is an increasingly common pattern in industrial societies. "For the majority of industrialized countries, the increase has ranged between 30 and 50 percent" since the early 1970s.[63]

It cannot be emphasized enough that we may be witnessing a shift from what was once small-scale pathology to now large-scale normality. Clearly few people see it that way, and clearly many people see its evident costs. Still, look around us. Precision in attributing particular causes is difficult. But change there is. Some of this happens; some of that happens; time passes. When does change occur? The specific moment is unavailable, but change there certainly is.

Marx predicted that the working classes would rebel and rise up against the capitalist masters of production. These young women are in Darwinian revolt against the controllers of reproduction.

While the reproductive analogy is imperfect, nevertheless we are witnessing a revolution of sorts—about kinship, not ownership; about mothers, not money; about fertility, not free trade; about maternity, not materialism. In both capitalist and communist communities there is ample premarital pregnancy and abortion. Even in relatively conservative rural and Catholic areas they are unstigmatized and seen as signs of growing up.[64] Are communities so lacking in ways for young women to feel adult that they must demonstrate they are good at something? Do they otherwise feel threatened by reproductive unemployment the way many European skinhead males appear to be threatened by productive unemployment? The fact is that countless young women are turning to an old way as they confront a new world during their fleeting years of youth.

CHAPTER SEVEN

The Second Sex

HERE ARE THE MEN of those mothers on their own? What's their role in producing a third of the babies born outside of marriage? Why were 76 percent of teenage American mothers in 1997 unmarried, an increase of over 500 percent since 1960?[1] Is something missing in the alloy of male and female so that it is difficult to sustain a vital bond?

We've seen that men have less and less domestic control over money and production, and hence over women. Women have more control over reproduction and income.[2] In these central matters women have gained greater independence of men. In the old days when a man and woman married, her father literally "gave the bride away." It was a financial and legal reality. She moved from her father's house, his budget, his name. In many cultures the father exercised stringent legal and religious control, which he then transferred to her new husband. In Orthodox Judaism with rabbinical approval a father could assign his eleven-year-old daughter to a mate through marriage to a male without even informing her or her mother of the potential groom's identity. The enabling phrase is in Deuteronomy 22:16: "I gave my daughter unto this man as wife." There was a court case about this in New York State in 1996.

Contemporary weddings may appear to mimic the traditional portrait, with traditional emotions swirling around the ceremony. But the reality is substantially different. Father may be at the wedding, perhaps cradling her arm, but Daughter carries her own tiara, perhaps in the form of a graduate degree, a sales territory, a gift for writing computer programs, a position coaching high school volleyball, or a second lieutenant's commission in the army.[3]

These are substantial changes in the conditions within which males and females encounter each other. There is declining commitment by both men and women to the principle that normal adult life involves a man supporting a wife and children—or so the clear reality of society suggests. Contemporary role models for young women are executives boarding helicopters, not mothers rocking babies. Sexual acrimony has been compounded by a broad and general antimale ideology tacitly accepted by the main body of commentators on these issues. Men have been handed an explicit burden of Original Sin. In one writers' organization, the nomination to an official position of a distinguished Russian woman writer was opposed by feminist members who complained that not only was she often late to meetings but that her brand of sexual politics was risible: She perceived that the men of Russia needed support, not antipathy. How could someone lacking commitment to the unvarying specter of malevolent males fairly serve a community of right-thinking writers?

Male behavior itself is treated as intrinsically questionable if not outright pathological, as seen in such examples as Natalie Angier's article "The Debilitating Malady Called Boyhood. Is There a Cure?" and the frequent diagnosis of attention-deficit hyperactivity disorder (ADHD) in boys, making it, in effect, a male disease.[4] Boys are decisively more likely to be defined as needing special education. Some commentators advocate an earnest effort to "raise [boys] in a sex-neutral way . . . and they'll be better people."[5] Meanwhile, in her peculiar inaugural address in 1994 as president of Barnard College, anthropologist Judith Shapiro defended single-sex educational institutions for women because they are important for self-esteem and professional advancement. Yet single-sex education for men (in military academies, for instance) is seen as producing degraded behavior.[6] We have already seen this opinion reflected in the comment on the matter by Ruth Ginsburg of the U.S. Supreme Court in the case concerning sexual integration in the Virginia Military Institute; all-female institutions were exempted.[7] Shapiro's self-satisfied opinion was offered as self-evident.

This may just reflect dyspeptic antimale bias by opportunistic and sentimental female commentators. It may reveal an effort at historical retribution. But something far more serious is at hand, linked directly to our roots in history and prehistory. The hyperactive male student in class no longer has any place for the rambunctious exploratory behavior of a young hunter. But that same restlessness would be a useful and even essential trait on a savannah where protein-hunting assignments do not emerge from a lesson plan but must be sought out and conquered through strategic and cooperative physical behavior.[8] Paleoanthropologists know that small physical and behavioral advantages can produce sharp advantages and disadvantages to competing groups of evolving humans. In the words of Ofer Bar-Yosef of Harvard and Mary Stiner of the University of Arizona, "Minor differences can make a major difference in determining what population is more successful than another."[9]

It is obvious why males are diagnosed with ADHD when they pay little attention to the educational tasks they are given. They are evolutionary specialists in different work that is by and large no longer available to them. Boys will spend endless hours playing sports and conversing eagerly about teams and players. They are rarely accused of

ADHD during recess or athletics. However, in an increasingly feminized workplace, they do increasingly poorly, another source of their declining economic capability. They are punished for who they are, as if they were a race or caste. Even in the seemingly harmless world of middle-class American summer camps, male athletic competitiveness has been curtailed to accommodate female campers and "ways for the less aggressive to be heard."[10] Modern males who want to become lovers, husbands, and fathers must compete with women not only for the jobs enabling them to do so but for jobs in which they may be less interested and to which many appear to bring discernibly restricted enthusiasm.

And then, of course, there is the vast matter of professional sports to which the overwhelming majority of men around the world pay avid, unremitting attention. Many newspapers provide as much news about sports as about the entire economy of the nation and the world. There is a reason for the wealth of fine athletes. Television permits them to enact the dreams of successful cooperative aggression of men around the globe. Television sport is to male personal achievement as videocassette pornography is to love.

This is another indicator that males are now the second sex, embedded in an already female-centered mammalian biological system in which the male is more vulnerable than the female. Women live longer. The healthier a society is, the greater the disparity between male and female life expectancy. In the United States the disparity has increased from 4.5 years in 1940 to 7 in 1995. Since 1993, though, the disparity has not increased but has begun to decline, if very slightly, especially among affluent groups. There is now an increase in the rate of mortality improvement of males greater than for females, from a lower base.[11]

The reasons for the large difference in longevity appear to be both physiological and cultural. TIAA-CREF is an insurance firm that provides pensions to college teachers, people for whom heavy lifting and physical danger are limited. The company was being compelled by U.S. legal changes in the 1980s to equalize pension payments per month to men and women even though women lived much longer. A major political basis for the legislation was the assumption that men died earlier because they worked more. The insurance company considered the legislation unfair and in violation of acceptable actuarial principles of insurance, and disagreed with the government's judgment about the cause of the differences. TIAA-CREF challenged the government by introducing facts that compared the longevity of women academics with similarly situated wives of academics. The latter lived *shorter* lives than the active workers. The government's argument was simply wrong.

Notwithstanding such evidence and all other accepted equitable practice, governments forced insurers to pay male and female pensions at the same rate. So now not only do men as a group continue to live shorter lives, but they get less of the pension money they are owed while women get more years and hence more money over time. It is an astonishingly large financial penalty—of which few people are aware, including its male victims—to satisfy a prevailing social value, especially when the average life expectancy for this particular population of college teachers is seventy-five for men and eighty-one for women.[12]

There are indications that the inequity in longevity in industrial communities will diminish somewhat as females, especially young ones, smoke more, drink more, and exercise less than men. Young women in the United Kingdom are now more likely to begin smoking than young men. More Swedish women smoke than men. English single women are twice as likely to be moderate to heavy drinkers than married women, and their numbers are growing.[13] There may be a subtle reproductive nihilism here as young women confront the problematic courtship situation we have been considering. Using nicotine to control appetite is likely to be another factor. As for men, the main diseases afflicting them, heart disease and lung cancer, are abating—the former because of medication, the latter because of a reduction in smoking. Nevertheless, a six- to seven-year gap remains overall.

Whatever the modern male of the species is doing or thinking and feeling, the female is likely to be mainly responsible for the children, if there are any, and to be working. She will be juggling obligations to employer, family, and community. She will be the principal or exclusive supervisor of arrangements for child care. And she will remain under personal and media-honed social pressure to comport herself as if she were also an elegant, leisured femme fatale without a care or diaper or deadline in the world.

Legal, political, and moral pressures for equitable access by females to the labor force heretofore dominated by males results in more women working harder at better and more jobs than ever. More men are supplying less money than ever to these same women. Men whose wives work earn less money than colleagues whose spouses stay at home.[14] For economic reasons as well as psychological and ethical ones, women have responded by demanding their fair share of the jobs through which men had acquired money in order to support their families on their single income.

Men Have Been Liberated

If liberation means the absence of unavoidable irrefutable obligation, women's liberation has backfired. It is men who have been liberated. They needn't be husbands or fathers to assure themselves of social status. They can be ex-husbands or part-time fathers. They are not required to support women and children for life. They may experience transient social and sexual variety with a range of partners. The contemporary nuptial scheme may be problematic or seem arduous to men and hence less likely to appeal to them. If so inclined, they may restrict their affectionate and sexual experience to other men, homosexuality having more acceptance than in remembered history.[15]

Two central patterns of traditional marriages, surrounding food and children, are far more unpredictable and perhaps unrewarding than ever for a man. He and his spouse may not have children because of external pressures of work, or choice or infertility problems. They may delay childbirth with clearly deleterious biological impacts, first on female fertility but eventually on both partners. Countless people endure late-age infertility and inhabit a gynecological gulag of clinics, drugs, and bitter regret.[16] The appointment books of successful fertility doctors are filled with small writing. The Chinese ideology of disparaging infant girls and the American delay of reproduction has led to a boomlet in the adoption of Chinese girls among older affluent Americans. In well-off parks of rich cities, convoys of twins in strollers advertise the power of drugs to augment otherwise declining fertility.

And what of food, that central value in the transaction between mammals? When I was growing up in the 40s and 50s, virtually all the food my father and I ate was prepared by my mother, including the lunches we carried to work and school. "Can she bake a cherry pie?" was a genuine question about life to come because of the division of domestic labor that prevailed. Since 1969 in the United States the average number of meals eaten out of the home has doubled to one out of two. The fast-food industry has expanded worldwide. McDonald's opened 530 restaurants in Japan in 1995 alone and 2,000 outlets in the United States, where over half of prepared food taken out—"home meal replacement," in industry jargon—is consumed at home.[17] Here is another sign of the bureaucratization of intimacy and a decline in the importance of domestic life. Not only have the transactions between men and women been curtailed, but they have been curtailed between children and adults in the same manner. As an indication of change in familial sharing, new products are designed so that children as young as seven can prepare their own dinner.[18] In May 1998 a major reversal of mammalian norms was announced in an ad for Kentucky Fried Chicken; it portrays a boy of perhaps eight cradling a bucket of prepared chicken and nuzzling with his mother who holds a plate of the food in her hand. The headline reads: HAVE DINNER WAITING WHEN MOM HITS HOME.[19] In response to marketplace pressures, producers of common home-prepared foods have reduced the recipes times from 30 to 20 minutes. The average number of ingredients has been cut from ten to six.[20] Even in restaurants there is increasing reliance on factory-prepared foods masquerading as fresh.[21] Other minor technical innovations such as wash-and-wear clothing, readily available bulk laundries, frozen and microwavable foods, and electronic entertainment have reduced the usefulness of traditional domestic arrangements.

The conditions apply to both males and females, but the loosening of

ties between men and women appears to have greater financial consequences for the latter.

"Men's liberation" presumably was not and is not the point of this
shift. It was certainly not the goal of the hardworking and endlessly beset
single mother or even the most traditional patriarch. But it has reduced
male responsibility and male contribution to the family system. In those
old days, men were able to regard their work and status as automatic
marks of esteem. There was strong and relatively durable reciprocity
between men and women. There was a sturdy connection between men
and their communities of work and public life, and between women and
the kinship and neighborhood networks that encompass and enable
private social life. These were sustained, however unfairly or falsely, by
an image of men as valued pillars of society. Men were the political elites,
the managers of wealth. They controlled male-centered laws that
excluded females from some privileged centers of social life.[22] Such
structures supported men in their conviction that what they did was
worth it. *They* were worth it.

Of course the power to actually control the conditions of their life
and work was minimal for the vast majority of individual men. Nearly
everyone was a midget worker in mighty systems over which they had
little if any command. In practice, nearly all men as well as nearly all
women were controlled by a few men. How could the Marxist notion of
a ruling class realistically incorporate half the population? Nonetheless,
the rebellion by women against the domination of all people by a few
men has been fierce. Even men without control are frequently defined as
the enemies of women by virtue of their sex. Because of affirmative
action, some contemporary young men must endure reduced opportunities compared with their sisters. Black American men feel this in
particular when hiring practices favor candidates who are both female
and minority; the employer improves two governmentally mandated lists
at once. The most prestigious art school in Toronto announced it would
hire no male members of faculty until the year 2000. When the U.S.
Supreme Court forbade positive discrimination on racial grounds for
contenders for federal contracts, the new regulations proposed in 1997

would continue to favor women over men. For example, in 1987 women were first considered "disadvantaged" in competing for Department of Transportation contracts and earned 20.4 percent of the dollars in the program. By 1996 it more than doubled, to 41.4 percent.[23] If such arrangements are comprehensible in the eyes of history, they may be far less so in the eyes of a young male artist or ambitious contractor.

The Americanization of Sexual Anger

Social and attitudinal changes supporting females and limiting males have led to an array of legal initiatives. Many have been modeled on and joined with the means used to combat the perversities of racism.[24] This is particularly so in the United States, but techniques abetting sociosexual change have been generalized to other societies. American social notions are "central to the American creed and central to the 'democratic values,' the export of which has been the avowed aim of every U.S. president since Franklin Delano Roosevelt . . . We have made ourselves at home in the world, characteristically, by regarding it as American in the making."[25] Because of the vast power of American mass media, the agenda of sociosexual renovation has been transmitted over the globe.[26]

There has been a positive impact on female economic interests in the public sphere because of affirmative action, mandates about equal pay, equal educational opportunity, and the like. More women can support themselves more interestingly and with fairer reward than ever. Although the longevity of existing employees and other obstacles continue to delay its completion, the engineering of the "level playing field," at least in North America, is headed firmly in the direction of equity. The number of women elected to state legislatures has nearly tripled since 1975. Women also hold one of four executive jobs.[27] The doctrine of the wholly open society prevails where it never has. Even the complex issue of the role of women in combat in the military has been as much affected by the desire to offer opportunities for occupational advancement in combat posts as by their danger and functional requirements.

Declining income from many jobs, including those husbands hold, as well as sharply rising costs and expectations make second incomes desirable. International competition from low-wage economies has made two incomes almost the norm in North America and Europe.[28] This has long been the case in Eastern Europe where planned economies made productivity the overriding goal, and reproduction was consciously contained by contraception and abortion.[29]

Let me continue to focus on the male side of the equation. Particularly in North America and Europe, the comparatively poor education and social preparation of underclass young men appear to condemn them either to jobs too poor to support married life or no jobs at all. In contrast, Asian societies decided to spend money on primary education for everyone instead of only on university opportunities for the elite. The low-paid jobs that unskilled American men could once regularly find have been exported abroad or made redundant by machines and more efficient management of time and resources. Lester Thurow estimated that the number of males who could not find work sufficient to support themselves and a family doubled between 1985 and 1995. They are simply unprepared for the new economy. They may never be unless successful government and private initiatives are introduced. Meanwhile, their means and status do not commend them to potential spouses and parents-in-law. They are threatened with both productive and reproductive oblivion.

The plans of many young males have become increasingly difficult to sustain. The alternative opportunities that could guide and sustain them are not yet in focus. In the United States three of four young people do not receive a college degree. Even a completed high school education fails to equip them adequately for available jobs. Columnist Bob Herbert wrote, "New York Telephone once tested 57,000 applicants before finding 2,100 who were qualified for entry-level technical jobs."[30]

Many of these thwarted men are from minority groups. They face dual major obstacles: They must find productive employment in a system that, first, may discriminate against them and, second, that they are not prepared for. The experience is not racially uniform. Among immigrant members of races that often suffer discrimination, some appear to prosper. By 1994 black residents of Queens Borough in New York had higher average incomes than white residents, mainly because of immigrant earnings. Culture, not skin color, was the issue. When Haitians in New York plan a demonstration at the United Nations, they schedule it for 6:30 in the evening, after work; African Americans with similar skin color demonstrate after lunch.[31] Black West Indians living in the United Kingdom show the highest per capita level of educational achievement of any immigrant group.

Men with difficult economic options, often in the African-American community, may seek reproductive opportunities with women, but they may choose or be forced to reproduce outside of marriage because of a welfare system that offers them little role—and may even discourage them from joining—in family life. We have also seen that young men in general acknowledge little responsibility for contraception. They are both stymied and irrelevant at once. There is even a social pattern that they call "sperming." Their frank intention is to copulate with as many women as possible. They obviously take no effective responsibility for any outcomes of their sport.[32] Nearly one-fourth of single U.S. black men state they have no intentions to marry.[33]

Women in poor sections of the population possess some clear-cut options that directly serve their reproductive agendas if only because they can secure some benefits from the welfare system. For males the problem is more abstract. It depends on factors and forces almost wholly out of their economic control. Certainly capable and determined individuals can overcome many obstacles, but countless young men continue to founder.[34] The dual stigmas of productive and reproductive unemployment characterize their youth and prejudice their prospects for the future. Among sixteen to nineteen year-old males in Detroit, Michigan, 47 percent are jobless. In Italy, even with its low birthrate, 30 percent lack jobs, and it's 25 percent in France.[35] Such large numbers of people cannot be considered simply marginal. The international nature of the situation strongly suggests a generic cause.

It is no surprise that young men in these thwarted groups act recklessly, often destructively. The most challenging test to industrial communities will be to provide acceptable and gratifying occupations for young males and the adults they become. No one can exaggerate the crucial importance of how a community engages the energies of young males. Young women can at least have babies. Many do so, married or not. Legitimate productive and reproductive prospects for males appear to recede implacably. Their energetic challenge to the overall community becomes sharper and harsher.[36]

Would You Like Your Daughter to Marry a Man?

In less than sixty years the number of American brides who were divorced and remarried increased 400 percent. There have also been striking changes in the complexity of private domestic arrangements.[37] The number of households containing kids under eighteen and headed by mothers more than doubled between 1970 and 1990. The matrilineal arrangement—single motherhood—is the predominant response to marital failure in some 80 percent of cases in the United States, Great Britain, and Australia.[38] Out-of-wedlock birth is rising fastest among women over twenty; seven of ten American single mothers are now over twenty. We have seen that this is a comprehensible reproductive strategy in view of the declining economic situation of men and the enhanced economic independence of women.[39] There is independence from the broader family as well. A strikingly smaller proportion of children than in the past went to live with relatives or joined their mothers living with family members after a divorce. No more. The extended family is no longer so extended.

Even when not split, the family in industrial societies has been declining in size for decades, with the exception of the few years after World War II. Sharp consequences have followed. Small families discourage their children from entering a celibate church, surely part of the cause of a dire shortage of Catholic priests. Citizens, except in the clearest danger, will resist sending their children into the military, to risk death. This has a surprisingly substantial impact on military planners, who are making zero-casualty assumptions.[40] Presumably, even in a populous society such as China with a preference for male children and an official one-child policy, demography will affect military strategy. Doting grandparents have fewer potential grandchildren.[41] Grandparents vote or at least have some political influence, even in China. Grandparents are more likely than in the past to support and care for grandchildren and to lobby for political and economic support to do so.[42]

We know grandparents are reproductive strategists. They are parents. They entered the game and stayed in it. This is important for communities whose young males find relatively little employment. They will not be considered promising candidates by potential parents-in-law. They have no prospects, to use the old-fashioned but still relevant term.

Economic and reproductive frailty overtakes countless modern males. They are the fellows standing in a clump on the street corner that you see on the way to work. Hopeless, they are drinking beer or fortified wine before lunch. There are legion other men, fired from downsizing companies, never employed, or never employable to begin with. Members of the traditional working class may still perform jobs when they exist, before they are mechanized or internationalized, but they remain apprehensive about their children and themselves. Even though millions of new jobs have been created in America at any rate, workers remain troubled by job insecurity rather than reassured by their prosperity. In Europe where economies are more rigid and unemployment higher, the situation is even more pronounced. In Japan downsizing has induced a surge of suicides among managers who must supervise it.[43] The far-reaching economic turbulence in Asia will involve ever more communities in a competitive, yet uncertain environment. Children of the professional and even upper class will be wary of downward mobility. There may be relatively few new slots for eye surgeons and general managers. Banking and finance houses are now international competitors with little interest in family lineage. Companies are looking to bright and avid people in cheaper countries who will do capable work, and the price is right: A month's salary for a U.S. software expert can buy a year's work from an equally capable Indian. Overall, it becomes very difficult for young men to sustain confidence that they will find work, a mate, earn enough money to support the entire family, and live happily ever after.

Certainly, as the twentieth century ebbs, North America is prosperous and promising. By world standards, so is much of Europe and growing sectors everywhere else. But predictions about the global future do not translate into confidence about one's personal economic future.

We can stare at the broad picture. Males down, females up, children on an often unpleasant carousel, with memories of a jerky ride that may persist for years. But with the bad news there is the good. It is remarkable how inventively and stubbornly people raise their children, often under terrible conditions. It is also remarkable how successfully nature's model, the human child, is able to extract from adults the goods, services, and affectionate interaction that it requires.

The child is a marketing design on a par with the baby panda bear, puppies, and kittens in evoking work on its behalf. As any parent knows, young children will do to them what they would tolerate from no one else. They throw up on tailored suits. They awaken two-job parents in the middle of the night. They fling oatmeal. They whine for an hour when they realize they aren't monarchs. But parents continue to perform duties, often fiercely, on behalf of their offspring.

The infant does not rely on charm alone but also on inner chemistry. We have seen that childbirth and fatherhood release hormones that predispose parents to act in uncommonly unselfish and devoted ways.[44] There is obviously much more to be learned about the chemistry of parenthood. It will elucidate one reason for the enormous success of our species over many millennia. We are physiologically primed and motivated to bear young, care for them, and attend to their needs in the broader social world that they must prepare to enter. But relying on inner biology takes us only part of the way, even if it is perhaps much of the journey.

Has our society reached a watershed so that there is more parenting work to be done than there are parents and others to do it? The world beyond the home may be perilous. If parents succeed in supporting their children in the intimate sphere, the wider community may fail them in the public setting.[45] Social indices of deprived children mount even in rich communities such as the United States and the United Kingdom.[46] In the United States the forces of community are even unable to protect children attending school from hazardous *gunfire*; one astonishing report about New York City students found that "one in five admits carrying a weapon."[47] In New Orleans a 1994 commitment to their families among barely teenaged criminals was to prepay their own funerals. With stunning if realistic nihilism, they did not expect to live beyond sixteen years of age.[48] In 1989 nearly four million American children over the age of twelve were crime victims in public schools in the span of six months. This particular condition partly reflects a dramatic and baffling American pathology about guns, but it also reveals the hazardous nature of the world that children must enter. It underlines the failure of adults to provide conditions for a safe and rewarding childhood and young adulthood. It suggests the extent of the problem that adults face when they aspire to show their children how to live competent and pleasurable lives as adults.

Canaries in the Mine

The experience of African Americans stands out, not because it is different in kind but in degree. They are farther along a path that other groups in industrial communities appear to be following also. As Andrew Hacker has asserted, all the indices of social disorganization that were commonly thought to be confined largely to the African-American community are in fact rising far more quickly in white communities.[49] The prevailing African-American situation is part of the American system, and its characteristics are shared in other countries.

The perils confronting African-American children may stand in sharp contrast to the extensive wealth of the society as a whole, but they are also an indication of common trends in all groups, especially among poor males. According to Brent Staples, "Black men between the ages of 15 and 24 are murdered at 10 *times* the national average."[50] However, white males are five times more likely to kill with a vehicle than blacks.[51] Crime and incarceration rates reflect the same crisis as those of unemployment and mortality.

By this standard the pattern in the United States verges on failure. The principal victims are male—80 percent of the victims of murder and 90 percent of the murderers—but so are their mothers and sisters and wives and companions, as well as the wider community which suffers repeated assault and demoralization.[52]

It is essential to emphasize that these trends have to do mainly with behavior, not with race. Race is a spurious and imprecise category that has nothing do with biogenetic competence.[53] The best demonstration of this is in the United States military, a representative American group. There, on a relatively level playing field, black males function as effectively as white and reveal no intrinsic difference from any other group in their skill and reliability. The military offers a set of worthwhile goals and appropriate ways of learning how to reach them. Through a detailed personnel system it pays attention to the personal development of individuals equally. It also supports a socially valued expression of competence to which young men appear to respond.

Success in the military cannot be defined as a "sellout" or a sign of personal "wimpiness." There is a fit between the young men and the mission that challenges them, whatever their color or tribe. People face and perform serious tasks connected to major contemporary technologies and human problems. And black men accomplish them as well as anyone.

Outside the military is another story. The African-American male is the first victim of the toxic socioeconomic environment. The large dimensions of this are suggested by the striking research conclusions of Signithia Fordham, formerly of Rutgers and now of the University of Maryland. In the 1980s she studied American inner-city high school students. Broadly, she found that when black females succeeded in the academic system, their peers considered that they were turning white. They were capitulating to white power. They were selling out their ethnic pride. But when black males succeeded in a comparable manner, their peers accused them of turning female. They had lost their maleness.[54] Earning good grades in algebra was not manly. The rigmarole of education was girlish, not masculine.

Race is skin deep, but sex is implicated in many fundamental human systems. From the evidence we have to assume that the overall social system is far less able to funnel males through the educational system into effective adult roles than females. In the black community over 60 percent of black college students are women, 65 percent of professionals, 52 percent of managers, and 57 percent of technical workers. The issue of success is sexual more than racial.

African-American males evidently suffer a dual handicap at school— that it largely reflects white and female values and skills—they perform less well than the women in their communities and the males and females in other communities. Some critical work involved in raising effective dark-skinned males doesn't get done. There is a gap in the reproductive assembly line. There are no adult males at home. There is no one for a child to observe leaving home to go to work and returning from it. The absent father produces a son who then becomes an absent father. It is a sharp rebuke to American complacency that the only large organization other than the military which has provided an effective and disciplined community for African-American men is the movement led by Louis Farrakhan—an organization accused of extraordinary doctrinal bigotry and the misogynistic restriction of women from many of its activities.

It is difficult to know what to do to raise effective and responsible youngsters when many seem extreme and peripheral. The very character of the society as a whole is affected in a tangible way. The distinguished historian William H. McNeill deplores that the "attenuation of familial nurture, which seems to have gone very far in modern cities, implies that institutions of all kind—public and private, governmental, religious and social—have been undermined." Good and effective societies depend on good and effective families.[55] It is difficult to define how it happens and what happens, but when members of a community are disconsolate about their young people, they are making a judgment about the kind of adults they will become. It takes twenty-one years to raise a good and effective twenty-one-year-old. It takes as long, although with less effort, skill, and care, to produce an adult unable to fend for himself in the existing world or unable to coexist effectively with other people. Especially in very complicated societies, the link between family life and national capability is difficult to draw with confidence. Nevertheless, basic education of children is clearly foundational to adult life. Skills with modern techniques such as computation, reading, data management, and statistical judgment are vital to effective modern economies.

We are proposing here that the industrial communities are beginning to do more poorly by their male children in the present as they did more poorly by their female children in the past.

The Bedrock Solution

What happens when the new arrangements founder? We have seen how women have begun to respond, by focusing and evidently relying on the mother-offspring connection. When other systems fail, that connection emerges as the default pattern in the industrial world, in the form of the single-mother family. Many women don't marry in the first place. When they do and marriages fail, single motherhood is the predominant response. It is hardly surprising that human beings return under pressure to the bedrock mammalian community of mother and child. But a major innovation has been added: money from the state. Call it welfare, applied Christianity, societal decadence, progressive policy, stark desperation, whatever you like, but bureaugamy is a genuinely new development.

In a deeply unsettled time it makes biological sense that our basic system for social survival relies on the individual with the clearest and earliest commitment to the child—the mother, not the father.

CHAPTER EIGHT

War, Games, and Fantasy

I HAVE BEEN DESCRIBING a kind of generic maleness associated with men, in addition to and interwoven with humanness, which most males are ready and willing to display most of the time. What happens to it, and to them, in the post-biological work environment that many men confront? What happens to it, and to them, when their relations with women are set within a new context of unclear rules and sharp sanctions? And what about organized respectable aggression, war, which has forever been a dramatic male speciality but is now rapidly becoming a female livelihood, too?

I suggest that, among others, there have been three large-scale behavioral responses by men to their new situation: sports, drugs, and pornography. In these milieus men try to replace what they experienced

before or what they think their ancestor males experienced before them.
All three have burgeoned into huge businesses. They have grown and
prospered at the same time as the experiences they mimic have been
curtailed. Of course there isn't a direct one-to-one connection between
the industries and the inner psychologies of those who patronize them.
But large social movements do not happen at random and for no
definable reason. And an indirect connection is still a connection.

"Sublimation" is an enduring Freudian concept. A person who can't
engage in one particular behavior redirects the pertinent energies to
another activity. Someone who can't experience sexual behavior would
turn to another form of assertive physical activity such as exercise—even
physical spiritualism such as that of the Shakers whose adherents actually
shook in religious praise.

It is difficult for industrial men to engage in the aggressive behavior
which in evolution influenced social and sexual success. Except during
relatively limited periods of formal warfare, such behavior is no longer
acceptable. There are few other respectable venues in which to engage in
it. Men have had to find other outlets for this element of their inherent
maleness. Assertive young American males spend their money adding
huge tires to their barely muffled pickup trucks; females in the same age
group will stereotypically apply these resources to personal grooming.
Males are decisively more likely to acquire and covet stereo equipment,
often the louder, the better. They pursue status, including sexual status,
through objects that create noise. The industrial setting provides a handy
tool kit for assembling a personal style. It recalls the bower bird, who
collects trinkets, glass, and bits of this and that to produce a seductive
nest for the females choosing a partner, as he perches expectantly on his
real estate. It is interesting that among birds it is the males who sing to
advertise their wonderful territories to the females, who then assess and
select or reject them. When male birds lose fights and territories, they
sing less or not at all.

A study of warbler birds by Swedish scientists using DNA finger-
printing reveals that female warblers seek copulation with males other
than their social mates. Their choices are based on how extensive the

repertoire is of a male's song. More generous singers attract more sex partners. Astonishingly, the fledglings of males with large repertoires survive more readily than the offspring of those with smaller song kits. There is no direct immediate benefit to females from the extracurricular males they choose, since they are already being provisioned and pro-tected by their mates. So the principal advantage in choosing prominent singers appears to be in providing their offspring with superior genetic representation in the gene pool of warblers.[1]

By and large, unless they are caged, birds continue to live in the kind of world in which they evolved. But modern humans do not. What do men do when they can't fight each other in groups? Does anything replace banging the skulls or piercing the hides of animals promising dinner? What does a man do when he cannot capture or seduce a promising female in order to lure her to his bower? Is it possible to sublimate the forces behind the endless, tense, and unreliable quest for food and safety? Can something modern summarize the ancient energies at the heart of sexual drama and reproductive zeal?

Dirty Pictures

One thing industrial men do is look at pornography. They watch displays of female nudity and provocative action. They buy magazines and videos and surf the Internet for sexual imagery. They drink costly beer in public places where they watch dancers expose their breasts and sometimes their genitalia.

The wealthiest man in England used to be the Duke of Westminster. For generations his family had enormous estates of vital rural land and owned large tracts of property in what became central London and the center of an empire. The family gave Westminster Abbey its name. Its wealth grew for generations. Its scion sits in the House of Lords. But the Duke of Westminster is no longer the wealthiest person in England.[2] Paul Raymond was until his recent death. Raymond owned a stable of strip clubs, porn shops, and related real estate in London's Soho district and elsewhere.

The shift in wealth at England's financial peak illustrates the changed world that men face. It is a novel world of legal permissiveness about sexual fantasy. Which came first, the liberal laws or the strenuous demand? Is this a matter of demand creating law in the way that the abortion laws were enacted after sexual turmoil made abortion necessary for otherwise law-abiding women?

Constitutional freedoms may or may not generate rich industries, but usually not industries involving products that are apparently deeply at odds with central moral and religious values. This one has. Conventional media of communication, such as films, recordings, and widely distributed cassettes, have all been affected. Even the cozy telephone has been pressed into service as an erotic instrument for a minute-by-minute price. Dozens of cities have a cavalcade of escort services, which provide various grades and flavors of sex to consumers. They are listed in telephone books, like roofers or locksmiths, with drawings of women in gowns exiting limousines.

The zest for this seems unstoppable. It takes advantage of what is purported to be the most contemporary and technologically innovative form of communication—the Internet and associated forms of telecommunication. The full array of contemporary media, either alone or combined with others, is involved in this burgeoning marketplace.

According to a 1997 report from *The Economist*, the Internet's "chief early colonization is by the erotic." The Playboy Entertainment site receives five million "hits" a day for its channel, which appears to consist almost exclusively of vignettes in which women expose their bodies and from time offer sexual autobiographies. In the United States *half* of the revenue for pay-per-view films in hotel rooms is for "adult entertainment." The emphasis is overwhelmingly on films catering to male fantasies. Twenty-five percent of the forty-five million corporate travelers in 1996 in the United States were women, an increase from 20 percent in 1991. This suggests either that many women choose these symbolic experiences or, more likely, that male travelers are even more avid consumers than the percentages suggest.[3] Three-quarters of the travelers choose the movies, half of which are explicitly sexual. To allow business travelers to charge the films to their employers' accounts without being detected, many hotels do not record film titles on receipts. In Germany adult films are 40 percent of the rental market. Germany also generates twenty million of the world's sixty million minutes of sex calls each month.[4] In the United States an Internet site, Amateur Hardcore, receives more "hits" per day than mainstream Web sites from providers such as the Disney Company and CNN. Sexual images are the most profitable products of Internet businesses.[5]

Hence the most sophisticated and seemingly impersonal forms of human communication are pressed into service to simulate the most intimate and primordial of interactions. A man in Osaka converses over a line routed through Guyana and a satellite to a woman in Rotterdam who is asked to remove her clothes. For this customers pay the equivalent of $6 a minute, with an average call costing $78. The woman receives $25 an hour. Search engines on the Internet will find references to any vulgar word, action, or erotic organ, literally in the hundreds of thousands. In 1997 the world's largest Internet service, America Online (AOL), was seriously considering providing their subscribers with an adults-only Web site. According to U.S. News & World Report, "It might have been structured like a multi-room house, with one . . . devoted to . . . discussions of sexuality, another to portraits of breasts, and a third to dialogues with prostitutes." AOL's trepidation about public backlash scuttled the project.[6] One of the widely watched programs on Home Box Office is its "Reel Sex" late-night show.

There are now wholly understandable concerns about the effect of pornography on children. Television programs, music videos, films, and the Internet transmit an unprecedented array of sexual images and acts into homes on a daily basis. They offer youngsters a menu of sights and sounds unimaginable several decades ago. Their creators and distributors would have been jailed. Once upon a time the mysteries of the body and its private behavior were at a seemingly impossible distance. They tantalized the ignorance of the young and the fantasies of the adult. They were available in only a few places, such as Paris, Amsterdam, and Hamburg. People obviously sought sexual connection for the pleasure and vitality of it in itself, but they also wanted to satisfy their curiosity about otherwise mysterious bodies. What did bodies look like? What did they do? The world inside clothes was unreachable, certainly for the young, and it was certainly not for public display.

Rules were strict. Perhaps because contraception was unreliable, if it was available at all, it presumably appeared responsible to reduce attention to erotic matters. Through its laws and censors, the industrial community sustained a sharp distinction between private sex and public display. It was remarkably successful in keeping from its citizens news and views of their own bodies. The sexual behavior of public figures was likewise under embargo—for example, the alliances of U.S. presidents Franklin Roosevelt and John Kennedy, or of private citizens such as Martin Luther King, Jr., or Rock Hudson. In the first half of the twentieth century public discourse about sex was very different indeed from what people were doing in private and certainly in fantasy. This was rather the way China presented itself at its close. Chairman Mao may have worn a puritanical Mao jacket, but the "dancing instructors" with whom he surrounded himself were invariably young attractive females.[7]

The frankest, most intimate sexual depictions are now widely available for purchase or rental for the price of an order of blueberry pancakes. The sexual liaisons of politicians, star performers, business executives, and even religious leaders have become general knowledge. More than ever, performers, especially female ones in film, may be nude or nearly so in the course of their work. If these images are recorded and available, then their images flash around the world on the Web and in publications specializing in such revelation. One group most interested in computers and the Web consists of young males who are also enthusiastic consumers of the sexual content now so colorfully and coolly available to them.

The male homosexual community is increasingly served visibly by male-oriented materials. However, women predominate decisively as performers in the porn industry. The first ever labor union contract for American strippers appears to focus exclusively on female performers.[8] Of course some women enjoy and participate in this industry as consumers, but it remains overwhelmingly dependent on the active male sex organ—the brain.[9]

Modern men manage symbols, peer at computers, negotiate zoning changes, plan the marketing of Sheetrock, make cold calls to sell strangers stocks and bonds. They are separated from nature and the natural use of the body in nature. Pornography is about icons and reverie. It doesn't involve exchange, touching, scents, probing, caresses. There is usually an embargo on actual contact between the provider and the consumer. An exception is the novel addition to the striptease industry in which a semi-naked woman writhes briefly for tips on a client's lap. As in the nightlife of Japan, the strongest bond may be between the men who attend the event rather than between customer and woman.[10]

While the rapid growth of pornography has to do with relaxed laws, it also reflects tenser relationships between men and women. Just as liberal abortion laws followed good contraception controlled by women, easy access to pornography followed the relaxation of the rules that men and women previously had to follow. The law led from behind. There is suddenly a far more open sexual market. The stakes and the costs are higher. The importance of personal attractiveness and behavior has increased. Drugs such as Viagra have brought to the surface once-concealed vulnerabilities. Sexual techniques, once deeply private, have become widely known. Intimate sexual acts such as oral sex have become acceptable subjects of party conversation. There are broadly available, even omnipresent, images of desirable or at least acceptable bodies in films, advertisements, and the like.

These changes have increased the emphasis placed on physical appearance by both men and women. The mating rigmarole requires some semblance of youthful physical effectiveness. Exercise clubs provide acceptable locations for sexual self-advertisement. Maintaining taut, attractive bodies is strenuous for people beyond the early twenties, and keeping thin is especially agonizing in wealthy countries with cheap, delicious fat food. People are marrying later so that more effort is required to approximate the lines of youth. Television commercials hawk exercise machines and videotaped programs to goad the body to perfection. Surefire diets supplant each other like monsoons in season.

The obligation to maintain and restore bodily appeal is especially felt by divorced people, who almost always seek another partner, often at an age when their memories of courtship fail to correspond to their bodily realities. The new candor about the appearance of bodies and broadly circulated standards of sexual skill have reduced inhibition and increased pressure at once. Intimacy becomes a performance art. It is possible that, among other things, pornography provides sexual instruction.

Play Ball!

The growth of the business of pornography has depended on opening up a private world, elements of which have often been associated with immorality and ill health. Another expanded business, sports, has always been utterly public, morally restorative, and widely considered healthy for mind and body. Yet it, too, may reveal a turbulent male preoccupation with competition and physical assertiveness that is no longer available to ordinary men. As a consequence, these ordinary men focus their often intense and unremitting attention on athletes, who are their surrogate performers in a complicated world of contest, personalities, and skill. The passion is international. Cricketers in Pakistan, footballers in Brazil, designated hitters in Detroit, center forwards in Slovakia—all enjoy similar adulation from their fellow citizens; for extraordinary performers, it comes from those in foreign countries, too.[11]

Newspapers have always devoted large amounts of space to sports results, often as much as business and economic news. Fans journey to sports auctions and spend a week's salary for an item of banal sports memorabilia. Each arena and stadium sells products related to the home team and the game—close cousins to the facilities near famous churches and shrines that stock items of religiosity. Never have athletes been so highly paid and their activities so widely chronicled as now. Everyone is familiar with athletes who earn $5 million to $20 million a year or more for their work, and additional revenue for endorsing products and lending their presence to social and business events. They are among the best-known people on the planet, indeed in history.

Franchises for sports in various cities and countries are bought and sold just as players are, often for vast sums. Teams flow like players to the better deal. Eager communities have been willing to subsidize with tax dollars the construction or improvement of venues for professional sports. The threat of abandoning one city for another with a better offer has been effective more often than not in shaking out millions from treasuries that often have more serious responsibilities to address. Fees paid by television networks to sports organizations for the opportunity to broadcast games have zoomed upward: In 1998, American networks dispensed no less than $17.6 billion to display various football contests to viewers.[12]

Hardly any players on a team are from the community in which they play. They may even be from a distant country—19 percent of 1997 major league baseball players in the United States were foreign born. There is constant movement of players from team to team. Nonetheless, after some initial resentment or awkwardness about a newcomer who may have replaced a once-favorite hero, the primordial loyalties tapped by sports come to the fore. A group of lavishly paid strangers becomes the elect band of local heroes. Their ascendancy is propelled by ceaseless reportage, interviews, game coverage, and similar propaganda. If they lose, there is second-guessing, mockery, and wistful glances at next year. If they win, there may be a ticker tape parade and a series of journalistic assertions that their host community is especially vivacious, colorful, and deserving. And while it is happening, it seems true. I've experienced in New York City three occasions on which somewhat improbable teams became champions: the Mets of 1969, the Rangers in 1994, and the Yankees of 1996. Each time a supposedly hard-hearted and impersonal city produced conviviality in unexpected quantities.

Much of the popularity of sports is linked directly to television and other media. They have permitted a small number of outstanding performers to be seen and followed by unprecedented numbers of people, often on a web of international communication. But they also become intensely local. For example, especially in North America, colleges and universities provide elaborate sports programs to their students but especially to alumni and fans whose loyalty is maintained by vigorous athletic competition. This often depends on an unending supply of young athletes lured by athletic scholarships, many of whom complete their athletic careers without gaining the degree that is the justification for their attendance in the first place. Only a minuscule proportion graduate to professional sports. The process degrades many institutions engaged in it who extract four years of athletic labor at very modest remuneration from students who do not graduate but who, if they are competent athletes, may help generate substantial revenue and attention for their institution. Especially in the United States and for African Americans, the youthful ardor of novice athletes is exploited while placed on their shoulders is a considerable burden of public performance. At Texas Tech, for example, only 17 percent of African-American football players on scholarship graduated.[13] Its ubiquity extends ever more the attention of the wider community to the ongoing skein of events called sports—the "male soap opera."[14]

The economics are clear, obvious, and increasingly dramatic. But something else is driving the industry of sports, something subtler, more interior, more psychologically complex. It addresses a need, an interior experience related to overt changes in the lives of fans. The core of it is that games and play and teams and heroes are real while real life itself is muffled and buffered. The indirect work world of most men is in direct contrast to the real-time, real-drama fact of sports and competition.

The ball is hit or missed. The fielder either catches it or doesn't. The goalie rebuffs the penalty play or doesn't. One runner has to run faster than the other. One diver must plunge more smoothly into the water than the other. There is no occasion for a seminar, for second thoughts, for a negotiation based on feelings, self-esteem, childhood deprivation, or character. Sporting events are tightly bound by time, physics, effort, effective cooperation. There is an indisputably definite result. The existence of such definition seems attractive to countless fans who choose to expose themselves to turbulent uncertainty.

The principal catalysts have been cable television and satellite transmission, which allow events to be flashed around the world as they are taking place. Competitive drama can be experienced with unprecedented and immediate coverage. Fans at opposite ends of countries or continents or the planet tune in to the same events, heroes, and failures, and share the same tension about outcomes.

These matters don't only involve men, of course. There are female fans, female athletes both amateur and professional, and increasing emphasis on contests between women in events such as the Olympics. An unexpectedly large number of women in the United States watch reruns of celebrated contests on the Classic Sports Network, especially tennis.[15] If only because of legal rulings that colleges and universities should support male and female athletics roughly in proportion to overall enrollment, there has been a consistent increase in the number and salience of women's sports.[16] It is unclear if the difference in emphasis and prosperity between male and female athletics will be reduced over time. Differences in male and female performance have been somewhat reduced by illegal but nonetheless omnipresent use of hormones to stimulate muscle mass. But under present conditions of relatively free choice and open markets, there remains a marked disparity. It may endure for a long time, especially in team sports in which the dynamics of aggressive social groups appear to be of interest in themselves.

Overall, sporting events are symbolic and emotional analogues of primitive contests, either with other fierce groups or prey animals—as reflected in team names such as the Bears, Panthers, Bulls, Arsenal, and the like. These involve often exorbitantly dramatic spectacles in which males have had a charter evolutionary interest. The most primal and unadorned is, of course, prizefighting, in which the most colorful outcome is the knockout, when the loser falls to the canvas with a brain concussion. There are almost incredible wrestling spectacles in Japan in which fighters are deliberately cut against modified barbed wire in the ring. They bleed copiously under the attentive stare of cameras and willing spectators.

These are perversions, more Roman than Spartan, but many sports events are astonishingly tense, with a clarity rarely equaled in daily life. The emotions that pulse through those riveted by them are physiologically and symbolically fundamental. They are memorable psychic experiences that become gripping and central. They reflect the agonized competitions between people and nature, and people and people. They recreate pivotal dramatic moments of our formative life in the Paleolithic age and before. Full-throated advocacy echoes the lost world of contests that formed us and to which we voluntarily return for a temporary haunting sense of it. Half the crowd supporting the loser will be more bereft in their minds, hearts, and in all their cells for no practical reason that they could have imagined before the contest. If they are males, their bodily levels of testosterone will actually drop while the winning fans enjoy an increase. Nevertheless, both sides will return for the next game, the next match, the next season, to experience the finite rigor of winning and losing. On the first day of the season all teams expect or at least hope to win, but only one will. Winning and losing are deep legacy emotions. Why else would so many people propel themselves into uncertain situations in which they will experience one or the other?

The world of sports recalls the turbulent, warlike world that made us. Contemporary people, especially men, inhabit a world largely cut off from such immediacy, and turn to sports instead.

Sex and the Military

Warfare, however, remains a grim and visceral connection between our evolutionary history and contemporary life. In wars, organized groups of people try to destroy the property, if not also the freedom and bodies, of people defined as enemies. Wars have existed in all manner of community, with all kinds of economies, religions, politics, and theories about violence. After the mighty carnage of World War II it seemed preposterous to look ahead to war ever again—the same dream as after World War I. However, there have since been dozens.

The tools, speed, tactics, and scope may have changed, but an irreducible feature of war is the violation of flesh, by flesh or metal or chemicals. The outcome is pain, injury, death.

Another irreducible feature has been the prominence of men in all this. Men are always drafted, women very rarely. Where they are, as in Israel, they must serve less time—one and a half years rather than three. Men serve in combat. Until recently, virtually only men were killed. In the archetypical Westerns, the hero always said, "Get the women and children out of here." When it has been necessary to place people in combat and harm's way, with a few exceptions, such as among the Israelis and the Vietcong, it is men who have had to go. Whether people have willingly entered warfare as a heroic and bold adventure or have been forced to endure it as virtual prisoners of the state, the overwhelming plurality of warriors has been men.

There have been exceptional female warriors and unusual historical cases, and certainly women have claimed their right to military careers and rewards. However, in general, they have not clamored to join in warfare. They have not made as strong appeals to fight as they have to vote or enjoy equity in employment—except in the United States where the political pressure to extend military life to women has been strong. The transformation was enabled and empowered in part by the civil rights movement. The reparation for slavery created an unshakable goal of equity and legal techniques to pursue it. A similar process has been applied to sex as it was to ethnicity, even though the functional differences between the impacts of skin shade and sex are enormous. With a level of success that gratified the community, the military was able to integrate groups seemingly diverse in ethnicity and skin shade. In the current U.S. Army most infantry are white-skinned while officers are disproportionately black.[17] It was convinced it could achieve similar results with men and women. This was a far-reaching misjudgment.

There were two other important historical reasons for the inclusion of women in the U.S. military. The first reflected the Vietnam War. As a result of profound public disillusion with the military in general, the U.S. draft was abandoned. An all-volunteer force was created in the mid-1970s. Previously, only men had been drafted. But who should be actively recruited? The American military projected its future requirements. Based on its test score requirements, the use of which the military had itself pioneered, it predicted how many young men and women were likely to be able to meet them.[18] Much of modern warfare requires relatively sophisticated skills. As I've noted, women perform better than men in the elementary and high school systems. Military planners decided that not only did they want to recruit women on ethical or political grounds, but they had to on functional grounds. They need so many people so regularly that they could not close down a major pool of reliable and effective recruits. They initially selected recruits based on their performance on written tests, the vital currency of occupational advancement in the society at large.[19] They did not select recruits based on some of the pertinent general characteristics broadly associated with maleness and femaleness, such as aggressiveness or physical caution.[20] Despite the fact that in the civilian economy half of all employed women leave the labor force for varying periods of time, especially early in their adulthood, military recruiters treated men and women as if they were more or less identically likely to serve out the traditional military career.[21] This is to say nothing of the "gender-norming," which was required to permit men and women equal opportunity for equal work, even though some traditional physical requirements of military life, such as upper-body strength in climbing and carrying packs, are differently distributed among men and women. Male Marines must complete a fifteen-mile march carrying a forty-pound pack and weapons in five hours, while women must march ten miles with twenty-five pounds and no weapons in three and a half hours.[22] The U.S. Marine Corps also has used a hand grenade that only 45 percent of females can throw far enough so they are not injured by its explosion. In addition, the issue of similar salary for dissimilar output rankles males in the military as much as it has women in civilian employment.

The second reason the military began recruiting women is connected with the first. The prevailing climate about women's rights and employ-ment changed markedly. Suddenly military service, at least in peacetime, was not an imposition but an opportunity. The same groups of politicians who during the Vietnam War were demonstrating and railing against the draft and warfare in general began to apply political pressure to open the military to women, at first with the understanding that they would not be sent into combat.[23] But then activists in the process sought to include combat posts in the agenda of women. The argument made in favor of this was a claim that only individuals who have served as effective warriors at the core of their service can scale the carefully controlled military hierarchy. Real combat produced real senior officers. The dramatic issue of the role of women in combat was therefore joined with broad notions of occupational equity. The grimmer issues of battle readiness and entry into mortal danger were set aside by the desire to offer opportunities for occupational advancement in combat posts. Danger and the functional demands of warfare had to reflect broad and general social policies not necessarily tied to strict military requirements.

The General Isn't Wearing a Uniform

For some feminists and policy makers, nothing less than equality if not similarity between what men and women do is acceptable. One commentator complained about a limited expansion of jobs open to women: "The new plan will allow women into some units that were previously off limits but will keep them in rear headquarters . . . and restrict their ability to compete for assignments that are necessary to rise to the Army's top ranks."[24] It is clear that the dramatic members of the military are those who fly the fighters, command the destroyers in sea battles, and lead infantry over the hill to face hostile fire. Those who reflect the traditional core function of the military, which is to protect homeland and defeat enemies, will attract the attention of promotion boards, to the disadvantage of noncombatants both female and male alike.

Achieving the American dream of entry into the elite is primary. The whole system focuses on the fair reward of ambition and competence. Similar concern about the effect of combat restrictions on women when they leave for civilian jobs has been expressed in Israel. Because of the central role of the military in Israel, and especially its technological nature, which translates into potential for civilian careers, females have complained that their noncombatant military experience places them at a disadvantage.[25]

At the same time, two new conditions in the American military are likely to lead to enriched opportunities for the promotion of women. The first is a systematic program of affirmative promotion of females wherever possible. With varying degrees of formality and explicitness this holds existing officers accountable in their promotions for how well they prepare female candidates for advancement. This effort reflects the recognition by military leaders that recruitment and retention of talented females requires both the perception and the reality of occupational equity. In addition, the military is under intense political pressure to conform to gender-neutral inputs and outcomes in all the services. The politically appointed secretaries of the services may be mandated by the administration to seek and achieve such gender neutrality. Therefore, ejector seats on fighter aircraft have to be reengineered to adapt to light female bodies; otherwise the explosive pressure may cause spinal damage. Naval vessels are reconfigured to provide separate living quarters for men and women. This means, for example, that if a female or male electronics technician has to leave ship, she or he must be replaced by a person of the same sex, a requirement that essentially adds to the personnel burdens on the service as a whole and especially so while it is reducing its personnel.

The second new condition is associated with the rapid expansion in American military activity of operations other than war. These may be humanitarian missions, as in Rwanda and Somalia, or policing functions, as in Haiti and Bosnia. Such activity is evidently regarded more favorably by females than males. Women are therefore inclined to join such missions, which are not defined as combat and therefore are as available to females as males. Successful duty in such activity obviously enhances opportunities for promotion. During periods of peacetime these missions occupy much of the time and resources of the military as a whole. Though for obvious political and career reasons it is unexpressed in public, serving officers are concerned that over time a corps of senior officers will emerge through these two processes—affirmative promotion and promotion within operations other than war—who have not faced the traditional combat conditions that have always preceded promotion to the highest ranks. This may or may not result in a decrement of military readiness, especially of equipment, though there are indications that operations other than warfare degrade military readiness in general.[26] It may also produce an enhanced capacity for a broad and relatively new range of military-linked activities. Yet the question must continue to be posed: If the military is the social group of last resort for societal defense, should those responsible for it be those most familiar with the central warrior functions that have always justified the existence and support of military institutions?

The issue has been joined in other countries.[27] In the military, the forward movement may be far more controversial, even among those who are supposedly its major beneficiaries. Women serving in the U.S. Army in Haiti, Bosnia, the Persian Gulf, and elsewhere were interviewed by Laura Miller of the University of California at Los Angeles. They offered firm opinions on females in front-line combat. They explicitly sought restrictions on roles in which they thought women would be at serious mortal risk. They thought their male colleagues would be imperiled, too.[28] Their principal complaint was not with their conditions of employment but with the usually feminist ideologues and politicians who helicoptered in with recipes for other people's lives and then reported back with satisfaction to fellow theorists in Greenwich Village, Georgetown, and congressional offices on Capitol Hill. For an explicit if fatuous and self-satisfied statement of this political position, see Linda Bird Francke's *Ground Zero* and a severe criticism by UCLA anthropologist Anna Simons.[29]

The U.S. military and civilians were convulsed by the case of Lieutenant Kelly Flinn who resigned her commission as a pilot of B52s carrying nuclear weapons after a threatened court-martial accusing her of adultery, lying to an officer, and disobeying an explicit order. The adultery charge was the most colorful in public debate, but the issue of insubordination by an officer flying nuclear weapons was the core of the military case, as well as the violation of a no-fraternization rule governing officers. The public discussion became surprisingly general, including vigorous consideration of all-female military units as a solution to any problems posed by sexual integration. This suggests broad public and political questions about the direction in which the military is marching.[30] Anna Simons has made a point of the issue in her study of Special Forces soldiers, in which she found resistance to integrated military groups by women.[31] For them a vital source of female solidarity and bonding emerges from candid and personal conversation, which becomes largely impossible when men are present.

Anyone who has any association with military commanders quickly learns that their overriding concerns are to achieve their military goals and also protect those under their command. To assume that resistance to females in various forms of combat results from bigotry and inexperience may be partly justified, but it also trivializes the deep concerns of the commanders involved who must complete often complex, treacherous, and dangerous military maneuvers with minimum casualties. Anything that supports this goal is desirable. Anything that degrades readiness and escalates risk is undesirable, whatever its source.

While there was initial resistance, often strong and bitter, to racial integration, it became clear that members of all races could perform equally well, and now the military exemplifies successful race-blindness in its operation. Skin shade is just that, a variation in pigment, and means nothing basic about people. But the sexes are and will continue to be different. Policy makers often adopt an opposite view, especially in the American legal system. For example, in college sports, courts ruled that any statistical differences between men and women, such as in rates of participation and financial and alumni support of programs, resulted from sexist social pathology. Did fewer women than men elect to play varsity sports? Were attendance and media coverage lower at their events? The cause had to be bad nurture, not recurrent nature. It reflected a coercive conspiracy, not free choice. No doubt this is partly correct, and the history of a work in progress has yet to be written.

Nevertheless, full legal action is the response to what also might be sexual differences in enthusiasm for competitive athletics and for male and female athletes.

Meanwhile, in military training or scores on tests or even in longevity, sexual differences are held to reflect imperfect opportunities for women. Therefore, as *The New York Times* advocates, it is justified to reset supposedly culture-free tests when females do less well than males on mathematics.[32] Females do better than males on verbal tests, but their scores are not adjusted. The well-meaning statistical zealots who navigate this issue pay this example far less attention.

But these and other differences between men and women are in some tangible sense derived from evolution. They are part of the human inheritance.[33] They reflect strengths and priorities that served us well during the overwhelmingly long history of hunting and gathering. When definable skills are masked or distorted, the community may be deprived of excellent mathematicians or skillful communicators because measures of ability have been gerrymandered. However, this appears to be less important than the appearance of equality and similarity.

For some tangled reason, public comfort flows from the claim that differences result from prejudice and other disreputable legacies of a sexist past, rather than from real differences based on evolutionary success. It assumes the worst of the past, the best of the future, with little attention to the choices made by people in the present. This is Icarus-like avoidance of reality. It cannot be sustained without great cost, if it can be sustained at all. For example, in training people to do dangerous and unsentimental work, such as in the U.S. Marine Corps, different ways are emerging of dealing with men and women. The traditional draconian immersion of young men in Marine culture is less successful for women. They do not prosper under it, enjoy it, or become effective contributors. Even with some downward adjustment of particular tasks involving upper-body strength, the dropout rate of women from the six-week Parris Island boot camp initiation is 60 percent higher than for men. The organization is responding by paying attention to the real organization of real people, not only to its tradition. They are listening to the women and men who have elected to join it. The leadership is responsible to them and for them. A politically appointed lawyer who had been advising the Secretary of the Army had to resign her post in 1998 when she called the Marine Corps "extreme" in their treatment of gender, but her views reflected prevailing political sentiment.

This is controversial, but the Marine commanders are acting practically rather than ideologically. This is not to say that females will be less useful or effective. They will carry their share of military responsibility. However the stark discipline of injury and death forces one to acknowledge sexual differences.[34] And for the future, intensely focused groups such as Special Forces and the Navy SEALs are anticipating the best use that can be made of the skills and interests of the female recruits who join them.

Meanwhile, a congressional commission led by Senator Nancy Kassebaum Baker recommended in 1997 that wholly integrated residential training for men and women be sharply curtailed because of its disruptive impact on unit cohesion and clarity of leadership. The Secretary of Defense largely rejected the report in principle, though in practice some of its recommendations about segregated residence were quietly supported. Laura Miller's report on Army women at ten U.S. facilities and in Germany, Somalia, Macedonia, and Haiti reveals a sharp gap between feminists who reflect their ideology and political goals, and women in the military itself. She concludes that "by treating gender differences as entirely socially constructed, activists have failed to equip military women with the tools to understand physical difference or to challenge arguments based on that difference. By focusing on women as victims of sexual harassment, activists have failed to recognize and pass along the strategies of women who have confronted and managed gender conflict despite the hostile environment. . . . They alienate women who simply do not find their male coworkers to be 'the enemy.' "[35] In addition, in an unusually interesting finding, after a year and half of living as an observer of Special Forces soldiers, Anna Simons reported, "A combat unit's very success depends on something that is hard to measure but too easy to discount: male bonding. . . . Male bonding is critical to the effectiveness of combat soldiers."[36] Simons emphasizes the vital importance of establishing trust among groups of twelve men who must rely on each other in dangerous situations. She suggests that discussing and boasting about sex is central to this trust: "Only discussions about sex allowed the men to define themselves separately, while not challenging the group's unity." Women in the group would not only be potential foci of sexual action but would affect its abstract discussion: "Men who are willing to put their lives on the line have their own way of communicating, and all the political pressure in the world can't change that." Simons also found that females in mixed units may also be unable to engage in the give-and-take discussions of social matters. Some writers such as the linguist Deborah Tannen have claimed that these discussions are characteristic of women in groups, so sexual integration will have an impact on women, too.

Maternity Uniforms

Men in all-male groups may achieve some effective solidarity from sexual discussion. Females in all-female groups also experience direct effect from their relationships with other women. However, heterosexuality itself continues to provide interruptions to heretofore normal military life. As Simons commented on the American television program *Hardball*, "It gums up the works." Its most tangible unarguable form is pregnancy, which occurs despite the fact that both contraception and sexual information are widely available and that their use is officially encouraged. Pregnancy occurs also despite the fact that there are legal barriers to sexual activity within the military. The possible serious consequences of violating them are well known—all of which makes the incidence of pregnancy the more puzzling. Among fertile young people not using contraception, pregnancy will occur after about two out of ten copulations. Spontaneous miscarriages occur rather frequently as well. It is therefore clear that a considerable amount of inappropriate behavior takes place despite the regulations, despite the awkward openness of the living situation, despite the concrete sanctions extending to dismissal and even prison. We also have to assume that many people use effective contraception because it is readily available, so the amount of sexual activity must be far larger than even the pregnancy data confirm. A senior Army general, while apologizing for anecdotal data, reported that during his command of a brigade every woman in the command became pregnant. His daughter, who is now an officer herself, evidently notes a similar trend in her group.

But would any sensible primatologist expect anything else? To keep healthy primates from sexual activity, they have to be kept in individual cages.

When naval women on board ship are identified as twenty weeks pregnant, they are removed from their ships, at considerable cost and often difficulty. They may have to leave small work groups, many of which are technically skillful and interdependent. Because of patterns of segregated quarters, a woman may only be replaced by another woman, ideally one trained to do her specific job. This has sharply affected the conduct of work. During 1996 I visited a Navy nuclear aircraft carrier at sea with a crew of 500 women and 4,500 men. It was clear that any number of departures in an intense work organization such as an aircraft carrier carries a financial and functional cost. It costs as much as $2 million to train a carrier fighter pilot. Departures are also likely to affect the unit cohesion and morale so vital to combat readiness and the drastic tasks a deployed military may be called on to perform.[37] Dependable staffing is a factor in avoiding injury and lethality and damage to vastly complex and costly equipment. A fighter aircraft may cost $75 million, and there are some eighty of them on a modern American carrier. These objects must be landed on a moving platform, often in the dark, at speeds around 170 miles an hour, to tailhook one of four cables set forty feet apart. The aircraft are catapulted off the ship with a force able to hurl a Volkswagen car thirteen miles. The vessel itself may cost close to $3.5 billion. It is an unimaginably large object.

The intensely cooperative ballet of the work involved in completing missions is utterly remarkable. It is dangerous, noisy, timed to split seconds, and associated with manufactured power and speeds almost beyond comprehension. It is seemingly at the extreme reaches of coordinated human action. Any possible interference with the safety and effectiveness of the process requires careful evaluation, which it receives.

There is an additional complexity, most coercively on board ship but also in the military in general. Incoming sailors are given sexual instruction and protection against disease and, presumably, pregnancy. At the same time there is an official prohibition against various romantic and sexual links between men and women and in specified circumstances. The prohibition is especially severe concerning liaisons between officers and enlisted personnel and people in the same chain of command. The system of public authority may too readily turn into private misconduct. The 1996 rape charges against Army drill sergeants at a training base exemplify the issue, and we have already noted the case of former B52 pilot Kelly Flinn.[38] In the Canadian military, similar charges and counter-charges about abusive sexuality have drawn intense public attention.[39]

The subject is hot to handle, but the question of female sexual adventure has also had to be confronted. For example, in the Flinn case, the initial public assumption was that Flinn was maltreated by a man who told her he was separating and divorcing. But the man's wife wrote to the Secretary of the Air Force describing visits by Flinn to their home in the enlisted person's neighborhood while they were together. She included the observation that Flinn wore her flight suit during these visits. It is difficult to convey to someone who has not been in a military environment involving dangerous flying how dramatically impressive pilots are when wearing flight suits. Their wearers almost reek of status, glamour, power, and accomplishment. Lieutenant Flinn in a flight suit was a provocation against which her sexual competitor had few defenses, including her marriage certificate.[40] Contemporary young woman have been raised to value their own sexual needs and rights. They are culturally empowered to express their independence intimately as well as occupationally. Does the general sexual equity in the wider culture make consensual and vigorous female initiatives more likely? Of course it does. What happens when the presumption of male original sin no longer applies when identifying the guilty party in a breach of rules?

An additional nightmarish issue is raised by the sexual abuse of female prisoners. During World War II the Japanese seized "comfort women" from Korea and China for prostitution purposes in connection with their military. This was part of a long-standing tradition. Impoverished, usually rural Japanese girls, called *karayuki*, were sold to brothel owners between 1890 and 1945, often to accompany Japanese military expansion.[41] Rape of civilian prisoners by occupying troops is endemic. An outstandingly vicious if contemporary innovation was the Serbian program in the former Yugoslavia of gang-raping Muslim civilians. Then they were sequestered beyond the time they could seek abortions. They would have to bear part-Serbian children. These innocent offspring face lives of gross abrasion because of the novel use of rape as a military tactic. Numerous Chinese mothers impregnated during the Rape of Nanking killed their newborn babies or themselves. Countless Bangladeshi and Pakistani women were abandoned by their own communities after they were raped and often impregnated by occupying infidel armies. Hutus and Tutsis alike raped women of the other group, who along with their children became degraded residents of a no-woman's land. One American female pilot was sexually violated by Iraqis during the 1991 Gulf War, though not raped because her injuries prevented removal of her flight suit.

There are indications that what actually happens in such cases is more vicious than what is revealed, if anything is revealed at all.[42] In early wars when women were more directly involved in close combat, Israelis found that when women were taken prisoner or wounded, their male colleagues would take militarily unwise risks to protect them. They would relax their military discipline and codes, for example, by abusing their own prisoners.

Because the issue stirs such deep passions, there has been little explicit public consideration of rape and sexual violence during wartime. But we have a telling clue about how people will react. The political sensitivities about sexual harassment within military units, *involving people on the same side and during peacetime*, foreshadows the intensity of response to the inevitable traumas that will occur when substantial numbers of women are in close contact with enemy troops. The legitimate and widespread outrage at sexual exploitation among fellow members of the same service prefigures the response that people will have to violations of vulnerable female prisoners in what are commonly violent and incendiary spasms of warfare unconfined by laws and norms of civility. And then what will happen? The public evasion of this issue is almost incomprehensible.

The daily lives of men and women in the military are affected in much less dramatic ways, too. In general, women tend to choose potential mates from socioeconomic echelons somewhat higher than their own. The rules prohibiting liaisons between officers and enlisted personnel directly interferes with enlisted women's mating opportunities with better-placed officers, particularly those of minority groups who may have less opportunity than more advantaged women to connect with steadily employed and reliable men. For example, it is in the military that African-American men have achieved the greatest occupational parity with men from other groups. This fact is presumably not lost on their potential mates. For them, military service may provide an unusually promising opportunity for both productive and reproductive activity. The prohibition of crossing lines of rank clearly affects the sexual civil liberties of male and female officers. What if they want to share their lives with a particular individual, whatever the person's rank and occupational circumstances?[43] Should they be required to leave the service? Sailors and soldiers may be isolated in camps or on ships for long periods of time. Their coworkers may be their only possible sex partners.

Unlike in civilian life where it is relatively common, adultery is an outright crime in the military. If convicted, a member of the military may endure dishonorable separation, reduction in rank, loss of earned pension benefits, or incarceration for life. Under Article 134 of the Military Code of Justice, fraternization merits prosecution because it damages "good order and discipline" of the organization. Surely this is so. But presumably the code reflects a time of history when military life was fully or nearly monastic. Now men and women are set next to each other as coworkers in often dramatic and demanding conditions. They must interact and cooperate under conditions of utmost interdependence. Yet they are severely restricted from those personal sexual dramas so colorfully at the core of the experience of life, especially of young unmated people. Are not the sexual harassers in this case those in charge who put relatively inexperienced and sexually exigent people in such a provocative environment?[44] Who subject them to cruel and unusual regular life?

The basic fact is that healthy people in the prime of sexual and reproductive life may spend a half year or more in relatively close physical proximity to each other. Unlike most other workers, they *sleep where they work*. Workers in the private sector are together perhaps forty hours a week; in the Marines it is often 168. Often these men and women are isolated from the wider community. It is clearly controversial and anomalous to expect that they will be celibate. And, of course, they are not. They send quick smiles across the workbench. They hold each other's bodies warmly. But the natural force that draws them together, the flood of the neurotransmittter dopamine that pleasingly floods the brain after sex, is defined as wild and unpatriotic. It is an occupational risk, a step to dishonor, disgrace, to personal ruin. Yet the wider community from which members of the military come and to which they will return becomes ever more sexualized. When they glance at the television set in the bunkhouse, they see famous actors lying together nude in bed. Channel X parades men and women performing every sexual caper short of visible penetration.

The military itself is becoming increasingly Victorian about sex. It stands on the premise that males will exploit females and that other combinations of infraction will occur, too. So all interactions must be controlled.[45] In an effort to do so, the Navy produced the now infamous advisory in which sexual contacts are graded like traffic: green for okay— mild compliments, shaking hands, earnest requests for dates; yellow for beware—touching the body, explicit references to sex organs or zones, importuning dialogue; and red—outright physical coercion, promises of occupational advantage in return for sex, disrobing without consent. Apart from its encapsulation of common sense and common decency, it is the product of enthusiasts for legal strategy, not sexual strategy. In the presence of her commanding officer and other leaders, one junior officer assured of protection described the entire initiative as ridiculous, one treated as risible by generally capable people engaged in their own normal lives. For most young people in the services this is likely to be the prevailing attitude. Yet it is also clear that for some individuals, and especially drunk ones, there is good reason to establish clear rules of sexual conduct.

The controllers of military life appear unaware of the extraordinarily close connection between dominance and sex among all primates, including humans. They are trying to stem fundamental tides of emotional association between exercising power and having sex. The tides flow both ways—from the dominant individual who is usually male to the dependent female, and from the subdominant individual, usually female, for whom the attraction of a high status partner may be intense. Insofar as women tend to marry men higher than they are in the status hierarchy, a sensible enhancement of life's options is wound up with illicit eroticism. And with more and more high-ranking women in the military, this sex-dominance link will be reversed and its impact heightened.

It appears to be assumed by military leaders that lesbian women have sexual eagerness for each other, but little attention is paid to animated sexual enthusiasm among women for men. Cosmetics are for sale at the base store, or women can bring a stash from their favorite Main Street salon. Women have been sexually empowered by contraception, public opinion, and moral freedom. They are not all merely victims overwhelmed by wretched men, even if some are. Will a military dominated by a political community committed to combating male original sin prosecute women who engage in consensual sex, even if they have consorted across the lines of rank? Will a new version of the sexual double standard emerge—one protecting women and their special occupational advantages?[46] The public dialogue about military homosexuals reveals confusions enough on sexual matters.[47] But it is just the iceberg's tip. The controversies about heterosexual troops are far more complex and perplexing, without even beginning to consider the potential *children* in all this turmoil.

And there is also the broad moral question: What rights should employers have over the sexuality, *and the only life cycles*, of their employees? Is there an issue of civil liberty here? The Royal Canadian Mounted Police used to insist that recruits remain single for seven years, a rule now abandoned. Rhodes scholars must not be married. The assumption is that sex interferes with accomplishment and mobility. General Patton removed pinups from his troops' barracks in order to focus their attention on war, not love. The residential military heightens the tense connection between sex and social action.

Another matter is both desperately banal and all too real. A man or woman leaves his or her spouse or companion for a tour of duty of six months, to live in a crowded facility where across a canvas flap may sleep men and women of similar age and interests. Those at home will have an understandable suspicion about the erotic loyalties of the person they are committed to love and trust. If for no other more emotionally elegant reason, they may depend on their spouse for income, housing, health benefits, and potentially irreplaceable pensions. Sexual misadventure and its discovery may jeopardize all these. The French navy is also integrating men and women, but because of the cost of total reconfiguration of bunks, male and female officers may share rooms, surely an added concern of spouses or partners at home. This may be why naval pilots operate a code of mutual protection. Sexual adventures outside home and hearth are never revealed, especially to wives or husbands. Other less glamorous members of the military presumably protect each other, too.[48] It is an old story, jacked up to a new intensity. Troops abroad have always had to muse about the fidelity of their partners at home.[49] But it is relatively novel to have sexual competitors living in the arena that heretofore has been all male and therefore less threatening. Of course a similar problem has always been faced by the companions of homosexual people serving away from home, in the military.

Churches that require celibacy of their ministers try to provide a direct answer and set of compensating rewards, with an array of protections, benefits, and privileges secular and sacred. Even so they appear decreasingly appealing to potential recruits.[50] The Roman Catholic faith has had to consider bending its rules as in the (presumably extreme) case of a Scottish bishop who, as reported in *The Times* of London, was told by the leader of his church that he "could remain a priest only if he gave up his long-standing friendship with his parishoner, a divorced mother of three. The two disappeared last Monday."[51]

Meanwhile, the U.S. military is becoming a vast commune. In an ironic historical twist, the effective victor of the cold war is the only functionally communist and *dirigiste* organization in the country. In classical Marxist terms it tries to provide to each according to his or her reproductive need while asking from each the productive best he or she can contribute. In 1971, 14 percent of entering Army recruits were married; fifteen years later, 73 percent were.[52] It is said that some junior service people contract marriages of convenience because they offer improved off-base housing. But because of restraints of budget, even they are provided for only minimally, even meanly. Most of the civilians who comment on military life do not comprehend the sharp economic restriction that service people experience. Domestic tensions are plentiful.[53] Are they relieved or augmented by sexual activity in an intimately coed military, especially one based abroad, in relative isolation? One in which men and women spend ever more time with each other? Even so, the political pressures on the military are enormous. It is expected to conform to gender-blind ways of recruiting, training, and deploying.

While I was exploring this issue, I was told by a respected senior officer that the Navy would deal with the issue of sexuality as it confronted drugs—with a policy of zero tolerance. But drug use is pathological, destructive, degrading, and illegal. Sexuality is normal. Even if naval and other regulations define it as a feature of human frailty and mishap, it is a predictable proof of thriving life. The drugs comparison is perversely misguided.[54] Techniques developed to control the deft transfer of illegal, tiny, and costly powders have little to do with the large turbulence of bodies and minds drawn as magnets to each other to engage in free and intense sociability. Such techniques don't and won't work with sex. In addition, the military simply fired people who took drugs, they didn't change them. But with sex?

Sexuality is inherently linked to reproduction. So sex can and occasionally does lead to pregnancy. A 1996 report by Patricia Thomas of the Navy Personnel Research and Development Center in San Diego described the sexual and reproductive patterns of several thousand women aboard fifty naval ships.[55] Their rates of pregnancy were about comparable to those of civilian women of the same age. Neither the strict legal barriers nor the relatively draconian conditions of the Navy had apparent impact in inhibiting a general American pattern.

Thomas did not find, as some critics had claimed, that women became pregnant in order to escape duty. Her evidence for this was necessarily indirect—there were similar responses to questions about stress and depression among pregnant and nonpregnant women—but her analysis is more respectful of her informants than one that defines them as malingerers. Perhaps some were. Then why would roughly the same number of Navy women become pregnant as civilian?

She found that 27 percent of pregnancies of women based on ships were planned, whereas nearly half shore-based ones were. More ship women used contraceptives than shore women, though, remarkably, 41 percent used none. One hypothesis offered by naval medical personnel is that the irregular schedules and strenuous work on board ship caused women to forget to take their contraceptive pills. This is obviously a risible reason for pregnancies, condescending and disrespectful.

The women involved appear to have a good grasp of what they are doing. They had clear reproductive strategies. Thirteen percent of the women interviewed hoped for pregnancy within a year. This just happens to correspond neatly with one of the higher estimates of shipboard pregnancies. It suggests capable self-management among women. The Navy and any other organization facing this issue should discard any overriding pejorative working assumption about their female and male members. They may well be as thoughtful and adept about their intimate emotional life as they are about the work life for which they were selected, trained, and retained.

In 1995 the Secretary of the Navy stated that "pregnancy and parenthood are compatible with a naval career." But achieving this goal is likely to require that shipboard pregnancy be conceptually normalized. It will have to be treated not as a traffic accident but as traffic.

At sea a half year or more, healthy people in the prime of sexual and reproductive life are spending the time in relatively close physical proximity. They are isolated from the wider community. They live in a gray-metal-enclosed world that is restricted and under constant pressure.

On board they are supposed to be celibate. They are not. The situation is echoed in the other services as well. The U.S. Army at its training camp in Aberdeen, and at camps elsewhere, has investigated dozens of complaints of sexual violations, often repeatedly by the same individuals. There is no question that violations did and do occur. At the same time there is a Rashomon or cubist quality to any sexual event.[56] Mostly, it is difficult to know who did what to whom, why, with what pressure or allure, with what deception and self-deception. And so hot lines can be called and criminal charges made and sustained, especially if judges define a forcible violation as any sex, consensual or no, between persons of different rank. In one Aberdeen case a woman charging harassment had driven her harasser in her car to their rendezvous on three occasions.

Certainly there is exploitation. Nonetheless, women are not simply victims. They may fancy an officer or a superior figure who represents success in the organization they chose to join. A female officer may find a man of lower rank appealing. Personal pride involving clothing or cosmetics or grooming often sends strong sexual messages. People in the military may sleep yards away from their legitimate fantasy.

The matter overall has been inadequately evaluated. A possible comparison is with the Israeli kibbutz. There the original ideologues, largely male, said parents should not live with their children. First chance they had, women overturned this anti-mammalian fantasy.[57] The military is trying to do with men and women what Israeli kibbutz settlers tried and failed to do with parents and children. The military may fail, too, if they haven't already.

This having been said, present indications are that the American policy of gender-blind military action will be sustained, certainly in a voluntary service, with whatever consequences, compensations, and advantages that may result. An alloy of moral righteousness and social scientific error overcomes norms of common sense. Officers in the military who may protest are silenced either by their own prudence or by superiors intimidated by fierce canons of political behavior. An unexpected number of officers, especially in the Navy, are resigning in part because they anticipate they will not survive promotion scrutiny under the new and retroactively puritanical rules. One service commander whose unit was due to be integrated sexually was advised to maintain his command for several months so that his record would reflect his leadership of an integrated group, but then he was advised to leave swiftly before the inevitable problems blemished that record. Politically savvy officers reserve discussion of issues surrounding sexuality for after hours and moments of candid privacy. There remains disagreement between advocates of gender neutrality as a principal military objective and those committed to untrammeled combat readiness, which they fear sexual integration will compromise.

Neither one or the other position may be correct. Some compromise may be reached. The changes under way involve revisions of traditional practice, but the new procedures depend on the realities of human emotions, sexuality, and the needs of children. In the United States the outlines of policy are likely to be sustained if only because opponents have been ridiculed or dismissed. There may be considerable cost as well as advantage to individuals and the wider community. The real long-term benefits for military readiness and effectiveness have yet to be examined objectively. It is not clear who wants to do so or can. From the White House on down, the order of the day appears to be "Keep marching straight ahead."

The changes in military life reflect the feminizing shift we have been tracking. Change is especially vivid in this classic area of potentially heroic male behavior—everywhere and forever identified explicitly with the lives of men. Merely half a generation ago the Army could advertise "Be a Man, Join the Army," and the Marines "We Want Just a Few Good Men." Now these slogans are absurd, to say nothing of illegal. The military used to be the most socially acceptable form of organized male aggression, often rewarded with commendation and social status. What happens when the quintessential male-only sign of super-maleness becomes open to perfectly capable females? What happens when military society is changed decisively?

To repeat Margaret Mead's simplified judgment, if nature makes women and cultures make men, how can this culture make our men? What variety of men will emerge? What will they share with each other?

What will they share with women? Who will marry them? What kind of fathers will they be if they have children and a structure for them? How will they vote and for whom? What kind of work will they want to do and be able to do? What will be their games and their nightmares?

In this chapter we've encountered three realms in which new questions about men have produced suggestive answers. In pornography, symbolic sexuality and unrealistic erotic access may either replace or render more gratifying the real sexual activities that men engage in. Whether they provide cathartic adventure or fantasized sexual dominance, the burgeoning pornographic trades may reveal not only the pull of newly available freedom of communication but also the push of thwarted and confused opportunities for real and robust sex and reproduction.

Pornography is about symbolic affection. Sports is a thriving world of symbolic conflict. It mainly involves men who identify with other men who are their psychic representatives when they perform physically skilled and elegant heroic actions. It usually stimulates commitment to teams or territories from which individuals receive secondhand affirmation of masculine effectiveness that they fail to experience more directly.

The third subject was warfare, all too real when it happens but also now an emblem of changes in technology, the nature of warfare, and, centrally, the meaning of sex to its main protagonists. If pornography and sports are metaphors of a changed environment of gender, warfare and the military are the altered thing itself.

To this list we can add yet another industry booming from severe perturbations in human arrangements: drugs. While countless women take drugs, illegal drug users are overwhelmingly male. The fantasies of omnipotence and invulnerability, and the reality of escape, that men purchase when they buy drugs have generated industries which have enriched and corrupted whole countries and caused radical convulsions in the flows of cash and wealth in the world. There have always been drugs, dealers, and users. But the combination of new agricultural skill and techniques of transport with an expanded market of needy consumers has proved combustibly dramatic.

The industries of drugs, sports, and pornography prosper due to men who lack confident connection with reality, their own reality, and whatever reveries of accomplishment they entertain. The numbers of their children and the richness of their families decline over time. So do their incomes and sense of confidence about work. They turn to other certainties even if they are illusions. But the businesses are real. The world they span is a changed place. Men have remained the same for hundreds of thousands of years. Now they try to do, and do, different things because they have to.

Conclusion: Global
Cooling and the New
Future of Two Old Sexes

A S T H E C E N T U R Y closes out, there is an ambient global sexual cooling, particularly in America. There emerges an atmospheric anti-maleness. Males are no longer conventionally celebrated as the princes of creation. As the bearers of male original sin they can be held responsible for many of the difficulties women decide they face.

There is one clear result in America: the political gender gap. It is unlikely that it is solely the subject *du jour* or will remain confined to America. It is emerging elsewhere, too, with variations in emphasis and tempo. It remains imprecise in character and changes over time and space. It takes different forms in different places. Each human community has its traditions, its economics, its special notions of men and women, so different factors will determine a variety of different outcomes.

But generally similar social forces operate virtually worldwide, and there is a relatively concrete and common result. Although men and women inhabit the same society, the same social class, and often even the same homes, increasingly they are defining political reality differently. Then they are voting accordingly.

Traditionally, women have voted much as their husbands or fathers did.[1] No more. What was a real or potential source of support and protection for them—marriage and the family—is being stripped away, and through their votes they seek a replacement because they know they need one, even if it's just the government. What is happening to their private lives does not serve their needs. They may never want to marry or be able to find someone they are willing to marry. We have seen how many decide to have children on their own despite burdensome difficulties writ large. The old system was failing them and seemed likely to continue to do so. It was alarming.

In the American case, especially in the 1996 election which turned out to be of watershed meaning, there was much talk by politicians and economists of restricting the safety net. A much more intangible virtue beckoned: balanced budgets. But what would be in place to give a hand with welfare, family leave, and medicare for the old? Not much was promised. Instead, people were expected to forgo benefits from the state and work in the private economy.

But women knew how difficult life was if they had children or other family responsibilities. They had had ample experience about questionable day care, busy hospital waiting rooms, and employers unwilling to accommodate the routines of work to the needs of domestic life. A United Nations report revealed that the United States was one of only six nations without a paid leave policy for mothers.[2] So they voted for candidates who promised to protect what they needed in a perilous environment. Particularly in white groups, they voted in sharp contrast to their husbands, fathers, brothers, coworkers, and sons, who in turn deserted the traditional political leader working-class males, the Democratic candidate.

This was new. It was the unmistakable and unprecedented message of the 1996 election in the United States. The number of women elected did not necessarily change in a significant way up or down, but the clarity of female political demands was aggressively enhanced and sharp. Many male politicians failed to comprehend what was happening in their general constituency, but others responded and were successful, such as Bill Clinton.[3]

The development is understandable. The world had to change—first for reasons of profound fairness, and second because more and more women want to and have to work. Opportunities have to be fairly and helpfully available. Women have to be able to compete not only with women in reproduction but with men in production. In the past they were often unable to do so or had to disguise what they were doing while they did it. At that time males were evidently considered too vulnerable to face the facts of real female economic life.

Now women must compete with men in production while perhaps cooperating with them in reproduction. This is a novel and problematic basis on which to operate a human system. Potential antagonists must not only work together but eat together, make love together, live together, raise young together, and share the unforgiving mortal coil. Here is a source of substantial tension.

The industrial community must engage in two massive endeavors at once. Battles are being fought on two fronts at the same time: in the workplace and at home. It must restructure the modern arrangements that are resulting from contemporary technology and patterns of business, and must reexamine its utterly primordial social patterns and perhaps move to the mammalian default mode—the matrilineal form of many of the chimpanzee communities.

Not that this is necessarily either good or bad. Many people immersed in it may have an opinion on it or a personal story to tell or a reverie about a better future. It is unquestionably a major matter. These are factors in a new kind of cold war. It is conducted in tiny skirmishes in private or semiprivate as well as massively—in courtrooms, lecture halls, and the floors of legislatures.

The species is being separated into the two largest possible armies: males and females.

Neither frail dreams of romance nor self-congratulatory announce-ments of moralists seem able to withstand the cavalcade of escalating demands on individual men and women. They must first acquire and husband their own resources—supply rent, ensure food and shoes, pay for cable and faxing—and only then can they reach out to exchange and share. They must give and withhold at once. Not that they are strangers to each other. One way they "give" is sexually. Revealingly, sexually transmitted diseases are the most prevalent of all illnesses in contempo-rary America and among the most punishing in the world.[4] Genital herpes grows in its impact on American populations, which betrays inattention to protected sex.

Noah's Ark in the Dark

Noah was given a set of instructions on how to prepare for the flood. He was advised to create a guest list of duos for his cruise—a male and a female of each flavor of living creature. Even in those days, before Darwin and Mendelian genetics, and despite the ruckus created by sex in Eden, it was clear that the continuity of life required both males and females. Often the resulting duet is enjoyable, fulfilling, and of shocking interest. It can also be irritating and confusingly provocative. But sexuality has never been trouble-free and crystal-clear. The two groups may often find their encounters arduous and occasionally impossible, but they are drawn together—at least during the permissive privacy of the night. The link between physical pleasure and evolutionary success is dramatically strong, even fierce. On the other hand, controlling sexual congress is invariably a far greater challenge than inducing individuals to enjoy it. There is never complete and open license to engage in sex on any occasion and with just anybody. Virtually always there is a set of complex and pervasive "thou shalt nots" designed to cause people to pause and look before they love. Nearly everywhere sexual contact between two individuals possesses status, significance, and even drama. Kevin MacDonald has shown most explicitly and influentially in Europe and then its colonies, how since the Middle Ages socially imposed monogamy has been part of a restrictive ideology that privileges the officially reproductive duet of husband and wife.[5] The sexual bond differs from the links between partners in work, politics, games, dining, or any other endeavor. It is of interest that an enormously success book, *The Rules*, about effective ways to conduct successful courtship advises women to withhold sexual access to men who provide no tangible signs of serious commitment.[6]

Members of our species are doomed to the process of sexuality that produced us, despite whatever its would-be controllers or opponents may wish to encourage instead. We remain what Norman Mailer called "prisoners of sex." But in this prison the bars keep people out, not crowd them in, and the conditions surrounding the prison and within it have changed dramatically from those that generated human sexuality in the first place. So it is understandable to find disagreement and anger as well as affection and cooperation in sexual matters.

In this book we have explored a host of these new conditions. We tried to connect them to private experience and the trends pointing to the future. We have to conclude by examining what is happening, what it means, and what may be done about it. It will help to stand back and take two points of view at once. One is as the benevolent dictator of the world who is responsible for understanding what is happening on his property. The dictator wants practical knowledge that will make it easier to provide an agreeable home for exigent complicated beings. The other point of view is as the evolutionary scientist who wants to identify the underlying biological forces animating what is happening. How will human beings be affected by the changes under way?

The two perspectives together should generate a new picture of at least two guests on Noah's ark. Perhaps they will explain why sex and the sexes has become such an absorbing issue as the twentieth century closes.

Social Lysenkoism

The origins of the problem are unexpected. They derive from some hidden matters of unexciting science. Until 1964, Trofim Lysenko dominated Russian biological science. He believed that changing the environment of a species or plant could change its genes in an unexpectedly rapid and permanent way. For example, he thought that particular strains of wheat could be induced environmentally to grow in the cold parts of the U.S.S.R. where wheat had always perished. A series of self-deluding experiments convinced him that he was right. In turn he convinced Nikita Khrushchev, the Soviet leader, to set in motion a costly program of planting wheat in frigid environments. The wheat died. Lysenko's radical environmentalist program was a nutritional, economic, and intellectual disaster for the country. Lysenko's notions of environmentalism eventually died after 1964, at least in serious biology, but it blighted Soviet science for decades.

But his notions did not die in social science, especially in North America. Theories of environmentalism continued to reign in the social sciences. There is a background to this. Lysenko was part of an exciting effort in Eastern Europe to overcome centuries of near-feudal inequity. It was time to create new social patterns founded on convivial opportunity and economic parity. The initiative was of unquestionable moral value. Its methods were largely plausible and practical. Its virtue attracted politicians and social scientists convinced that there were no important fixed elements in human social life. Inequality was unnecessary, fairness was practical, opportunity could be for everyone, inheritance could be curtailed and eventually disappear. Surely well-meaning and ardent people could create lustrous new societies out of a renovated and emancipated *Homo sapiens*. They could combat notions of genetic racial superiority. There was no reason to tolerate any barrier from nature to enthusiastic planning for the brightest of futures.

The message of Lysenko found support in the psychology of Pavlov in the U.S.S.R. It resonated in the work of B. F. Skinner in the United States. They were both convinced that managing the environment of an animal would constrain its behavior. The experimental work was done on dogs, mice, rats, and pigeons. The principles of the learning theory on which it relied were confidently transferred from these relatively simple species to our own, far more complex one. It is very puzzling that this far-reaching translation was often accepted by the same people who denied the role of primatology in human life!

But learning theory had intrinsic and reassuring merit. It focused on what we could do for ourselves rather than on the fixed inheritance of our nature. It promised social freedom and political opportunity. It rewarded the zest for experiment. It was supported by the impressive ability of science and technology to plumb an ever-growing array of baffling matters.

The most recent and most important manifestation of this Lysenkoist environmentalism pertains to sex.

Nature? Nurture? The argument about the cause of our social nature has been endless, but it is no longer of much interest because the answer is not one or the other. Bodies are indisputably managed by natural programs. That's why they die. And a body cannot act except within a community of other individuals. The nature-nurture dialogue is especially uninteresting scientifically. The argument is settled. Neither can exist without the other. The challenge now is to understand the stew of factors that compose social life.

For public policy, however, the conclusion is different. The preeminent working assumption is that social emphasis must be on nurture. This suits the modern industrial notion of progress. It is consistent with the most appealing claims of politicians and reformers. Its emphasis has been sharpened by feminist assertions about the decisive impact of environments. They have won the day. They have also won the last three decades and the century. In many political circles it remains hazardous to a commentator's well-being to contemplate biological elements of sex differences. The orthodoxy is firm, well meaning, and altogether entrenched, rather like Marxism in its heyday and with many similar ways of crushing critics; they may be subjected to extraordinary personal and academic censure. For example, based on his own review of the material, the Austrialian anthropologist Derek Freeman challenged the quality and meaning of Margaret Mead's work on Samoa and was with dazzling sanctimony formally censured by the American Anthropological Association.[7] Even people who understand the importance of biological factors in social organization may hesitate to draw direct conclusions from what they know is true.[8]

Consequences flow. An important one is in the American legal system. It takes as a given that any statistical differences between men and women reveal faulty arrangements. It takes as a given that with good will, stern law, and remedial craft these differences can be eliminated, prejudice can be excised, and equity can be ensured. Any deviation from this is the result of bad nurture, not recurrent nature. In military training or scores on tests or even in longevity, differences are held to reflect imperfect opportunities for women or resistant hostile action by men or a complex combination of similar factors.[9]

"Male" and "female" are vital intellectual signposts. They are defined and treated differently in each society. Nonetheless, there is great overlap. The bodies and behavior of each flow into the other, and there are some regularities. To understand them we have been using both traditional social analysis as well as the new biology that has become available. This may help us discover what is going on in our whole species.

The beginning of the century was Marx's apex of analysis and influence. Darwin presides intellectually over its ending but his insights and message remain strangely and widely unpopular. No other body of science bears such a formidable burden as the collective weight of various fundamentalist religious assertions against it. Darwin needs our help in sketching the meaning of his incisive proposal for our life and times.

My own effort to reintroduce Darwin into a community that acknowledged him but effectively rejected his implication for practical social matters involved the use of sex—the category—to understand biology, the science of social events. I had been teaching about sex differences in political behavior. There was much to learn about how primates formed and operated social groups. I traveled during a summer to London, where there was an active group pursuing a Darwinian program. One of the first calls I made was to Desmond Morris, who was then the curator of mammals at the London Zoo and was soon to write *The Naked Ape*. I told Morris that I wanted to study the behavior of males in groups. He replied that this was a fascinating subject and that primatologist colleagues were baffled by the high mortality rate among male monkeys in several communities, especially Cayo Santiago off Cuba where some 80 percent of males perished, often of tetanus from cuts and wounds resulting from fights with dominating males. Morris invited me to return the following year as a social scientist in residence at the zoo.

More than thirty years later I appear to be wondering still about what is happening to the males.

In November 1996 two specific events occurred. They symbolized the massive changes in the lives of men and women we have been inspecting in this book. One was national but significant beyond particular borders. The other was international, species-wide, everywhere. Together they bear important news.

The first event was unusual differences in the voting patterns of men and women in the presidential election. The differences revealed, among other things, increasingly divergent underlying reproductive and productive strategies of males and females. It reflected and established their different expectations, fears, and wishes of the future.

The second event was the announcement by a United Nations statistical agency that the growth of population in the world had begun to level off for the first time this century.[10] Women in many countries had begun to plan their lives and limit their reproduction for a variety of reasons. Many were empowered to do so for the first time both by family planning initiatives and "more economic power and social status." In 1996 the average Mexican woman had three children, compared with 6.8 twenty years earlier.[11] To demographers this is a classic sign of a decisive shift. It portends that a cascade of substantial changes will occur well beyond the birthrate itself.

The news overall is that women are taking firmer control of their destinies. We've already seen that in once conservative Poland women sharply reduced births by 30 percent and marriages by 20 percent during the nine years following the collapse of the Communist government in 1989. Women are beginning to shape the direction of their lives and societies in new and explicit ways. They are more able and willing to conduct their lives on their own terms and by themselves. They have babies on their own. They operate their own businesses. Some define themselves skillfully and opportunistically as members of a kind of functional minority group despite the fact that women are the majority. They have taken firm advantage of legislation initially designed to compensate groups such as ex-slaves whose conditions of deprivation were far different and more punitive than theirs. (The indignity of slavery was largely based on total exclusion from dignified life, whereas women were relegated primarily to the domestic sphere rather than the public. Indeed, white-skinned women benefitted from slavery along with their men.) With astonishing speed they have shifted from being defined as vulnerable or amoral temptresses (Eve and Delilah) to fiercely demanding moral exemplars (the Virgin Mary, Joan of Arc, and Eleanor Roosevelt).

On the other hand, as a loose but palpable group, men are unclear and confused. What is weakness and what is power? What is responsibility and what is personal failure? What can they do and what must they not? Which words may they use in public and which only in private?

Men may not like or agree with many of the public demands made by women. They may not know how to respond to women who decorate and carry themselves in a potently attractive manner but become potentially litigious if men respond in a sexy manner. They may be bewildered when they join work groups like armies, universities, or companies and are handed a manual of stern and detailed operating procedures with which to discipline their emotions about women. Or they may be required—for example, by organizations eager to clothe their posteriors against possible law suits—to endure bizarre ministrations of so-called sensitivity consultants. In one Fortune 500 company a consultant guided employees through this puerile exercise: "I want all of the men to sit down on the floor in the center of the room. You are not allowed to speak while sitting down. The women are to stand around the men in a circle and begin to whistle and make sexist comments about the appearance and anatomy of the men."[12] Men are hence made to feel vaguely but personally culpable for general male sexual misdemeanors. They have to accept a reverse inheritance from their father's generation and watch women appear to enjoy legal advantages in the hunt for jobs, at least for some jobs. They can no longer influence women by pregnancy and marriage, by putting a woman "in the family way." Here may be one reason that they appear to resent those welfare payments and other bureaugamous fixtures that permit women to raise children without their help and certainly without their control. Assigned by women to a "patriarchy" not of their choosing, men nevertheless look about for the concrete signs of their presumed kingly status. But when they look in the mirror, there is no crown to be seen.

In a few short years, when DNA paternity testing becomes common, they will face yet another new challenge: Courts may hold them responsible for supporting children they may not have wanted to father or could have caused to be aborted if they had remained in contact with their partner. Chemistry, not morality, will constrain them. In the aberrant but not insignificant case we've mentioned, a fifteen-year-old boy was raped by an adult woman who became pregnant; the boy is the father, and the courts have held him and his family responsible for the financial welfare of his child.[13] A mother controls her own body; a father may not share that control, but he will be responsible for the result whether or not he wanted it or even knew that a pregnancy was possible during a "one night stand" sexual episode that may have seemed intentionally casual. English journalists Matthew Campbell and Jack Grimston report that, in the United States where paternity tests may be conducted by mail, there is a paternity test pending for one out of every 100 children.[14]

Men may stew and grouse in private, but except on the issue of abortion and occasionally about affirmative action, hardly any of them in public life are able or willing or sufficiently intrepid to challenge the legal and political demands of women. They remain silent and cowed in the face of seemingly unassailable moral orthodoxies. This is certainly almost universal in the university community and, more or less, in the liberal governments.

Privately, but usually only privately, they may respond with some bitterness to clear discrimination. A young man told me his Wall Street employer was sending a recruiter to his alma mater, to help hire the next crop of employees. I assumed he was going along since he was in fine standing among his peers. He scorned the suggestion. Only a female, probably with dark skin, would be sent to this elite institution, not a white male.

The response of men may be quiet consternation, but they are not the only people with problems and uncertainties. There are more than enough to go around for everybody. Nearly everyone in the system will have to navigate a particular barrier or window of advantage or some other new factor. The pattern and force of the shift is not yet precise, but the fact of change is clear enough to the people held in its thrall.

This change is not ubiquitous or near total; in fact, it is sharply inadequate. Countless women remain in harsh constraint established by religions, families, doctors, husbands, the police, needy children, the court of public and private opinion, their own beliefs and prudence. The caste system in India coerces the entire population within a stringent scheme, one especially onerous for poor women.[15] With remarkable bravery two dozen women in Somalia publicly bared their breasts to protest their subservient positions. But they were not even given the respect implied by serious punishment—their male relatives were.[16] The Chinese government carefully manipulated an international meeting about women to isolate potential Chinese feminist dissidents and gather international support at the United Nations.[17] It is common and almost acceptable for South Korean men to beat their wives, who are also chronically pressured to bear male, not female children.[18] As we have seen amniocentesis and abortion have driven the ratio of male-to-female births in China to profound imbalance.[19]

Whole nations sustain overt and often harsh restrictions on their women. They do not permit them to vote, own property, show their mouths, hold public office, drive cars, shop alone, or caress or even touch male friends without danger. In many places there is no expectation that women should earn the same as men for the same work. There is no effort to ensure that women receive opportunities to be educated, if only because it may make life more interesting for them and their work more rewarding. Young women can be sold into sexual slavery by families or abused for free by sexual opportunists with a safe exit.[20] Like members of ancient feudal estates, many women in many countries see no options for themselves other than the narrow sliver of one they have been handed. Perhaps they heard of the revolution. But it happened elsewhere.

Their lives are very different from those of the relatively independent and sophisticated women who have been defined, by themselves and journalists, as the modern standard of vigorous effectiveness.[21] Other women, the current majority in the world, may enjoy lives of intensely traditional familial reciprocity even if they don't choose them explicitly. They may relish the stateliness of living at the classic pace of the whole life cycle: youth, growing up, marriage, children, their marriages, bustle, grandchildren, seniority, pop off, end of story. No independent initiatives, no bravado, no separate bank accounts, no family bust-out, no psychotherapeutic dramas, no disruptions of the universe. A friend who is a well-published feminist told me with equal reluctance and enthusiasm how much she envied the lives of the women in the Scorcese godfather films. They were protected, and had untroubled duties and expectations. Since they couldn't question, they had no need to worry about answers.

Of course, Mafia kinship is no solution to anything, but it is important not to be bedazzled by the promise and drama of radical sexual change. There is no virtue in denying the value of the lives that countless women have lived and live. Many women choose to emphasize reproduction, perhaps to the exclusion of nearly all other nonfamilial matters. This is hardly eccentric in the cold biologist's eye of Mother Nature, but it is plausible that "having it all"—children, job, mate, attractiveness, warm household enjoyments—remains the ideal that nearly all women will define in public if not in print.[22] However, for what one woman's experience is worth, one response to this issue is "Many of my friends say they want the traditional setup more but would never admit it in public." Whatever the private opinion, in public countless women do and will struggle with the complex demands of contemporary mother-hood and work. An ad for *Redbook* magazine said, "We go for the Juggler." One of the most effective, well-staffed, and powerful of entertainers, Madonna, said after she had a baby, "Now I'm late for everything."[23]

Women are now subject to double jeopardy. Those without children may have to accept a sense of loss of one of life's fundamental experiences. Those without work may endure the same loss. A rapidly increasing proportion of women must face a newly emphasized and widespread dilemma—the apparent choice between love and work, and all the compromises that choice involves, which are at the core of modern social life.

Male Men

Thirty years ago I published my first book, *Men in Groups*, which developed the idea of male bonding. I linked it to human evolution as a cooperative hunter-gatherer. I described how men courted and chose other men as working and fighting partners, and as recreational companions, and how one feature of male bonding was the exclusion of females. The cross-cultural evidence was overwhelming concerning the ubiquity of the division of labor in human communities. It was reflected in the extraordinary predominance of men in forms of public life ranging from church to army to sport to legislature to business to law enforcement. It also prospered in secret societies, mysterious social groups cutting across all sectors of social life. Who knew for sure what they did and to whom? Secret shenanigans heightened the sense of the omnipresent potency of men in groups.

Rapid substantial change seemed doubtful in any of these systems. They were undergirded by a time-honored array of biosocial imperatives associated with marriage and the relatively large extended families then still found in the industrial communities.[24] Women as well as men appeared to have an enduring stake in the system. For example, in the arranged marriages among Iranians, women were the ones who deter-mined family action and who competed with one another. Anthropolo-gist Paula Ardeheli describes opposing groups of women who would deploy crass stratagems, such as covertly spiking a rival hostess's cooking with excessive spices in order to shame another family, thereby elevating theirs. Women were mainly in charge of family affairs. Men were permitted to provide approval after the fact.[25] Iranians who moved to the United States after the revolution in 1979 continued their patterns of matchmaking. They adapted ancient exchanges of property to the shopping malls of New Jersey—so many dresses from Macy's each year, a chandelier of at least twenty-four inches in width, a bedroom set of walnut, and so forth.[26] The business of family was carried on as usual even in a radically different environment, on a different continent.

But could the changes have been predicted? There were relatively few early signs. I had some inkling that the contraceptive pill would make a substantial difference to society and said as much in an *Observer* (London) essay that appeared near the publication of the book.[27] But this was obviously too tentative in light of the medication's complex power over users and the societies in which it played a major, even defining, sexual role.

I had no idea change could or would occur as rapidly as it has in the industrial countries. Wasn't biology a durably influential feature of human motivation? How could a system of million years' standing ebb and flow in the flash of a few decades?

Hindsight makes it obvious that fundamental change in a fundamen-tal process would produce still more fundamental change. It has. But it remains unusual and controversial to analyze social change with the benefit of biology. In many political precincts it is simply unacceptable morally. Not only does a biosocial argument have to be effective or plausible, but it has to justify its very existence. It remains unnecessary to know a shred of biology to hold down a policy job involving biological matters like families and sex. When I gave a talk on these matters in 1997 at the Nitze School of International Affairs at John Hopkins University, one attendee, a senior advisor in the White House, asked,

"How come we don't know any of this?" It is even difficult to receive government approval for research on the matter, let alone funds.[28] The first subject mentioned for possible funded research by the Sexuality Research Program of the Social Science Research Council in the U.S. in 1998 was "social construction analysis of sexuality," which is, in essence, academic code for antibiological approaches. A veil of ignorance separates the facts and the discussion of them. Pundits discuss logic that is specialized and isolated but not biologic, which is omnipresent and ongoing. Social commentators are generally comfortable with superficial but plausible social explanations, so they connect family size with jobs and houses, male behavior in school with television, and female pregnancy with sultry movie stars. They are able to ignore the inner processes. They discuss steam with no knowledge or mention of the physics of heat.

Even with the comfort of hindsight it remains difficult to grasp how decisively the changes effected by women have affected men. It would have seemed crude and heartless to predict how rapidly male resistance would grow to marrying pregnant partners. Who could have tracked in advance the rate at which women themselves would seek other remedies? Who would have proposed the counterintuitive idea that effective contraception would enhance the legal status of abortion and spur single motherhood?[29]

Now we can better acknowledge the firm link between female sexual independence, which hardly existed at the time, and economic independence. Without this understanding it would have seemed reckless and uninformed to anticipate how rapidly women would enter the educational and economic systems, establish their own businesses, and demand public attention to their needs once largely confined to the private realm. Women have been very efficient. They recognized very quickly that although they may from time to time, or even for a long time or lifetime, be protected by the family system, they nevertheless have to be competent independent contractors to the economy. They must be able to support themselves. They must be able to support offspring if they have them.

Females are the sex with the greater responsibility for the conduct of individual lives. They appear to have less choice in what to do about families and divorce, but they have rapidly begun to meet their challenges. In the United States, 59 percent of mothers of young children doubled their jobs in the economy between 1979 and 1984.[30] By 1996 over half of English women with children under ten were at work. This is a major reason that domestic service is the fastest growing category of consumer spending by English people. It doubled between 1985 and 1996.[31] We have already seen from the work of Arline Geronimus and her colleagues that unmarried women with children attack the labor market better than their childless sisters. Predominantly, these women are not the economic elite of their communities. Further-more, their decision to bear children early demonstrates biologic if not logic.[32] They must often struggle for years, surviving on a weak cocktail of unreliable sources of income. Against stacked odds, the decisive majority of them conduct and complete their obligations as parents.

Nonetheless, the single-mother system continues. It is a paradox if only because of the availability of effective contraception. Its very ubiquity alarms many onlookers, which at the same time may attest to its effectiveness.

These players at the casino are dealt a hand of very poor cards. Yet they play them with skill and persistence. A substantial majority do not leave the casino broke. Of course these mothers have restricted oppor-tunity to prepare their children for the grand agendas of societies lured by upward mobility. Nevertheless, they grasp their small moment of private history. They play their cards stubbornly. Presumably, they and their children do not regret they are alive, whatever abrasion, indignity, and barriers they confront.

The Feminist International

These and other women somehow benefit from the global cooling I have discussed. As a loosely connected but definable group, women in general have fomented a philosophical change in manners, morals, and laws that favors their interests. They have extended this to areas such as the military and diplomacy, which would have been inconceivable three decades before. The majority of incoming elite foreign officers in the United Kingdom are women, and 30 percent of senior American officials are women, including Madeleine Albright, the U.S. Secretary of State since 1997.[33] Though from a small base, the fastest growing movement of women into traditionally male jobs in the United States is in the construction industry, especially as managers and owners of start-up firms. Also in the United States, women have earned 55 percent of all doctorates in anthropology[34] and approach that level in the social and psychological sciences and humanities overall. Fifty-four percent of the entering class in 1996 of Yale Medical School was female, while women have outnumbered men in graduate school since the mid-1980s.[35] In 1975, 18 percent of Harvard Law School was female; twenty-two years later that number had risen to 42 percent.

As we have seen, men in this new environment have lost jobs and virtually any publicly acceptable sense of entitlement. They can look forward to a sharply reduced portion of places in colleges and professional schools. Scenes of formerly all-male drama such as the military, the police, and fire departments now have casts of females, too. They are often first shoe-horned in by legal obligations against resistance, sometimes despite sabotage. But finally they are there, on the scene. Again, legal instruments designed to integrate races that are not biologically different in any important way have been wielded on behalf of women who are biologically different in very important ways from men. But these different biologies play a minor, even negative, role in forming social policy even if they affect behavior.

An inevitable result is that men receive a smaller slice of the money pie than in the past. Single men earn the most contempt among recipients of welfare. They are relatively unlikely to be given it. Men under fifty are educated less as a class than women. The benefits as well as wages of unskilled workers in the United States continue to decline.[36] Men under thirty commit 90 percent of violent crimes, often against each other, and males often congregate in dangerous groups.[37] Income differences with women are likely to grow because males perform comparatively poorly in the educational system and are less numerous and effective in it.

Finally, no one attached to the traditional image of authoritarian patriarchy could imagine the consternation men endure. They have suffered an unexpected blow to the emotional quality of their lives. Its gravity has not been calculated. They have far fewer reliable links than women to the classic currents of family life. They are alienated not only, as Marx said, from the means of production but also from the means of reproduction.

Sex and the Engines of History

Marx and his associates were convinced that the communist revolution was inevitable. It would follow self-evident laws. It would be stimulated by mature urban working classes, such as in Germany, educated enough to appreciate the value of the Marxist proposal. Instead, agricultural Russia led the way in Communism. Ideas of radical change elsewhere affected other populations in unexpected ways, too. The agents of change were unpredictable, but change there was. Who could know what would coerce the future?

Are there guidelines here for the modern-day equivalent of the communist internationale—feminism? As with Communism, are the changes occurring because of feminism not the changes predicted? I don't want to overargue either the parallel or the similarity of the two movements or imply a moral judgment, which I am not making, but there is a plausible connection to explore.

We are confronting populations no less massive and heterogeneous than those of the whole world. Usually we divide populations of people into nations, blocs, religions, ethnic interests, and myriad other forms of human affiliation. Usually we examine who has the money in a society—the elite, the clans, the government? We examine what its form of government is—democratic, fascist, communist? We examine its commanding ethical system—Christian, Muslim, atheist? We even examine its attitude toward environmental nature—exploititively industrial, cautiously Buddhist, scientifically agnostic? We examine any other useful contemporary metric. But I want to look at countries, the alliances they sustain, and the international policies they pursue through a wholly different lens. I want to use sex—not sex in the personal erotic sense or sex as a form of personal self-expression, but sex as a master organizing principle of a society. I think it will be directly and unexpectedly helpful in anticipating international social change and the sources of unanticipated human tensions.

An analogy about a large historical matter may help. In my opinion, human beings are not very skillful at macro-rationalism, which is the quality of intellectual skill necessary to operate complicated communities with the complete big-picture planning of classical Communism. In fact, it is against human nature. We may call ourselves *Homo sapiens*, but we cannot know everything at once and respond to every force and all people all the time. Communism failed as an organizational device. It was a failure of macro-rationalism. The human brain and sense organs are simply not up to the challenge of integrating the kaleidoscopic information and social initiatives generated by an industrial system.

Except for periods of full-bore mobilization and seriously dangerous warfare, it is better and also easier to decentralize social process. Smaller groups of buyers, makers, and sellers can make limited deals with one another. They can satisfy one another directly rather than through an independent plan. An overarching economic scheme such as Communism may seem intellectually elegant and more promisingly predictable than the erratic angularity of markets. But repeated experience shows it is unlikely to be sensitive enough to the people involved—what they can do, what they won't do, and what they want.

Its anti-nature was the principal reason Communism failed, certainly in the forms it was tried.[38] This was not because of its originally lustrous ideals and aspirations, which continue to be understandably appealing nearly everywhere in the world. There was excellent reason for its attractiveness in many countries that embraced it, such as China and Russia. Still, to carry it off required the discipline of an exotic circus-brand performance. You can teach a bear to tango on a barrel but his enthusiasm and performance are limited and brief. He will prefer to do something else unless you continue to needle and bribe him.

This is not to say that Communism's stereotypical opposite, capitalism, is natural instead. The priest-theologian of capitalism, Adam Smith, wrote the famous *The Wealth of Nations* about achieving productivity, but he also published a more complex and interesting book, *The Theory of Moral Sentiments*, that was about achieving moral fairness and decency. Cooperative hunters and gatherers focused on nothing less.[39] Moral sentiments not only made them feel better but were essential in small-scale communities tied to the land and to each other. Cooperation was natural. It still is.

The Politics of Alluring Flesh

And what has all this to do with sex? Communities that violate human sexual nature will experience the same kind of problems that communists had. To try to solve them, communists had to impose their ideology, often viciously, on largely unwilling populations. Remember all that fatuous hypocrisy about communist parties being the people's vanguard (even if the health and morale of those in charge required access to subsidized stores providing tasty foreign food)? And remember the example of the kibbutz, which failed in its utopian schemes about love and families but succeeded fully with politics and money?

It means that communities, whether industrial or otherwise, will have to come to terms with the male and female behavior that is produced in the wealthy nations. Like good blue jeans, their liberal ideas are attractive, fit comfortably, and are a signal of complex personal sophistication. It is especially likely that norms of female life developed and held up for emulation in the rich countries will cross borders. They are appealing to women, plausible, and empowering. They suggest the most volatile departure from the restricting past, and they offer the largest menu of options. The 1996 United Nations Population Fund's report noted that by the year 2006 more than half of the world's people will be living in cities. Cities historically present fewer obstacles and provide greater opportunity for women. Women enjoy more room to maneuver there than in the rural regions from which they stream.[40]

New images of female life will diffuse in a variety of ways. They will permeate other countries through the deliberate action of feminist politicians. Concernocrats will work through international organizations. The mass media will sketch new patterns of social choice as well as intensely private ones. Going to the movies, hearing rap, balancing checkbooks, and watching television, to say nothing of travel, have and will change women's lives. Even in the heretofore rigidly controlled arena of public behavior by Islamic women in traditionalist communities, there has been assertive activity by various groups, including the Sisterhood Is Global Institute based in Maryland. Its leaders claim they do not wish to be confrontational. They assert their fealty to "Islam-based" values. Nonetheless, it is clear they pose a challenge to the fundamentalist communities in which they live or from which they are exiled.[41]

It is and will be increasingly difficult for resistant governments to prevent access to the flood of liberating stimuli that swirls around the world at electric speed. Maintaining old patterns in new conditions will require ever more draconian restrictions. Women will continue to make direct and personal choices. For example, at one time relatively closed countries such as China promoted quite stringent norms of public modesty, especially about revealing the body. But as soon as they were able, mainly female entrepreneurs began to provide cosmetics and lively clothing, and did very well. How did fifty years of vaunted role models evaporate so rapidly? The same is true in Russia.[42] Despite decades of the button-up New Socialist Woman, the Russian female is liberated when it comes to her physical appearance if she can afford to be—again despite decades of strenuously stern propaganda. Elsewhere, during the time of the shah of Iran, traditional Iranian women attending the university would be chaperoned to its gates where they abandoned their black chadors and donned jeans and T-shirts, the new garb of their sex and their generation. They crossed the line even if they had to go back.

In some places or periods of history, women may be unable to do this, especially where contraception is unavailable or imperfect and sexuality therefore may have major consequences. But the wish for sexual self-expression is neither extinguished nor very deeply hidden. The quick cadence of contemporary social change produces an absorbing kaleido-scope of personal possibilities. Television satellites make borders nearly irrelevant. To maintain their current arrangements governments will have to censor and restrict behavior and information the way the communists did. Some will succeed, such as the mullahs in Iran or orthodox rabbis in Jerusalem or Farrakhanites in the United States, if only for a while. Politicians may call the problem of women's independence a symptom of the Great Satan. Moralists may define it as the decline of the West or the East. Historians may see it as the conflict of civilizations. However it is described, the idea that women can be free of traditional restrictions is as subtle and yet volatile as an idea can be. United in a flash are Eve, Lady Chatterley, Margaret Sanger, Rosa Luxembourg, Eartha Kitt, and Eleanor Roosevelt.

It is increasingly questionable that any government, especially one largely operated by men with conventional male priorities, will produce communal arrangements accommodating Mother Nature and Father Nature for any length of time. The overriding requirement will have to be that family systems are robust and resourceful enough to provide women with suitable conditions for both production and reproduction within a tolerable zone of comfort. Otherwise there will be constant pressure for tectonic-style shifts in the links between public and private life, and between men and women in their various modes of relationship. Not only has the personal become political, but the political system has come to encompass experiences and forces for which it is intellectually and even morally unprepared.

Marx has been turned on his head. Class struggle, of course, continues. But the boil and froth of primary elemental history is now the account of the struggle between sexuality and public life—the struggle of sexual classes.

Can it be that Charles Darwin diagrammed the central political challenges to the twenty-first century?

Ideology and Utopia

The sociologist Karl Mannheim showed many years ago that ideologies had their origin in the fertile soil of problematic social conditions. They were cries of pain and ardor rather than independent dreams. They reflected what was currently hostile, irritating, and erosive rather than pure thought in the service of perfection.[43] Will a new master theory of social behavior like utilitarianism or socialism or democracy or communism emerge to respond to new issues that have rather suddenly become apparent to people everywhere? Will Wordsworth's "rulers of the present day" be able to "deal with the domestic affections of the lower orders" as well the other strata, too?

During much of the twentieth century, societies were often defined by their economies—capitalist, communist, developed, third world, so forth. They will continue to be defined this way. How people earn and use resources—how they are productive—is an irreplaceably vital feature of their lives. But we have to add a new and broadly consequential category, too. How are they reproductive? Have they a positive or negative birthrate? Do they help fertile people or leave them to their own devices? Do they restrict fertility as in China or promote it as in France and Singapore? Do they perceive immigration as a factor in positive or negative population levels? Is there any discernible way in which citizens relate their own family experience to the future of their community? For example, in Russia after the abandonment of Communism there were sharp decrements in health and fertility (so that deaths far outpaced births)[44] that, along with political convulsions, affected social spirit overall. Of course, in the long run of any community's history, reproductive élan or its absence will have substantial diplomatic and military impact.

The Politics of
Reproductive Strategy

On a planet with countless people and ever greater consciousness of crowding and limitations on resources, the issue of fertility will assume ever greater prominence. It will concern marketers anticipating customers, moralists struggling about belief and abortion, and generals conjuring up platoons. Communities largely formed of one ethnic group will consider whether or not because of their neighborhood they are a particular society and how to reflect the answer for immigration.[45] Societies with high reproductive rates and low productive rates will have to search for ways to provide, against enormous odds, dignified and potentially reproductive life cycles to large numbers of young males. They may legislate dowry subsidies, as they do in the United Arab Emirates, or proffer fundamentalist religious promises about the future.[46] Japan has sought to confront low birthrates and long-standing restrictions on immigration by embracing automation and robots. But Japan may have to go beyond this, perhaps locating its production offshore, if there are too few Japanese at home to perform the work economically. And we can predict that the government's 1996 decision to legalize the contraceptive pill will generate unexpectedly rapid and far-reaching changes at the core of Japanese social and economic life should the pill become widespread; using it goes against the wishes of physicians who profit from the abortions they perform. A relatively conservative and brittle society will be pushed into unfamiliar turmoil about private emotions. Suddenly, individual passions and ardor will surface as novel issues for public policy. Meanwhile, what will be the long-term population of a nation such as Italy where the birthrate of 1.19 children per female will produce a nearly depopulated Italy in fifty years? And what of Spain, Germany, Portugal, Russia, Austria, and Bulgaria, which among other European communities show a birthrate around 1.60 per female?

How communities respond politically and economically to the reproductive strategies of women will be crucial. These may be articulated as political realities or perceived as psychological forces. What has been called feminism is largely the result of an array of initiatives, demands, explorations, and dialogues arising from the unexpectedly rapid rewriting of the script of the human reproductive drama. Compared with men, women have responded first and most directly to the changes. They are more accustomed to consider these matters. They are as individuals more directly and consciously in thrall to time. Their biological clock is wound more tightly and accurately. And they have been supported by an unprecedentedly general and innovative set of political moves—often supported by males themselves. For example, in preparation for the 1997 general election, which at the end of 1996 the Labour Party was expected to win decisively, the party nominated a large number of women candidates in nearly half of the nearly certain Labour constituencies.[47] The result was that the new Parliament contained 106 women, up from 23.

Lost Males

Nothing males have done as a self-conscious gender group is remotely comparable, thorough, or effective.[48] Men in groups do not appear to perceive themselves as men in a group. They do not define themselves as members of an assembly with a collective interest. To the extent that they are conscious at all of any problems they face, men seem to assume these will be solved in the traditional public way. Their fantasy is, all they have to do is behave in reasonably civil, even gentlemanly ways. Everything will turn out peaceably and well.

But they are enduring illusion and self-deception.[49] In truth, "they just don't get it" and don't get what they're about not to have. They fail to understand the implacably coercive breadth of what is in their faces. What is under way is so imprecise but so general and atmospheric they do not realize what is happening to them. In response, men pursue a strategy that they barely realize is a strategy, perhaps because it is a failure. To maintain agreeable lives, they will use traditional tools and modes of power. But this strategy is also one that is clearly foundering. It is accelerating the decline of men. The new outcome for men is not yet clear. Nevertheless, their disorganized passivity may embolden governments and bureaucrats to devise schemes that work against them, such as the British plan to demand common child support payments from all divorced fathers, to be redistributed by the government, or the even more demented suggestion in 1998 that divorced fathers be obligated to pay for the opportunity to visit their children.

Earlier on we confronted the fact that males and females have different reproductive strategies. These are in many respects at odds. Yes, there must be contact, intimate contact, at least between men and women, at least between those traditionalists who do not take advantage of modern techniques of insemination. But otherwise it is possible, as has happened in many communities, for male groups and female groups to carry on with considerable apartness. There can even be some real hostility as in physical violence, legal action, or political assertion, to say nothing of the symbolic or sardonic variety. What traditionally connects the male group and the female group and mediates any discordance between them is what we call the kinship system. To maintain it requires much effort, many resources, people who know how it works, who want it to work, and who care about it. With smaller families and more broken and disheveled ones, there are fewer skilled and available personnel to carry on family business. The family organization chart is thinning out. Middle management of family life is disappearing and spending nearly all its time and energy at the office. The kinship system is at risk and in some precincts near extinction.

Contrasting and competitive sexual strategies have been magnified beyond calculation by new technology. What might have been considered benign or at least neutral technological adventures have become sharply leveraged tools in the ancient sexual arms race. Because of the existence of safe and effective contraception controlled by females, perhaps for the first time in mammalian life, certainly for the first time in human history, one sex can control reproduction. This has given enormous general power to women that has been translated beyond the family sphere.

At the same time there have emerged relatively inexpensive, easy, and accurate DNA tests of paternity.[50] These will be increasingly used both for legal and affectionate reasons. At its grimmest, the test will reduce women's ability to deceive their partners and themselves. At the same time it will restrict men's opportunity to escape from responsibility. Governments are already using the test for public welfare purposes. Should governments require mothers applying for welfare for children to define the fathers of their children with tests as authoritative as DNA, the mere existence of the test will have some effect on the bureaugamic process.

At the personal level, we can expect that a test about the outcome of making love will have impact on the intensity of courtship and marriage. It is difficult to predict the impact, just as it was impossible to have predicted that the contraceptive pill would be followed by increased abortion and skyrocketing single motherhood. Pharmaceuticals may reintroduce one feature of the social controls that the discredited double standard was designed to impose. And although pre-parental, the paternity test has some of the character of a prenuptial agreement, with all the understandable but inhibiting calculation and self-protectiveness such agreements often encompass.[51]

Suddenly there is genuinely unprecedented biological novelty and hence adventure. Here is technology's next fundamental intervention into the core behavioral essence of human life. Now we are immersed in and challenged by its consequences. We have lost the complex innocence of having no freedom. Now there is the lure of plausible control. But there has been no Socrates, Aristotle, Jefferson, Rousseau, or Magna Carta to define the rules of such luxury. No one has convincingly announced the obligations of the sexually renovated citizenry. Independence has been achieved without a declaration, without a revolution, even without an explicit goal or explicit foe other than the absence of choice.

Feuds about abortion are bitterly real in themselves. They also are symptoms of a large struggle about biological freedom and constraint. They reveal a form of war between the tidal flow of feelings and the explicit private plans people often sketch.

What happens now? It can't be partisan. Half of mothers have sons. Half have daughters. They all share interest in the future of sex and gender. What arrangements can be made? What will feel right and be doable?

A young man dated a young woman at a New York college with a lively women's studies program, of which she was an enthusiastic accomplished member. One evening he was present when some of its students discussed their futures. They turned to the subject of children. With warmth and anticipation they spoke of the books they would read to their daughters, the role models they would be to growing girls, the anti-sexist upbringing they would provide daughters. The young man destroyed their reverie with: "But what if you have sons?"

An ideology devoted to one sex won't suffice.

The Declaration of Dependence

Let me identify some principles to underlay useful and practical social policy. These are controversial, though not deliberately so. Many current practices would be controversial, too, if they were newly proposed, and my few illustrative suggestions may seem recklessly impractical. But wasn't sending military mothers of six-week-old infants to Saudi Arabia in 1991 also recklessly impractical? So what if it was done for reasonable reasons. Is the current system of work, family, and the like practical? It exists, but is existence an excuse, a moral claim, an anesthetic?

So let's see what happens if we envision a few basic priorities. Whether bold, visionary, stupid, puerile, or whatever, they are directed to the heart of the issue.

(1) One priority is raising capable and congenial children and valuing families and what they do.

(2) Another priority is providing adult men and women and their communities with sufficient and varied tasks and rewards so that all members will give and receive with a sense of fairness and effectiveness. This means that if men and women end up living their lives in more or less different ways, as many do and surely will, the reason is not simply prejudice or restriction.

(3) A third emphasis should be fostering a set of ideas and styles of cordiality so that men and women have ways of mediating their real ancient and new differences as groups. They will do better without the acrimony and self-righteousness of the First World Gender War. A truce and then a peace are desirable. These are, after all, two groups that often willingly, even eagerly, exchange enormous physical intimacy, to say nothing of sharing nests together for decades on end.

Governments and the communities in which they are embedded face a variety of questions that are very pressing at the same time as they are very general. They are at once public and private.

Children

Who will raise children? It is best to begin with the mammalian fact that small children should be raised by their mothers. That is Mother Nature's plan. Of course, in modern times it can't always be followed. It is nonetheless a sturdy, well-tested scheme. It is supported by intricate physiology and lots of contemporary evidence, to say nothing of millions of years of luxurious and successful mammalian encounter. The old mammalian plan should be the basis for new proposals, not because it is logical or ideological but because it is biological. As even the gloommeister Anton Chekhov observed, "Man will be better when he finds out what he is like."

Some families don't want both parents to work. They prefer that one parent, usually the mother, spend some time after birth at home with the child.[52] The dimensions of the population able to choose this option are unclear because economic need drives many women from the nursery, while others can hardly wait to return to the work they leave temporarily even if the money they earn is marginal to their needs. Perhaps this is directly shown in the fact that the number of women at home, even with infants and small children, is in steady decline. Nevertheless, many women crave the opportunity to remain with their child or children. They regard the obligation or necessity to work as a negative factor in their lives. To them, "Take your daughter to work" is the psychological equivalent of a tour of the salt mines.

The notion of "quality time" is for many parents and onlookers no substitute for full participation in the unpaced schedule of a child's life. Some women appear to regard the time they steal from the workplace to be with their offspring as a secret indulgence, a version of parental adultery. At the other extreme are demanding stay-at-home mothers who endlessly rush youngsters from activity to activity—hoping to "improve" their preparation, which occurs from the cradle on, for graduate schools of business.[53]

The general issue of how much time and how much fun, to say nothing of how much love, women in particular and parents in general have with their children is frequently dismissed or avoided by commentators on the role of women in modern economies. The index of feminist writer Naomi Wolf's *Fire with Fire*, which purports to nourish feminist analysis, does not contain the word "mother." But this word remains vital in the lives of many women, despite how insistently public behavior is defined as the source of personal worth and social equity. Women facing these matters are far more likely in private than in public to express bitterness about current arrangements. Workers in American child care centers earn less per hour than hamburger handlers at fast-food restaurants.[54] In the United States there are between one and three million full-time nannies providing child care, many supplied by one of the five-hundred nanny placement agencies. Parents who interview potential child-minders are discourage by increasingly draconian legal regulations governing prejudice which restrict them from asking about precisely those personal and family experiences which may affect a person's capacity to care for a child.[55] Uncertainty about the quality of their work—to say nothing about fear for the safety of the children they watch—has stimulated some parents to monitor their homes with secret cameras and to inscribe formal legal contracts.[56] In essence this turns a domestic space into a bureaucratized one. It becomes the location of an in-house bureaugamy this time among the affluent with quarterly tax payments, employer liability, and formal privacy agreements—another example of the bureaucratization of intimacy so characteristic of contemporary family life.

There have been a host of family alternatives suggested. They range from the understandably sentimental "Daddy should be as involved as Mommy" to the bureaucratically idiotic "it is best for children to be in day care or children's houses because it is better for their psychological development."[57] Practical compromises will always be necessary; some will be desirable. For example, a simple and provident social policy could bend provisions of law and custom so that small babies can remain in close contact with their mothers for some time, rather than not being in contact, as in the savage requirement that military mothers leave newborns after six weeks when their units are deployed. Some current legal arrangements will have to be changed to make mother-infant contact easy, sweet, and convenient. Amitai Etzioni has suggested that expanding federal government income in the United States can be used "to allow mothers of infants to remain on welfare."[58] Now it is virtually illegal in a variety of circumstances, and for pregnant women to claim maternity benefits, they have to apply for what are called disability benefits. Otherwise fatuously, men are deprived of a public right to get maternity benefits, too.

Perhaps infants do not enjoy formal legal rights, but they have unshakable needs that are obvious to those who love them. These are largely made secondary to the public obligations of parents to the labor force. If many mothers decide to remain at home with their children—or to have them as close as possible, as women in the kibbutz chose—this should be treated as an adult choice by empowered people, not a distasteful primordial legacy.[59]

Valuing Families

The second broad challenge will be to consider supplying extra money to workers with spouses and children for some phases of the work and life cycle—even men with wives and children. In the old days men often got more money when they were "family men." New babies bumped up pay. These benefits were not acts of nobility or special male privilege. They acknowledged the fact that the only income a family had was from the husband, and it cost more to be a parent. Through its legal system, the community decided there was nothing wrong with that. It was discriminatory, yes, but pay raises were not given to people who bought Ferraris which were expensive to service. We have seen how difficult it is for many men, especially poorly educated and poor ones, to find work that allows them to contemplate marriage and fatherhood with some measure of autonomy.

Without conscious attention to the matter of income linked to family, we will replicate the communist countries. They were sufficiently interested in production that they set salaries so that one income was not enough to live on. The consequent requirement that all women and wives work was called the emancipation of women by those who imposed it. Perhaps it was, but it also had an impact on the experience of children and how many were born. In Europe and America the two-income family is virtually universal. Birthrates are very low. This obviously is desirable from various points of view but presumably not in the opinion of those who are reproductively unemployed or underemployed.

I am suggesting here that there should be a pro-biology, pro-family bias in pay schemes during appropriate phases of the life cycle of a first marriage. One version of that is the decision of the United Arab Emirates to provide a dowry of $20,000 to local men who marry local women but cannot afford the ritual and bride-price obligations they must assume.[60] Treating everybody, especially men, as independent contractors may induce or coerce many more of them to remain independent from the community. They just stand aside. A pro-family decision will have to be made, certainly in a revised context of legal equity, and it may well be against the objections of childless citizens who may regard paying school taxes as more than enough levy on their money.

Civilized Bureaugamy

Another broad decision the community has to make concerns supplying adequate support to unmarried women who have small children. This is widely available now, as we have seen; however, there exists the attitude that this is not a good thing. Efforts persist to make a mother of young children leave them—for example, to take care of another mother's young children for money. Working for money is seen as redemptive. Mothering for money is acceptable only if done with an inheritance or a husband's cash. This is heartless, senseless, economically picayune as a formal policy and, in my opinion, morally questionable. It is also stupid biology. No zookeeper would have Monkey Mother A take care of Monkey Mother B's baby and vice versa. What can concernocrats be thinking when they devise their legislative schemes?

An Apartment of Her Own

Finally, there should be in place protections for any female who wants to make her life on her own, whether or not she is married. There should be no presumption of female dependency or diminished need. Legal systems and, more important, personal, social, and economic behavior should allow females to live their lives with competence, aplomb, and the same comfort zone as males. We have already seen that women are achieving parity with men in many walks of life, which is as it should be. If 55 percent of college students are already women, are affirmative schemes still necessary? Should the number be 80 percent? And, again, even if statistical differences do emerge in how men and women live and in what they do, this is no less than anyone should expect from a species such as ours. Shepher and I found that the Israeli kibbutz, a setting of examplary economic and political parity, produced differences between men and women greater than in the rest of Israeli society. Anthropologist Melford Spiro of the University of California at San Diego has indicated that his updated study of the kibbutz as well as Shepher's and mine have "the dubious distinction of having virtually never been cited or referenced in the veritable library . . . dealing with the comparative study of women and gender."[61] The fact that men and women who have the freedom to do so may decide to act differently from each other appears to cause ideological commentators on this matter to avert their eyes almost completely. If they were medical practitioners, they would be charged with malpractice for burying evidence centrally relevant to their assertions.

And Don't Ignore Reality

Both studies—ours and Spiro's—attended to underlying biology. Both were icily dismissed by nearly all the writers claiming to seek understanding of these issues. The fact is that realities ignored are realities corrupted. Just as in war truth is the first casualty, so it has been in the gender war—one good reason for an armistice. This may be wrenching and sobering for those who derive jobs, money, position, and a sense of mission from pursuing a now conventional cause. But their accomplishments are in place. Now they should turn in a different direction because their ideas are outmoded.

* * *

I have explored a profound and exceptionally intricate and important change in how men and women live in contemporary times. I focused first on men and saw that their options in life, their income, and their comfort zone have been sharply restricted by changes in the productive and reproductive activities of women. We saw how the parental connection between men and women has been stretched by modern circumstances to such an extent that it sometimes breaks. This leads to a novel pattern of kinship in which men are decreasingly vigorous and effective. In a haunting way the new social form throws shadows of our past and represents a return to human genetic roots, to an older, safer, primate pattern focused on mothers and offspring. It is rather like the bonobo chimpanzee communities now so well understood by scientists who have studied them over generations to learn that females are sexually active in the context of political power.

The changes we have explored affect people in the privacy of their bedrooms, at the table where they write checks to pay their bills, and at work when they are gossiping and politicking during lunch hour. They also affect national politics, and I have predicted that once we are more familiar with the forces in place, we will see how they affect international politics, too.

From the blight of pollutants and the lessons of the environmental movement, we know that there are limits to what human beings can tolerate healthfully when they come into contact with nature. We also have an inner environment. Call it human nature. Exploring the inner environment has been the agenda here, with particular emphasis on sex. While the sexes differ and may have differences that are sharp, men and women nevertheless have a great deal in common. They share two immense realities: the same world and everyone's unfolding lives.

What will women and men do?

Notes

Chapter One

1. Molly Haskell, *Holding My Own in No Man's Land: Women and Men and Film and Feminism* (New York: Oxford University Press, 1997).
2. Steven Holmes, "Census Says Women Surpass Men in Schooling," *New York Times*, June 30, 1998.
3. There are, of course, considerable international variations. For example, in Germany some "73% of German women are still wholly or partly economically dependent on husbands or social security checks": Alan Cowell, "Germany's Anguish: History, Identity, and Shopping," *New York Times*, May 19, 1996. The sharply restricted hours of shopping in that country, which are close to the same as working hours, press at least one member of a family to be available as purchasing agent during part of the day.
4. Simone de Beauvoir, *The Second Sex* (New York: Alfred Knopf, 1953).
5. Betty Friedan, Presentation at Wellesley Women's Center, New York, January 30, 1997.
6. Bruce Little, "40 Hours: A Workweek on the Skids," *Toronto Globe and Mail*, September 2, 1996.
7. Ellen Graham and Cynthia Crossen, "Too Many Things to Do, Too Little Time to Do Them," *Wall Street Journal*, March 8, 1996. Driving is defined as the principal time-waster by respondents to a survey.
8. Diane Eyer, *Motherguilt* (New York: Times Books, 1996), p. 32.
9. Gail Sheehy, *Understanding Men's Passages* (New York: Random House, 1998), p. 18.
10. Robin Davis Miller, "From the Home Office," *Authors Guild Bulletin*, Fall 1995, p. 5.
11. The coinage is by Shulamith Firestone.
12. Robert Schoen, et al., "Why Do Americans Want Children?" *Population and Development Review* 23:2 (June 1997).
13. Sylvia Ann Hewlett and Cornel West, "A Parents' Bill of Rights Would End a 30-Year War," *New York Times*, April 12, 1998.
14. "The Family," *The Economist*, September 9, 1995.
15. Darren Becker, "Stats No Surprise to Students," *Montreal Gazette*, May 4, 1998.
16. See Clinton Esser, *Fierce and Tender Men: Sociological Aspects of the Men's Movement* (Westport, CT: Praeger, 1996). The wanness of such assessments is

unfortunately explicable. It is very difficult to discuss males in a robust manner in an academic context because to do so suggests opposition to feminism. This is no help to young scholars seeking university posts. There has been for several decades self-censorship by people interested in these matters and whose views of them may depart from ambient sentimentality.

It is pointless to spend more words on the issue of political correctness. While it may well be overestimated as an intellectual force, it is underestimated as a practical feature of university politics. I have had tenure for a long time and know for certain that without it I would have had a less interesting and fair academic career than I am willing to boast I've had.

17. Gustav Neibuhr, "Men's Group to Lay Off Entire Staff," *New York Times*, February 20, 1998.

18. Henrietta Moore, "Balancing Acts: Gender at the Turn of the Century," *London School of Economics Magazine*, Summer 1996.

19. Susan Faludi, *Backlash: The Undeclared War Against American Women* (New York: Doubleday, 1991).

20. Megan Rosenfeld, "What Nobody Ever Bothered to Ask About Boys," *International Herald Tribune*, March 27, 1998.

21. Susan Chira, "Nursing Becomes a Feminist Battlefield," *New York Times*, October 10, 1993.

22. See Lionel Tiger, *The Manufacture of Evil: Ethics, Evolution, and the Industrial System* (New York: Harper & Row, 1987) which describes the radical individualism of the industrial way and the accompanying "psycho-industrial complex."

23. Friedrich Engels, "The Part Played by Labor in the Transition from Ape to Man," in *The Origin of the Family, Private Property and the State* (New York: International Publishers, 1972).

24. For a fair and learned discussion of the broader issue of the politics of biology, see Mel Konner, *The Tangled Wing: Biological Constraints on the Human Spirit* (New York: Harper Colophon, 1983), pp. 439–46.

25. Edward Shorter, *The Making of the Modern Family* (New York: Basic Books, 1975).

26. Christopher George, "As Welfare Rolls Drop, Changes Big and Small Hit a Housing Project," *Wall Street Journal*, December 19, 1997. "Among the four women, three of whom say they suffered through abusive relationship, none expected, or even desired, to marry the fathers of their children. . . . 'There was no advantage to being married.'"

27. A basic account of this is in Lionel Tiger and Robin Fox, *The Imperial Animal* (New York: Henry Holt, 1971 and 1987) and Robin Fox, *Kinship and Marriage: An Anthropological Perspective* (London: Penguin, 1967; 2nd ed., New York: Cambridge University Press, 1983). See also Robin Fox's, *Reproduction and Succession: Studies in Anthropology, Law, and Society* (New Brunswick, NJ: Transaction Publishers, 1993).

28. New York State Document MV-2LX (9/95), Part 3.

29. Orna Landau, "Bedroom Politics," *Ha'aretz*, July 2, 1998, p. 6.
30. See Sylvia Hewlett Warner and Cornel West, *The War Against Parents* (Boston: Houghton Mifflin, 1998).
31. An effective early study that identified the underlying trend, though without relating it to behavioral biology, was by Mikhail Bernstam and Peter Swan, "The State As the Marriage Partner of Last Resort: New Findings on Minimum Wage, Youth Joblessness, Welfare, and Single Motherhood in the United States, 1960–1980" (Palo Alto, CA: Domestic Studies Program, Hoover Institution, Stanford University, 1986), p. 32.
32. It is interesting that Joseph was not made a saint until 1729.

Chapter Two

1. John Noble Wilford, "In Australia, Signs of Artists Who Predate Homo Sapiens," *New York Times*, September 21, 1996. It is likely that even earlier dates for human-like activity will be found—that has been the scholarly pattern for decades. The definition of human may have to be expanded to include human behavior as well as or instead of human form. It appears appropriate to redefine the species as a behavioral, not just a physical, entity. As Darwin understood, a species' form is the product of its behavior. A drawing may be as significant as a femur.
2. Random Samples, "Early Music," *Science* 276 (April 11, 1997):205.
3. Michael Balter, "Cave Structure Boosts Neanderthal Image," *Science* 271 (January 26, 1996).
4. P. McGovern et al., "Neolithic Resinated Wine," *Nature* 381 (1966).
5. Delwen Samuel, "Investigation of Ancient Egyptian Baking and Brewing Methods by Correlative Microscopy," *Science* 273 (July 26, 1996):488.
6. Meave Leakey and Alan Walker, "Early Hominid Fossils from Africa," *Scientific American* June 1997.
7. Jacques Monod, *Chance and Necessity: An Essay on the Natural Philosophy of Human Biology* (New York: Knopf, 1971).
8. William Wordsworth, cited in Humphrey Jennings, *Pandemonium: The Coming of the Machine as Seen by Contemporary Observers, 1660–1886*, (New York: The Free Press, 1985), p. 114.
9. Jennifer Steinhauer, "Study Finds Little Male Responsibility in Birth Control," *New York Times*, May 23, 1995.
10. Associated Press, "Research Finds Genital Herpes Soaring Among Young Whites," *New York Times*, October 16, 1997.
11. Kristin Luker, *Taking Chances: Abortion and the Decision Not to Contracept* (Berkeley: University of California Press, 1975).
12. Peter Laslett, "Introduction: Comparing Illegitimacy Over Time and Between

Cultures," in Peter Laslett, Karla Oosterveen, and Richard Smith, eds., *Bastardy and Its Comparative History* (Cambridge, MA: Harvard University Press, 1980), pp. 54–85.

13. Susan Harari and Maris Vinovis, "Adolescent Sexuality in the Past," in Annette Lawson and Deborah Rhode, eds., *The Politics of Pregnancy: Adolescent Sexuality and Public Policy* (New Haven, CT: Yale University Press, 1993), pp. 26–46.

14. "Outlook," *U.S. News & World Report*, September 25, 1995.

15. Personal Communication, Robin Kennedy, Tampa Preparatory School. I am grateful for permission to cite this vivid hypothesis about possible links between contraception and sperm counts.

   This remains controversial, if only because it is difficult to be confident about the historical levels of sperm count against which contemporary data have to be contrasted. There appears to be no doubt that one completely real index of sperm effectiveness, fertility, poses problems to large numbers of people. There are also regional differences in sperm count that are perplexing, such as the much higher level in New York compared to Los Angeles. One English study found a decline in sperm counts over time as a direct function of quality of drinking water downstream of a polluting industry; since people are 70 percent water, perhaps this is a factor, though it remains unclear what the mechanism may be for the changes. Nonetheless, something is happening. For example, over a twenty-year period a French sperm bank found an annual decrease of concentration of 2 percent a year, similar to the result of a Scottish study of six hundred men. As well, testicular cancer in many industrial countries has doubled and quadrupled since World War II. Experimental data about other mammalian species confirms a serious reproductive result of environmental conditions. For a roundup of materials see Betsy Carpenter, "Investigating the Next 'Silent Spring': Why Are Sperm Counts Falling So Precipitously?" *U.S. News & World Report*, March 11, 1996.

16. Robin Baker and Mark Bellis, "Human Sperm Competition: Ejaculate Adjustment by Males and the Function of Masturbation," *Animal Behavior* 45 (1993). See also Robin Baker and Mark Bellis, "Human Sperm Competition: Ejaculate Manipulation by Females and a Function for the Female Orgasm," *Animal Behavior* 46 (1993).

17. Virginia Morrell, "Starting Species with Third Parties and Sex Wars," *Science* 273 (September 11, 1996).

18. Carol Kaesuk Yoon, "The Biggest Evolutionary Challenge May Be the Other Half of the Species," *New York Times*, June 18, 1996.

   There are also data about other species in which spermatozoa are affected by the widely used chemical components of plastics. These encourage the production of estrogen, which in turn appears to cause birth of feminized offspring with small testicles and low sperm counts. See "Are Men Necessary?" *The Economist*, December 23, 1995–January 5, 1996.

19. Lionel Tiger, "Male Bonding and the Exclusion of Females," *New York Magazine*, June 1969; *The Observer of London*, June 1969.

20. Anna Quindlen, "If You're Pregnant, Men Look and Move On," *New York Times*, October 6, 1988.

21. H. Steklis et al. "Effects of Medroxyprogesterone Acetate on Socio-Sexual Behavior of Stumptail Macaques," *Physiology and Behavior* 28 (1982):535–44.

   H. Steklis et al. "Progesterone and Socio-Sexual Behavior in Stumptailed Macaques (Macaca Arctoides): Hormonal and Socio-Environmental Interactions," in H. Steklis and A. Kling, eds., *Hormones, Drugs, and Social Behavior in Primates* (New York: SP Medical and Scientific Books, 1983).

22. Meredith Small, "Female Choice in Nonhuman Primates," *Yearbook of Physical Anthropology* 32 (1989):113.

23. Very recently inventive and substantial work on the subject has begun to see publication. For example, one recent study showed that women preferred the odor of particular males who for complex chemical/genetic reasons were likely to be desirable mates. However, using the oral contraceptive *reversed* their preferences. This is precisely analogous to the results of my colleagues and me. See Claus Wedekind et al., "MHC-dependent Mate Preferences in Humans," *Proceeedings of the Royal Society of London* B260 (1995):245–49. See also the work of Karl Grammer of the University of Vienna.

   A review is by D. W. Stoddart, *The Scented Ape: The Biology and Culture of Human Odour* (Cambridge: Cambridge University Press, 1991).

   An early discussion is by G. Beauchamp et al., "The Pheromone Concept in Mammalian Chemical Communication: A Critique," in R. Doty, ed., *Mammalian Olfaction, Reproductive Process and Behavior* (New York: Academic Press, 1976).

   Milos Novotny, "The Importance of Chemical Messengers in Mammalian Reproduction," in June Reinisch, Leonard Rosenblum, and Stephanie Sanders, eds., *Masculinity/Femininity: Basic Perspectives* (New York: Oxford University Press, 1987).

24. Barbara Seaman, *The Doctor's Case Against the Pill*, (Hunter House, 1995).

25. The most thorough recent study of links between hormones and status is the remarkable book by Thomas Kemper, *Testosterone and Social Structure* (New Brunswick, NJ: Rutgers University Press, 1994).

   Also, Alan Booth and James Dabbs, "Testosterone and Chess Competition," *Social Psychology Quarterly* 55, no. 1 (1992):70–77.

   For a good recent review see chapter 7 of Deborah Blum, *Sex on the Brain: The Biological Differences Between Men and Women* (New York: Viking, 1997).

   R. L. Doty, M. Preti, and G. Huggins, "Changes in the Intensity and Pleasantness of Human Vaginal Odors During the Menstrual Cycle," *Science* 190 (1975):1316–18.

26. S. Matteo and E. F. Rissman, "Increased Sexual Activity During the Midcycle Portion of the Human Menstrual Cycle," *Hormones and Behavior* 18 (1984):249–55.

27. Allan Mazur and Alan Booth, "Testosterone and Dominance in Men," ms, 1997.

28. Tara J. Chavanne and Gordon G. Gallup, "Variation in Risk Taking Behavior Among Female College Students as a Function of the Menstrual Cycle," *Evolution and Human Behavior* 19 (January 1998):1.

29. L. Tiger, "A Comment on Cross-Specific Comparison of the Effects of Progesterone Treatment on Social Behavior," in H. Steklis and A. Kling, eds., *Hormones, Drugs*, pp. 135–39.

30. Martha McClintock, "Menstrual Synchrony and Suppression," *Nature* 229 (1971):244–45.

31. Claus Wedekind, et al., "MHC-dependent Mate. Preferences."

32. Natalie Angier, "Study Finds Signs of Elusive Pheromone in Humans," *New York Times*, March 12, 1998.

33. Lionel Tiger and Joseph Shepher, *Women in the Kibbutz* (New York: Harcourt Brace Jovanovich, 1975).

34. The improved health of working class children surely helped stimulate the explosion of energy, talent, and assertiveness reflected most colorfully in the music and fashion of the time, but also the emergence of both artistic and then commercial representatives of a heretofore depressed and repressed class of society. It is fascinating that the moment World War II was over the British population rejected its heroic war leader, Winston Churchill, in favor of the Labour Party, which attended to such matters as orange juice for pregnant women and milk for children. There was also the baby boom, of course, which had a host of far-reaching impacts on the balance of power between adults and youngsters. See Robin Fox's comments in Frank Miele, *op. cit.* 1996, and also a comment on the representativeness of the Beatles during this time by Lionel Tiger in "Why, It Was Fun," *Rolling Stone*, February 16, 1984.

    See also Philip Norman, *Shout: The Beatles in Their Generation* (New York: Simon and Schuster, 1981).

35. Perhaps I choose restaurants poorly or choose ones with odd clientele, but I am helpless in face of the urge to recall yet another overheard conversation about a year later in which a woman described to her companion the number of her friends who "did guys they met on the Internet." Her disapproval was matched by my naïveté about the matter.

36. John Tierney, "New York's Parallel Lives," *New York Times Magazine*, October 19, 1997.

37. "Viagra Triage," *Wall Street Journal*, Editorial, September 17, 1998.

38. Paula Ardaheli, *Arranging Marriages in Iran*, Ph.D. Dissertation, Rutgers University, 1986.

39. Warren Cohen, "Kid Looks Like the Mailman? Genetic Labs Boom as the Nation Wonders Who's Daddy," *U.S. News & World Report*, January 27, 1997.

40. Maggie Gallagher, "And Baby Makes Two: For Celebrities, Fathers Are Dispensable. Anybody Have a Problem with That?" *Wall Street Journal*, August 7, 1998.

41. J. Balsdon, *Roman Women* (New York: John Day Company, 1963), pp. 75–76.

42. Ibid.

43. James Davidson, *Courtesans and Fishcakes: The Consuming Passions of Classical Athens* (New York: St. Martin's Press, 1998).

44. Michael Moffatt, *Growing Up in New Jersey* (New Brunswick, NJ: Rutgers University Press, 1988).

45. Samuel G. Freedman, "Yeshivish at Yale: Five Religious Freshmen Refused to Live in Yale's 'Immoral' Dormitories—and Opened a Schism between Orthodox Jewry and the Very Idea of a Liberal University," *New York Times Magazine*, May 24, 1998.

46. Michael Moffatt, *Growing Up.*

47. "The Family," *The Economist*, September 9, 1995.

48. Sheryl WuDunn, "Stigma Curtails Single Motherhood in Japan," *New York Times*, March 13, 1996.

49. There is anecdotal lore, however, about the sexual willingness of adult Japanese women when they are free from their home country, which apparently stimulates an otherwise disproportionate interest in contacts with foreign males.

50. Andrew Pollack, "In Japan, Equality Has Its Price: Women Take On Burden as Opportunities Open in Job Market," *International Herald Tribune*, July 9, 1997.

 Also, Steven Butler, "Japan's baby bust: Are unmarried 30-somethings 'parasites' on society?" *US News and World Report*, October 5, 1998.

51. Annette Lawson and Deborah Rhode, eds., *The Politics of Pregnancy*, p. 2.

52. Ibid., p. 6.

53. Mellisa Ludtke, "Sometimes, One Parent Is Better Than Two," *New York Times*, August 16, 1997.

54. Celestine Bohlen, "At 30-Something, Leave Home? Mamma Mia, No," *New York Times*, March 1, 1996.

55. Patricia Steinhoff, et al., "Characteristics and Motivations of Women Receiving Abortions," *Sociological Symposium* 111, (Spring 1972).

 Wendell Watters, *Compulsory Parenthood*, (Toronto: McClelland & Stewart, 1976).

56. Heather Remoff, *Sexual Choice: A Woman's Decision: Why and How Women Choose the Men They Do As Sexual Partners*, (New York: Dutton/Lewis Publishing, 1984).

57. Clifford Krauss, "Abortion Debated in Chile, Where It's Always a Crime," *New York Times*, August 9, 1998.

58. See Igor Kon, *The Sexual Revolution in Russia: From the Age of the Czars to Today*, trans. by James Riordan (New York: The Free Press, 1995).

59. Nicholas Eberstadt, "Marx and Mortality: A Mystery," *New York Times*, April 6, 1994.

60. James Riordan, introduction to *Sex and Russian Society*, edited by Igor Kon and James Riordan (Bloomington: Indiana University Press, 1993), pp. 5–6.

61. In general, legal decisions are uninformed by contemporary biological theory, but this one accords well with responsible knowledge in the field. Lawyers often deal with the bedrock of human behavior. They must make many important assumptions about human biological nature, but too often they are simply wrong.

In only a handful of American law schools—University of Washington, Arizona State, Vermont Law School, Wayne State, UCLA, and Yale—are students expected to learn some basic biology, just as they are routinely taught economics, politics, and ecological issues. If they focus on anything, it is on Marx, not Darwin; money, not love.

62. See Lionel Tiger, "Trump the Race Card," *Wall Street Journal*, February 23, 1996.

63. Jonathan Wright and Peter Cotton, "Experimentally-Induced Sex Differences in Parental Care: An Effect of Certainty of Paternity?" *Animal Behavior* 47 (1994):1311–22.

64. Sarah Hrdy, *The Langurs of Abu: Female and Male Strategies of Reproduction*, (Cambridge, MA: Harvard University Press, 1977).

65. Steven Gaulin and Alice Schlegel, "Paternal Confidence and Paternal Investment: A Cross-Cultural Test of a Sociobiological Hypothesis," *Ethology and Sociobiology* 1 (1980):301–9.

66. Martin Daly and Margo Wilson, "Child Abuse and Other Risks of Not Living with Both Parents," *Ethology and Sociobiology* 6 (1985):197–210. See also Martin Daly and Margo Wilson, *Homicide* (Hawthorne, NY: Aldine de Gruyter, 1988).

67. Margaret Mead, *Male and Female: A Study of the Sexes in a Changing World* (New York: William Morrow, 1975).

68. See also chapter 19 of Jane Howard's *Margaret Mead: A Life* (New York: Simon & Schuster, 1984).

69. David Popenoe, *Life Without Father* (New York: The Free Press, 1996), p. 4.

70. Jasper Gerrand, "'Jane' Bond," *The Times of London*, July 17, 1998.

71. Mellisa Ludkte, "Sometimes, One Parent."

72. Haya El Nasser, "Unmarried Dads a Surging Social Phenomenon," *USA Today*, June 12, 1997.

73. Christina Duff, "Mothers' Jobs Spurred 25 Increase in Couples' Income from 1969 to 1996," *Wall Street Journal*, September 1, 1998.

74. Associated Press, "Female Sterilization Not Foolproof, Study Says," *New York Times*, April 25, 1996.

75. Michelle Ingrassia, "Still Fumbling in the Dark," *U.S. News & World Report*, March 13, 1995.

Chapter Three

1. Kate Millett, *Sexual Politics* (Garden City: NY: Doubleday, 1970). The book is unfortunately, and surprisingly, out of print. Someone should reissue it.

2. Andrea Dworkin, *Intercourse* (New York: The Free Press, 1988).

3. Phyllis Chesler, *About Men* (New York: Simon and Schuster, 1978).
4. Marilyn French, *The New York Times* (Long Island Edition), July 9, 1995.
5. For an example of advocacy social science in the service of a sentimental notion that masculinity reflects nothing more than a peculiar American "chronically anxious, temperamentally restless manhood—a manhood that carries with it the constant burden of proof" see Michael Kimmel, *Manhood in America: A Cultural History* (New York: The Free Press, 1996). Kimmel generalizes about a parochial assertion: what disturbs him politically about his own community is in effect a characteristic of the species as a whole. He and others are able to make such an elision because on basic principles they reject the notion of human nature—one of the frailest of contemporary sociological assumptions.
6. Maureen Dowd, "The Fall of Man," *New York Times*, January 21, 1996.
   Anabolic steroids often stop or reduce sperm production and shrink testicles. See Caitlin Liu, "Drug Makers Tap Anabolic Steroid Market," *New York Times*, August 3, 1966. Many users are male and female professional athletes who are aware of the performance- and bulk-enhancing effects of these drugs. On the other hand, in the United States alone there are some half-million users, mostly non-athletes and mostly young male. It is plausible to assume they use drugs to enhance their reproductive attractiveness—in effect, a form of internal plastic surgery.
7. Joshua Davis, "Feminists Don't Seek Equality," Rutgers *Targum*, November 20, 1996.
8. For flavor of this see Marilyn Shuster and Susan Van Dyne, eds., *Women's Place in the Academy: Transforming the Liberal Arts Curriculum* (Totowa, NJ: Rowman and Allanheld, 1985).
9. The Canadian feminist Donna Laframboise has lamented for its churlishness and impracticality elements of the feminist position in *The Princess at the Window: Toward a New Gender Morality* (Toronto: Penguin Canada, 1996).
10. For a thoughtful review see Catherine Stimpson, "Women's Studies and Its Discontents," *Dissent* 43, no. 1 (Winter 1996).
11. Anne Roiphe, *Fruitful: A Real Mother in the Modern World* (Boston: Houghton Mifflin Company, 1996), p. 233.
12. "Corporations Under Fire," *New York Times*, February 25, 1996.
13. "A Wealth of Working Women," *The Economist*, June 8, 1996.
14. Barbara Beck, "Women and Work: For Better, for Worse," *The Economist*, July 18, 1998.
15. This is part of a larger matter that in my opinion reflects the ultimate triumph of the Protestant commitment to work and the Calvinist association of material with spiritual value. We cannot and need not here rehearse the classic arguments such as Max Weber's 1904 *The Protestant Ethic and the Spirit of Capitalism* (English translation 1930 by Talcott Parsons), Earnest Troeltsch's 1931 *The Social Teaching of the Christian Churches*, R. H. Tawney's *Religion and the Rise of Capitalism* (New York: Harcourt, Brace & Co., 1926), and C. B. Macpherson's *The Political Theory of Possessive Individualism: Hobbes to Locke* (London: Oxford University Press, 1962). I have also dealt somewhat

elaborately with the issue in *The Manufacture of Evil: Ethics, Evolution, and the Industrial System* (New York: Harper & Row, 1987). The central point is that the entire world has embraced the task of securing material goods and comfort, which is reflected in a multitude of international and bilateral efforts at development. I make no judgment here, only a comment that this differs markedly from the non-Protestant world prior to the modern period. There is still severe disagreement about the relative value of spirit versus money, but the latter appears to prevail. For a spirited and appropriately searching analysis see Benjamin Barber, *MacJob vs. MacWorld*, 1995. For an assertion about the ideal role of government in private life see Jacob Weisberg, *In Defense of Government: The Fall and Rise of Public Trust* (New York: Scribner, 1996).

16. Advertisement, *The Times (London)* July 9, 1997.

17. *New York Times*, August 2, 1996.

18. See Lionel Tiger, "Taxed for Living," *New York Press*, July 23, 1998.

19. Betty Friedan, *The Feminine Mystique*, (New York: Dell, 1963).

20. Jeffrey Rosen "Single-Sex Schools and Double Standards," *New York Times*, July 3, 1996.

21. Karen de Witt, "For Black Clubwomen, a New Era Dawns," *New York Times*, August 4, 1996.

22. Richard Stevenson, "Job Discrimination in Europe: Affirmative Laissez Faire," *New York Times*, November 26, 1996.

23. Kingsley Browne, "Biology, Equality, and the Law: The Legal Significance of Biological Sex Differences," *Southwestern Law Journal* 38, no. 2 (June 1984). Also see Browne's "An Evolutionary Approach to Sexual Harassment," *Journal of Contemporary Legal Issues*, Autumn 1997. Both of these are remarkably comprehensive and judicious essays.

24. Denise Grady, "Girl Talk Starts in Womb?" *New York Times*, December 23, 1997.

25. Deborah Tannen, *You Just Don't Understand: Women and Men in Conversation* (New York: Ballantine, 1990). Tannen makes no comment about possible biogenic sources of conversational strategies. Like Carol Gilligan, she discovers a biological regularity without biology.

26. The hypothesis has been presented by Myra and David Sadker that teachers prefer and favor males, an assertion founded principally on a study sponsored by the American Association of University Women; their methods and results have been decisively refuted by Christina Sommers. See Myra and David Sadker, 1992 and Christina Hoff Sommers, *Who Stole Feminism?* (New York: Simon and Shuster, 1993). A central conjecture of the Sadker essay is that females are essentially impressionable, victims whose choices and behavior mainly reflect societal, that is male, inequities and male standards of value.

27. Jacques Steinberg, *New York Times*, August 19, 1996.
    See also the comment by Anne Roiphe, "A.C.L.U. Sports the Wrong School Tie," *New York Observer*, August 19, 1996, which supports single-sex schooling for girls.

28. John O'Leary, "A-Level Analysis Finds Boys Do Better in Single-Sex Schools," *The Times* (London), July 14, 1997.

29. Lionel Tiger and Joseph Shepher, *Women in the Kibbutz* (New York: Harcourt, Brace, 1975).

30. Ray Raphael, *The Men from the Boys: Rites of Passage in Male America* (Lincoln: University of Nebraska Press, 1988).

31. Kristen Hawkes, "Showing Off: Tests of an Hypothesis about Men's Foraging Goals," *Ethology and Sociobiology* 12, no. 1 (January 1991). See also Matt Ridley, "Why Should Males Exist? The Reason Men Are That Way Is That Women Bred Them to Be That Way," *U.S. News & World Report*, August 25, 1997.

32. The classic report and analysis is Napoleon Chagnon, "Life Histories, Blood Revenge, and Warfare in a Tribal Population," *Science* 239 (February 26, 1988).

33. Ibid, p. 987.

34. The pattern can exist in fantasy as well as reality not only in movies but political ideology. For an analysis of the links between sex and fascism see the foreword by Barbara Ehrenreich in Klaus Theweleit, *Male Fantasies* (Minneapolis: University of Minnesota Press, 1987). The links between sex and draconian hierarchy in drastic cults is also pertinent, for example in the *droits de seigneur* of David Koresh in the Waco group and the castration of males in the Heaven's Gate suicide.

35. See Lionel Tiger, "Introduction," in Lionel Tiger and Heather Fowler, eds., *Female Hierarchies* (Chicago: Beresford Book Service, 1978). See also in this work Ernst Caspari, "The Biological Basis of Female Hierarchies," pp. 87–122, and Virginia Abernathy, "Female Hierarchy: An Evolutionary Perspective," pp. 123–35.

36. Michael Kimmel, *Manhood in America*.

37. Because of my interest in these matters I have from time to time spoken to or consulted with American college fraternities about the impact on their organizations of hazing and similar potentially dangerous patterns. Almost invariably it was difficult to establish the point that any efforts at remedy would have to be renewed each year. Each new class of members is vulnerable to dangerous and hectic excess because it is essentially the same as the one before: postadolescent males. This also poses a chronic problem in the military.

38. Douglas Martin, "Taking the Faithful to Prison Gates," *New York Times*, August 6, 1995.

39. Warren Leary, "Young People Who Try Suicide May Be Succeeding More Often," *New York Times*, April 21, 1995.

40. Brownmiller, *op. cit.*

41. Paul Taylor, "A South African Rite's Slow, Painful Change," *International Herald Tribune*, January 17, 1995. In his autobiography Mandela describes the excruciating pain of circumcision at sixteen but then the sense of adult capacity for the chief's role he was destined to assume.

There are also, of course, explicit analogues among other primates and especially chimpanzees during hunting, which they do essentially in all-male groups much like humans. See Craig Stanford, *op. cit.*

42. Richard Wrangham and Dale Peterson, *Demonic Males: Apes and the Origins of Human Violence* (Boston: Houghton Mifflin, 1996).

43. See Warren Farrell, *The Myth of Male Power* (New York: Simon and Shuster, 1992).

   See also Martin Kramer, "Hizbullah: The Calculus of Jihad," *Bulletin of the American Academy of Arts and Sciences* 47, no. 8 (May 1994).

44. While the signals became less obvious for obvious reasons, in the beginning of the *Intifada* Islamic martyrs attacking Israelis were assured their families would receive significant wealth and benefits. However, the sudden appearance of new vehicles, appliances, houses, and so forth, betrayed the identity of martyrs to Israeli authorities, who then destroyed the houses and other wages of dramatic death; nonetheless, the prevailing religious system provided the certainty of privileged residence in Heaven—presumably a sign of immense social esteem although necessary to be taken on faith. I am grateful to Professor Martin Kramer of Tel Aviv University for data about the military interaction.

45. Lionel Tiger, "Hazed and Confused," *The New Yorker*, February 17, 1997.

46. Shoshana Zuboff, *In the Age of the Smart Machine: The Future of Work and Power* (New York: Basic Books, 1988), p. 63.

47. Patricia Sexton, *The Feminized Male* (New York: Harper and Row, 1969).

   Ann Douglas, *The Feminization of American Culture* (New York: Doubleday, 1977).

   Lexington, "Meet Auntie Sam," *The Economist*, September 14, 1996.

   Elinor Lenz and Barbara Meyerhoff, *The Feminization of America*, (Los Angeles: Tarcher, 1985).

48. Robert Winkler, "Wildlife Participation Is Holding Steady," *New York Times*, February 8, 1998.

49. Of course many women hunt, too, many with their husbands or other male companions and not typically in all-female groups. There is an interesting growth in the number of single mothers of boys who want to provide guidance in this classic male recreation. See Mary Zeiss Stange, *Woman the Hunter* (Boston: Beacon Press, 1997).

50. J. C. Herz, "In the Mainstream: Dead Deer, Not Demons," *New York Times*, April 30, 1998.

51. So-called extreme fighting in which opponents may use a periously wide range of assaults has been outlawed in many American communities, but sufficient interest remains in this depressing spectacle to encourage promoters to find sympathetic venues for the bouts, which are then televised for a fee to willing buyers. It appears that some people are bloodthirsty at least some of the time.

52. Diane McGuinness, "Behavior in Pre-School Boys and Girls," *Learning and Individual Differences* 322 (1990).

53. Natalie Angier, "The Debilitating Malady Called Boyhood: Is There a Cure?" *New York Times*, July 24, 1994.

54. See Sandra Lipsitz Bem, "Masculinity and Femininity Exist Only in the Mind of the Perceiver," in June Reinisch, et al., eds., *Masculinity/Femininity: Basic Perspectives* (New York: Oxford University Press, 1987).

55. See John Leo, "Boy, Girl, Boy Again," *U.S. News & World Report*, March 31, 1997.

56. Natalie Angier, "Sexual Identity Not Pliable, After All, Report Says," *New York Times*, March 14, 1997.

57. Carol Gilligan, *In a Different Voice: Psychological Theory and Women's Development* (Cambridge, MA: Harvard University Press, 1982).

58. See Katha Pollitt, *Reasonable Creatures* (New York: Knopf, 1994).
     Also, Christina Hoff Sommers, *Who Stole Feminism?* and K. Roiphe *op cit.*

59. There have also been broad complaints that women with high status in corporations do not adequately support junior females, possibly for lack of time. See Amy Saltzman, "Woman Versus Woman: Why Aren't More Female Executives Mentoring Their Junior Counterparts?" *U.S. News & World Report*, March 25, 1996.
     For a report on the operational styles of female leaders in the communications industry, see Ken Auletta, "In the Company of Women," *The New Yorker*, April 20, 1998.
     See also, Barbara Beck, "Women and Work," p. 11.

60. Francis Fukuyama, "Women and the Evolution of World Politics," *Foreign Affairs*, September/October 1998, p. 36.

61. Gail Sheehy, "Angry Men, Resilient Women," *New York Times*, June 19, 1995.

62. Hugh Sebag-Montefiore, "Britain's Highest Earning Women," *The Mail on Sunday*, July 13, 1997.

63. Lisa Foderaro, "Metro Business," *New York Times*, March 27, 1997.

64. Marilyn Frazier Pollock, *Controlling Their Own Success: Women and Business Ownership*, Ph.D. Thesis, Rutgers University, 1988.

65. Cited in Christina Hoff Sommers, *Who Stole Feminism?*, p. 303.

66. "A Wealth of Working Women," *The Economist*, June 8, 1996.

67. "On My Mind," *Forbes*, July 7, 1997, p. 22.

68. Barbara Beck, "Women and Work," p. 9.

69. To my knowledge no man has gained access to female locker rooms.

70. From a study conducted by *The New York Times*, it turns out that, on average, the better golfer a CEO is, the more likely his company is to generate better economic results than those led by poorer golfers. See Adam Bryant, "Duffers Need Not Apply: Data Show That Good Golfers Make the Best C.E.O's," *New York Times*, May 31, 1998.

71. Christopher Kimball, "Busy Bees," *Cook's Illustrated*, September-October, 1998.

72. Sue Shellenbarger, "Marriages Go Begging for Care as Focus Turns to Kids and Jobs," *Wall Street Journal*, December 24, 1997.

73. Elinor Ochs, Clotilde Pontecorvo, and Allesandra Fasulo, "Socializing Taste," ms. May 1996.

Chapter Four

1. Among other discussions of this see the following: Lionel Tiger, *The Manufacture of Evil: Ethics, Evolution, and the Industrial System* (New York: Harper & Row, 1987); Richard Alexander, *The Biology of Moral Systems* Hawthorne, Aldine de Gruyter, (NY: 1987); Robert Wright, *The Moral Animal* (New York: Random House, 1992); Franz de Waal, *Good Natured* (Cambridge, MA: Harvard University Press, 1996).

2. David Haig, "Genetic Conflicts in Human Pregnancy," *Quarterly Review of Biology* 68, no. 4, (December 1993).

3. Mary Batten, *Sexual Strategies: How Females Choose Their Mates* (New York: Putnam, 1992).

   Tim Birkhead, "Mechanisms of Sperm Competition in Birds," *American Scientist* 84 May-June 1996:254–62.

4. Robin Baker and Mark Bellis, "Human Sperm Competition: Ejaculate Adjustment by Males and the Function of Masturbation," *Animal Behavior* 45 (1993). Carol Kalsuk Yoon, "The Biggest Evolutionary Challenge May Be the Other Half of the Species," *New York Times*, June 18, 1996.

5. *The World's Women 1995: Trends and Statistics* (New York: United Nations, 1995), p. 3.

   There has recently been the first sign of narrowing of sex differences in life expectancy in twelve industrial nations, in part because male work has become less dangerous, men smoke less and exercise more while women smoke more, and there is better health care overall. See Frank Trovato and N. M. Lalu, "Narrowing Sex Differentials in Life Expectancy in the Industrialized World: Early 1970's to Early 1990's," *Social Biology* 43 (1996):1–2.

6. Increased female and reduced male smoking over a generation appear to narrow the difference in age at time of death. The effect may be especially marked because when women smoke at the same rate as men, their smaller body size increases their risk. See Frank Trovato and N. M. Lalu, "Narrowing Sex Differentials."

7. June Reinisch and Stephanie Sanders, "Early Barbiturate Exposure: The Brain, Sexually Dimorphic Behavior and Learning," *Neuroscience and Biobehavioral Reviews* 6 (1982):311–19.

8. Andrew Cherlin, *Marriage, Divorce, Remarriage* (Cambridge, MA: Harvard University Press, 1992), p. 22.

9. Glenn Collins, "A New Kind of Detective for the Longer Goodbye," *New York Times*, April 4, 1997. However, the divorce rate in New York State continues to rise, perhaps because of the population density of mobile affluent people confronted by elaborate life choices and of independent women willing and able to initiate divorce.

10. "The Other Woman in China," *The Economist*, March 14, 1992.

11. I am grateful for these estimates to Dr. Jean-Claude Chesnais, who is Senior Research Fellow at the Institut National d'Etudes Démographiques.
12. Jean Veevers, "Voluntary Childlessness: A Critical Assessment of the Research," in Eleanor Macklin and Roger Rubin, eds., *Contemporary Families and Alternative Lifestyles: Handbook on Research and Theory* (Beverly Hills, CA: Sage, 1983).
13. Robin Fox, "Introduction," *Biosocial Anthropology* (New York: Halstead Press, 1975).
14. Carol Kaesuk Yoon, "Within Nest, Egret Chicks Are Natural Born Killers," *New York Times*, August 10, 1996.
15. James Weinrich, "New sociobiological theory of homosexuality applicable to societies with universal marriage," *Ethology and Sociobiology*, 8:1, 1987.
   Deborah Blum, *Sex on the Brain: The Biological Differences Between Men and Women* (New York: Viking, 1997), provides a responsible and lively account, especially in chapter 5.
16. N. Chomsky, *Language and Mind*, 2nd ed. (New York: Harcourt Brace Jovanovich, 1973).
   Steven Pinker, *The Language Instinct: How the Mind Creates Language* (New York: William Morrow, 1994).
17. Mark Flinn, "Culture and the Evolution of Social Learning," *Evolution and Human Behavior* 18 (1997):23–67.
18. An early and seminal paper on the ease of learning hypothesis is by David Hamburg, "Evolution of Emotional Responses: Evidence from Recent Research on Nonhuman Primates," *Science and Psychoanalysis* 12 (1968).
19. Lionel Tiger and Robin Fox, *The Imperial Animal* (New York: Henry Holt 1971).
20. Robin Fox, *Encounter with Anthropology* (New York: Penguin, 1973).
21. Andrew Cherlin, *Marriage, Divorce, Remarriage*, p. 28.
22. Roger Ulrich, "Human Responses to Vegetation and Landscapes," *Landscape and Urban Planning* 13 (1982):29–44. See also Roger Ulrich et al., "Psychophysiological Indicators of Leisure Consequences," *Journal of Leisure Research* 22:3 (1990).
   Lionel Tiger, *The Pursuit of Pleasure* 1992, pp. 207–22.
23. Apologies for reusing an image from *The Pursuit of Pleasure*, but it has been effective and efficient in making a basic point.
24. Randy Nesse, "Evolutionary Explanations of Emotions," *Human Nature* 1 (1990):261–89; see also Randy Nesse and G. C. Williams, *Why We Get Sick* (New York: Random House, 1994), an arresting evolutionary approach to contemporary medicine.
   Del Theissen, *Bittersweet Destiny: The Stormy Evolution of Human Behavior* (New Brunswick, NJ: Transaction Publishers, 1996).
25. Michael McGuire and Alfonso Troisi, *Darwinian Psychiatry* (New York: Oxford University Press, 1988). This is a remarkably thorough and provocative addition to medicine as well as social science.
26. Helen Fisher, *Anatomy of Love* (New York: Norton, 1992).

27. Phyllis Dolhinow, "Tactics of Primate Immaturity," in Michael Robinson and Lionel Tiger, pp. 139–57, 1991.
28. Natalie Angier, "What Makes a Parent Put Up with It All?" *New York Times*, November 2, 1993.

    C. Sue Carter and Lowell Getz, "Monogamy and the Prairie Vole," *Scientific American* (June 1993).
29. For an early statement of this that has proved quite durable see Lionel Tiger, "Somatic Factors and Social Behavior," in Robin Fox, ed., *Biosocial Anthropology* (New York: John Wiley, 1975).
30. Martin Daly and Margo Wilson, *Homicide* (Hawthorne, NY: Aldine de Gruyter, 1988).

    Also, Martin Daly and Margo Wilson, *The Truth About Cinderella* (London: Weidenfeld and Nicholson, 1998).
31. Sarah Blaffer Hrdy, "Infanticide Among Animals: A Review, Classification, and Examination of the Implications for the Reproductive Strategies of Females," *Ethology and Sociobiology* 1 (1979).
32. Cited in Robert Pear, "Health Panel Backs Cost Based on Size of Families," *New York Times*, March 18, 1994.
33. Lena Williams, "Childless Workers Demanding Equity in Corporate World," *New York Times*, May 29, 1994.

    Kathleen Murray, "The Childless Feel Left Out When Parents Get a Lift," *New York Times*, December 1, 1996.
34. See the remarkable study by Joseph Carroll of the relationship between contemporary biological theory, literary analysis, and the recurrent themes of human kinship and society: *Evolution and Literary Theory* (Bloomington: Indiana University Press, 1994).

    Vernon Reynolds and Ralph Tanner, *The Social Ecology of Religion*, Longman, 1983.

    Also see my review article: Lionel Tiger, "Survival of the Faithful," *The Sciences*, March-April 1985.
35. William Wordsworth, in Humphrey Jennings, ed., *Pandemonium: The Coming of the Machine as Seen by Contemporary Observers, 1660–1886* (New York: The Free Press, 1985).
36. See the excellent essay on the real and intellectual links between Marx and Darwin by Paul Heyer, *Nature, Human Nature, and Society* (Westport, CT: Greenwood, 1975).
37. Guido Ruggiero, p. 71.

    Richard Parker, *Bodies, Pleasures, and Passions: Sexual Culture in Contemporary Brazil* (Boston: Beacon Press, 1991), p. 70.
38. Again, see Lionel Tiger, *The Manufacture of Evil*.
39. Robert Wright, *The Moral Animal*, and Del Theissen, *Bittersweet Destiny*.
40. William Julius Wilson, *New York Times Magazine*, August 17, 1996.
41. "The Home Front," *The Economist*, December 11, 1993.
42. Christy Casamassima, "Love and Work," *Psychology Today*, March-April 1995.

    Gail Sheehy, *Understanding Men's Passages* (New York: Random House, 1998), p. 18.

43. Matrilineal systems are those in which children derive their family descent through their mothers and uncles, as in West Africa. This is a quite common pattern. A matriarchal system is one in which females essentially make the principal decisions governing not only kinship but other features of society, too. This is rare, even to the vanishing point. It is a favorite fantasy of theorists of ancient amazonian cultures, but until recent control of reproductive activity by women, it has remained a fantasy.

44. Signithia Fordham, University of Maryland, *personal communication*. Again, females who succeed are accused by their peers of turning white; males of turning female.

45. Elijah Anderson, "The Code of the Streets," *The Atlantic Monthly*, May 1994.

46. Ibid.

47. Sam Roberts, "Black Women Graduates Outpace Male Counterparts: Income Disparity Seen as Marriage Threat," *New York Times*, October 31, 1994.

48. Y. Spencer-Booth and Robert Hinde, "Effects of Six Days' Separation from Mother on 18-to-32-Week-Old Rhesus Monkeys," *Animal Behavior* 19 (1971):174–91.

49. Margaret Talbot, "Attachment Theory: The Ultimate Experiment," *New York Times Magazine*, May 24, 1998. The report is based on the difficulties experienced by adopted children who were previously raised in severely deficient orphanages in Romania and the former Soviet Union.

50. "Consensus Versus Jobs," *The Economist*, February 1, 1997.

51. David Popenoe, "The Evolution of Marriage and the Problem of Stepfamilies," *National Symposium on Stepfamilies*, Pennsylvania State University, University Park, Pennsylvania, October 1993.

52. David Popenoe, "The Controversial Truth: Two-Parent Families Are Better," *New York Times*, December 26, 1992.

53. Barbara Dafoe Whitehead, "Dan Quayle Was Right," *The Atlantic Monthly*, April 1993.

54. Francoise Barret-Ducrocq, *Love in the Time of Victoria: Sexuality and Desire Among Working-Class Men and Women in Nineteenth-Century London*, trans. by John Howe (New York: Penguin Books, 1992).

55. Judith Wallerstein and Sandra Blakeslee, *Second Chances: Men, Women and Children a Decade After Divorce* (New York, Ticknor and Fields, 1989).

56. Alan Otten, "Divorce Can Lead to Unexpected Splits," *Wall Street Journal*, 1993.

57. Margaret Talbot, "Attachment Theory."

58. A brief paper on the subject was Lionel Tiger, "Human Rights Are a Sub-form of Animal Rights," American Anthropological Association, Annual Meeting, Atlanta, Georgia, December 1994.

59. James Lincoln Collier, *The Rise of Selfishness in America* (New York: Oxford University Press, 1991).

60. Janet Daley, "Most People Now Accept That Marriage Has Been Devalued, and Wish to Rebuild It," *The Times* (London) February 10, 1994.

61. T. R. Balakrishnan, Evelyne Lapierre-Adamczyck, and Karol K. Krotki, *Family*

and Childbearing in Canada: A Demographic Analysis (Toronto: University of Toronto Press, 1993), p. 163.

62. "The Home Front, *The Economist*, December 11, 1993.
63. Jessie Bernard, "No News, but New Ideas," in Paul Bohannan, ed., *Divorce and After* (New York: Anchor Books, 1971).
64. Lionel Tiger, "Omnigamy: The New Kinship System," *Psychology Today*, July 1978.
65. David Cooper, *The Death of the Family* (New York: Pantheon, 1970).
    Gloria Steinem, "What If Freud Were Phyllis?" in *Moving Beyond Words* (New York: Simon and Shuster, 1994).
    Betty Friedan, *The Feminine Mystique* (New York: Norton, 1963).
    Jane Howard, *Families* (New York: Simon and Schuster, 1983).
66. Daniel Goleman, "Studies Find No Disadvantage in Growing Up in a Gay Home," *New York Times*, December 2, 1992.
67. Ibid.

Chapter Five

1. David Miller, "Graf Struggles to Maintain Final Progress," *The Times* (London), July 6, 1996.
2. Alan Feingold, "Gender Differences in Male Selection Preferences: A Test of the Parental Investment Model," *Psychological Bulletin* 112:1 (1992).
3. Glenn Burkins, "Work Week," *Wall Street Journal*, August 11, 1998.
4. Stefan Kanfer, "A Cartel More Durable Than Diamonds," *New York Times*, September 26, 1993.
5. Edward Jay Epstein, *The Rise and Fall of Diamonds: The Shattering of a Brilliant Illusion* (New York: Simon and Schuster, 1985).
6. But while a "diamond lasts forever," its value does not, once it leaves the retail store. So she shouldn't expect to receive more than two weeks' worth of her ex's premarital salary should she enter the open diamond market to try to liquidate the jewel. It is a simple, though legal and conventional, fraud. *Anything* goes to discipline those males even if it becomes necessary to persuade them to waste their money completely.
7. The establishing paper in anthropology is G. P. Murdock, "Comparative Data on the Division of Labor by Sex," *Social Forces* 15:4 (1937).
8. Lesley Lovett Doust and Jon Lovett Doust, "Gender Chauvinism and the Division of Labor in Humans," *Perspectives in Biology and Medicine* 28:4 (Summer 1985).
9. There is a huge literature too compendious and also well known to rehearse here on the certainties and controversies surrounding the sexual division of labor. From Mill to Engels to de Beauvoir in classical literature and in virtually any discussion of sex in modern times there is discussion of the link between ancient

biology and contemporary work. I avoid the exegisis not with trepidation but because I've written about it unduly elsewhere and also because in this matter it seems more useful to identify what is new in the situation than negotiate anew what is old. Obviously the prehistory of modern times is significant, but perhaps for purposes of this narrative we can take it for granted and examine principally what is plainly problematic.

10. *Academe*, September-October 1996, p. 8.

11. Diana Furchtgott-Roth and Christine Stolba, *Women's Figures: The Economic Progress of Women in America* (Arlington, VA: Independent Women's Forum, 1996), p. 18.

12. Kingsley Browne has shown that the evident overall differences in male and female income result from different schedules and patterns of work. Women who work as long and consistently as men earn about the same money. But we have seen that women are more willing and even interested in taking part-time work, which has an impact on both their skills and seniority. Kingsley Browne, "Sex and Temperament in Modern Society: A Darwinian View of the Glass Ceiling and the Gender Gap," *Arizona Law Review*, 37:4 (Winter 1995).

13. Robin Pogrebin, "Magazines Learning to Take Not-So-Clueless (and Monied) Teen-Agers More Seriously," *New York Times*, November 4, 1997.

14. Diana Furchtgott-Roth and Christine Stolba, *Women's Figures*, pp. 12–14.

15. Again, Kingsley Browne ("Sex and Temperament in Modern Society," 1995) makes this case authoritatively.

16. Jane Brody, "Women Under Stress," *New York Times*, June 11, 1997.

17. Janet Douglas, "Cold Comfort for Working Moms," *U.S. News & World Report*, August 4, 1997.

18. Halimah Abdullah, "Balancing the Babies and the Books: Forget the Student Center; It's the Day Care Center That Counts," *New York Times*, Education Life supplement, July 1997.

19. Margot Slade, "Have Pump, Will Travel: Combining Breast Feeding and a Career," *New York Times*, December 14, 1997.

20. Stephanie Mehta, "More Women Quit Lucrative Jobs to Start Their Own Businesses: Cathy Dawson's New Firm Gives Her a Lot Less Pay, More Time for Family: The Kids Stuff Envelopes," *Wall Street Journal*, November 11, 1996.

21. "The Wall in the Heads," *The Economist*, November 9, 1996.

22. Helen Trickett, "Covering New Ground: Businesswomen Can Operate Successfully in the Islamic World As Long As They Follow Some Simple Guidelines," *Business Traveler*, April 1997.

23. Though obviously the fierce antifamilial patterns of slavery decisively coerced the system, it is provocative to consider how much of African-American kinship has been influenced by West African matrilineal roots. If West African foods, gestures, music, languages, and the like have found expression in North America and the Caribbean, it is plausible that forms of social life have as well.

24. Lester Thurow, "Companies Merge; Families Break Up," *New York Times*, September 3, 1995.

25. Marcia Barinaga, "New Insights into How Babies Learn Language," *Science* 277 (August 1, 1997):641.

26. Since Benizir Bhutto's father had been a national leader before her, in a sense he also chose her job, though of course she was elected in the normal manner.

27. Vijayendra Rao, "India's Dowry Problem," *New York Times*, January 14, 1994.

28. In the words of an Egyptian farmer: "Am I supposed to stand around while my daughter chases men? . . . You know what honor is in Egypt. . . . If a woman is more passive it is in her interest, it is in her father's interest and in her husband's interest." Some two million girls are subject to mutilation each year. Neil MacFarquhar, "Mutilation of Egyptian Girls: Despite Ban, It Goes On," *New York Times*, August 8, 1996. Another perplexing feature of the system is the role of mothers, aunts, sisters, and other female relatives in performing the mutilation and sustaining its role in marriage in the community.

29. A report of an autumn 1996 wedding in New York quoted the marriage vows of the bride. She "promised not only to share Mr. Ruben's life but also to remain true to herself. 'Although we journey on the same path,' she said, 'your journey will always be your own, and my journey will always be my own.'" Lois Smith Brady, "Gordon Bakoulis and Alan Ruben," *New York Times*, November 3, 1996. A fascinating study of modern courtship is John Townsend's *What Women Want—What Men Want*, Oxford University Press New York, 1998.

30. Mildred Dickemann, "The Ecology of Mating Systems in Hypergamous Dowry Societies," *Social Science Information* 18 (1979):163–95.
    Also, Mildred Dickemann's "Female Infanticide, Reproductive Strategies, and Social Stratification: A Preliminary Model," in *Evolutionary Biology and Human Social Behavior*, N. Chagnon and W. Irons, eds. (North Scituate, MA: Duxbury Press, 1979).

31. I am grateful to Wendy Gimbel for her description of the extraordinary ceremonies of commitment to religious order of contemporary daughters of wealthy Catholics in American colleges.

32. Bob Herbert, "China's Missing Girls," *New York Times*, October 30, 1997.

33. Nicholas Eberstadt, "Asia Tomorrow, Gray and Male," *The National Interest*, 53, Fall 1998.

34. South Korea, "Statistics Office Project Demographic Figures for 2010," *EAS-97-006*, January 9, 1997.

35. Matthews Hamabata, *Crested Kimona: Power and Love in the Japanese Business Family* (Ithaca, NY: Cornell University Press, 1990).

36. Ibid, p. 43.

37. Ibid, p. 45.

38. Philip Kan Gotanda, *Ballad of Yachiyo*, New York Public Theater, November 1997.

39. Sheryl WuDunn, "The Prisoner of Japan's Great Expectations," *New York Times*, September 21, 1996.

40. Kevin Sullivan and Mary Jordan, "A Japanese Pioneer to Retire from Tennis: Kimiko Date Blazed Trail for Women," *International Herald Tribune*, September 23, 1996.

41. Andrew Pollack, "In Japan, Equality Has Its Price: Women Take On Burdens As Opportunities Open in Job Market," *International Herald Tribune*, July 9, 1997.

42. Laura Tyson, "Lure of Career Seduces Taiwan Women: High-Income Professionals Are Delaying Marriage and Motherhood," *Financial Times*, February 19, 1995.

43. In *The Manufacture of Evil* I detail the forces abetting individualism and their impact on people, so there is no need to account for them here. But the independent contractor is a historically novel figure, and while these contractors are principally defined by their economic activity, nevertheless, since lives are of a piece, most of their other endeavors are involved as well, such as marriage or its absence.

44. In this particular case there was the factor of not only love that challenged the verities of social class in England but also unexpectedly graphic sexual description that excited the interest of both British and American authorities. By contemporary standards these were tame erotic histories—as tame as the famously censored paintings by D. H. Lawrence that were exiled from Great Britain and now are on display in the office of the owner of The Taos Inn where Lawrence and his Frieda, as well as other artists, made a haven. You pay the desk clerk $3, and he lets you into the boss's office to see the half-dozen or so paintings.

45. Bob Herbert, moderator and commentator of panel discussion, "Who Will Help the Black Male?" *New York Times Magazine*, December 4, 1994.

46. "The War Between the Sexes," *The Economist*, March 5, 1994.

47. "Are Men Necessary?" *The Economist*, January 5, 1996.

48. Susan Gal, "Peasant Men Can't Get Wives: Language Change and Sex Roles in a Bilingual Community," *Language Society* 7:1–16.

49. William Stevens, "Poor Lands' Success in Cutting Birth Rates Upsets Old Theories," *New York Times*, Jan 2, 1994.

50. Lester Thurow, "Companies Merge; Families Break Up," *New York Times*, September 3, 1995.

51. William Leuchtenburg, *The Perils of Prosperity* (Chicago: University of Chicago Press, 1958).

52. Michael Young and Peter Willmott, *Family and Kinship in East London* (London: Routledge, 1957).
    Norman Dennis, *Coal Is Our Life: An Analysis of a Yorkshire Mining Community* (London: Tavistock Press, 1956).

53. See Benita Eisler's spirited essay *Private Lives: Men and Women of the Fifties* (New York: Franklin Watts, 1986).
    J. Ronald Oakley, *God's Country: America in the Fifties* (New York: Dembner Books, 1986).

54. Lionel Tiger, "Why, It Was Fun," *Rolling Stone*, February 16, 1984.
    Philip Norman, *Shout: The Beatles in Their Generation* (New York: Fireside/Simon and Schuster, 1981).

55. Gene Koretz, "An Education Edge for Women," *Business Week*, September 30, 1996.

56. Vijayendra Rao, "India's Dowry Problem," *New York Times*, January 16, 1994.
57. Sylvia Nasar, 1994.
58. Steven Holmes, "Income Gap Persists for Blacks and Whites," *New York Times*, February 23, 1995.
59. Robin Knight, "Gender, Jobs and Economic Survival," *U.S. News & World Report*, September 19, 1994.
60. Andrew Hacker, "We All Drink the Same Water," *Transition: An International Review* 5:2 (Summer 1995).
61. Catherine Manegold, "Fewer Men Earn Doctorates, Particularly Among Blacks," *New York Times*, January 18, 1994.
62. "The War Between the Sexes," *The Economist*, March 5, 1994.
63. Diane Crispell, "A Mother's Work Never Seems to End," *Wall Street Journal*, July 24, 1994.
64. Anne Cronin, "When the Juniors Are Senior," *New York Times*, August 17, 1994.
65. "Sweden: Judgement Day," *The Economist*, February 18, 1995.
66. Organization for Economic Co-Operation and Development, *The OECD Jobs Study*, 1994.
67. Victor Keegan, "Women Rise to Top of UK Jobs Market," *Guardian Weekly*, April 17, 1994.
68. Christa Worthington, "Of Dolls, Karma and the Pursuit of Motherhood," *New York Times*, November 30, 1997.
69. Juliet Schor, *The Overworked American* (New York: Basic Books, 1993).
70. Sue Shellenbarger, "Work and Family," *The Wall Street Journal*, August 3, 1994.
71. See also, Schorr, *op. cit.*
72. *New York Times*, August 2, 1996.
73. Lester Thurow, "Companies Merge," 1995.
74. The Carnegie Corporation of New York, *Starting Points*, New York, 1994.
75. "On the Home Front," *The Economist*, March 5, 1994.
76. Susan Chira, "Care at Child Day Centers Is Rated As Poor," *New York Times*, February 7, 1995.

    Tony Marcano, "Accreditation Is No Guarantee on Day Care Centers, Study Says," *New York Times*, April 20, 1997.
77. "That Sinking Feeling," *The Economist*, January 24, 1994.
78. Kim Lockhart, "Hints from Ottawa Spur Wealth Transfer Measures," *The Globe and Mail*, January 11, 1994.
79. "Gimme Daddy's Dough," *The Economist*, November 15, 1997.
80. Mary Rowland, "It's Tough to Keep It in the Family," *New York Times*, December 26, 1993.
81. Debra Judge and Sarah Blaffer Hrdy, "Allocation of Accumulated Resources Among Close Kin: Inheritance in Sacramento, California, 1890–1984," *Ethology and Sociobiology* 13:5/6 (1992).
82. Miki Tanikawa, "Japanese Weddings: Long and Lavish (Boss Is Invited)," *New York Times*, February 26, 1995.

83. Gordon Getty, "Fitness Accounting," in Michael McGuire, ed., *Human Nature and the New Europe*, (Boulder, CO: Westview Press, 1993). Also see Gordon Getty, "The Hunt for *r*: One-Factor and Transfer Theories," *Social Science Information* 28 (1989):385–428.

Chapter Six

1. A friend who lived in Aspen, Colorado, and pursued adultery frequently described the problem of living in a sexualized mountain community in which partners had to drive everywhere and everyone's vehicle was as well known as their faces. Where could you park your car? Evidently a form of adult carpooling developed in which chums would ferry each other to assignations and retrieve each other after a considerate interval.
2. Amy Schwartz, "Ataturk's Daughters," *Wilson Quarterly*, Autumn 1995.
3. Kristin Luker, *Dubious Conceptions: The Politics of Teenage Pregnancy* (Cambridge, MA: Harvard University Press, p. 18.
4. Helen Fisher, "Monogamy, Adultery, and Divorce in Cross-Species Perspective," in Michael Robinson and Lionel Tiger, eds., *Man and Beast Revisited*, (Washington, DC: Smithsonian Institution Press, 1991).
5. The information regarding the United Kingdom is from Michael Jones, "Wedded to Welfare," *The Sunday Times*, July 11, 1993.
6. "Will You Join Me in Civil Unionlock?" *The Economist*, May 2, 1992.
7. Amelia Gentleman, "Britain's Top for Single Teenage Mothers," *Guardian Weekly*, May 27, 1998.
8. A foundation executive in Canada, Bob Couchman, with experience in these matters, predicts that the Canadian statistics will begin to resemble those of the United States. Nevertheless, see his Letter to the Editor, *The Atlantic Monthly*, January 1995.
9. See letter noted in preceding footnote.
10. David Popenoe, "American Family Decline, 1960–1990: A Review and Appraisal," *American Journal of Marriage and the Family*, 55:3 (August 1993).
11. Adam Clymer, "Moynihan on Health: Cure Social Ills," *New York Times*, October 20, 1993.
12. Eugene Brody, *Sex, Contraception, and Motherhood in Jamaica* (Cambridge, MA: Harvard University Press, 1981), pp. 253–55.
13. Jessica Davies, "I Have a Child Nearly Every Year, but I've Never Met a Girl I'd Want to Marry," *Daily Mail*, July 17, 1993.
14. David Popenoe, "Beyond the Nuclear Family: A Statistical Portrait of the Changing Family in Sweden," *Journal of Marriage and the Family*, 49 (February 1987): 173–83.
15. I've already cited one geneticist working with these tests who offered, but only

off the record, one reason for the resistance to their widespread use. In a fairly large Canadian survey, the number of children not the offspring of their legal acknowledged fathers ranged from 5 to 15 percent.

16. See the memoir about his own father and family life by John Edgar Wideman, *Fatheralong: A Meditation on Fathers and Sons, Race and Society* (New York: Pantheon, 1994).

17. There is confusion about terms here, which may also reveal ambiguity about the human behavior involved. For example, when it was revealed that President Mitterrand of France had a daughter with a woman not his wife, she was called "a natural child." Likewise, scandal sheets are fond of calling children born to unmarried entertainment stars "love children." Are the children of married people unnatural? Hate children? Other kinship systems have clear terms for such offspring. The Euro-American community has not yet acknowledged the social reality of its reproductive behavior and hence has not developed conventional terminology for it.

18. "Singular Rise of the Fallen Tory Woman," *Sunday Times News Review*, January 2, 1994.

19. Lena Williams, "Pregnant Teen-Agers Are Outcasts No Longer," *New York Times*, December 3, 1993. The same is true in once-conventional suburbs, as Cohen (*op. cit.*, 1998) reported for the Washington area.

20. Sally MacIntyre and Sarah Cunningham-Burley, "Teen-age Pregnancy as a Social Problem: A Perspective from the United Kingdom," in Lawson and Rhode, *op. cit.*, pp. 70–71.

21. Lionel Tiger, "Production and Reproduction in Industrial Societies," in *Sexual Differences in Mating Strategies: The Interface of Culture, Law, and Biology*, Meeting of the American Association for the Advancement of Science, Seattle, Washington, February 1997.

22. Peter Gumbel, "Italy's Birthrate, the World's Lowest, Is a Vexing Anomaly," *Wall Street Journal*, June 18, 1993.

23. Tamala Edwards, "Incite to Abort," *Time*, June 22, 1998.

24. Richard Posner, *Overcoming Law* (Cambridge, MA: Harvard University Press, 1996); see especially chapter 16.

25. Martin Daly and Margo Wilson, *Homicide* (Hawthorne, NY: Aldine de Gruyter, 1983).
    Martin Daly and Margo Wilson, "Evolutionary Social Psychology and Family Homicide," *Science* 242 (October 28, 1988): 519–24.

26. Frank Furstenberg, Jr., and Kathleen Harris, "When Fathers Matter/Why Fathers Matter: The Impact of Paternal Involvement on the Offspring of Adolescent Mothers," in Lawson and Rhode, *op. cit.*, p. 193.

27. Myron Magnet, "Problem No 1: The Children," *New York Times*, November 25, 1994. Magnet proposes that mothers on welfare live in state hostels that provide enriched educational opportunities for both women and their children. This is a realistic extension of the government's current assumption of responsibility, but it also focuses strategically on influencing behavior as well as providing sustenance.

28. David S. Landes, *The Wealth and Poverty of Nations: Why Some Are So Rich and Some So Poor* (New York: W.W. Norton, 1998), p. 412.
29. "Feminism Reaches Japan," *The Economist*, June 1, 1996.
30. Stephen Kinzer, "$650 a Baby: Germany to Pay to Stem Decline in Births," *New York Times*, November 25, 1995.
31. Clyde Farnsworth, "Quebec Bets on Subsidized Milk, Mother's Kind," *New York Times*, April 5, 1994.
32. Andre Picard, "Quebec Birth Rate Multiplies: Paying Parents Has Desired Effect," *Toronto Globe and Mail*, May 1, 1991. There has long been in Quebec a pro-natal policy, partly as a matter of Francophone ethnic assertion in face of the Anglophone majority. This aggressive pro-natality accompanies a renewed drive for political separation of Quebec from the Canadian federation.
33. Michael Valpy, "Clever Societies Look After the Children," *The Globe and Mail*, January 11, 1994.
34. Associated Press, January 14, 1994.
35. "That Sinking Feeling," *The Economist*, January 29, 1994.
36. Peter Marks, "The Slice of the American Dream: Single Mothers Ready New Lives as Homeowners on L.I.," *New York Times*, September 26, 1993.
37. *The Economist*, October 16, 1993, *op. cit.*
38. David Hale, senior economist at Zurich Kemper Investments, Chicago, Illinois, personal communication.
39. Louis Uchitelle, "370,000 Jobs Added to Rolls in December," *New York Times*, January 10, 1998.
40. Mikhail Bernstam and Peter Swan, "The State as the Marriage Partner of Last Resort: New Findings on Minimum Wage, Youth Joblessness, Welfare, and Single Motherhood in the United States" (Palo Alto, CA: Hoover Institution, Stanford University, 1986).
41. William Julius Wilson, *op. cit.*
42. James Baron, "Urban League Cites Pressure on Black Men," *New York Times*, August 1, 1984.
43. Reuters, "Nearly 7 percent of Adult Black Men Were Inmates in '94, Study Says," *New York Times*, December 4, 1995.
    The overwhelming ratio of the increase has been among men. But the number of women in prisons and jails increased from 25,000 in 1980 to 116,000 in 1995. See Steven Holmes, "With More Women in Prison, Sexual Abuse by Guards Becomes Greater Concern," *New York Times*, December 27, 1996.
44. Bob Herbert, moderator and commentator of panel discussion, "Who Will Help the Black Male?" *New York Times Magazine*, December 4, 1994.
45. Cherry Norton, "Black women 'left behind' as men marry out," London *Sunday Times*, July 19, 1998.
46. Sylvia Nasar, "More Men in Prime of Life Spend Less Time Working," *New York Times*, December 1, 1994.
47. David Hale, senior economist at Zurich Kemper Securities, Chicago, Illinois, personal communication.

48. Irving Kristol, "The Feminization of the Democrats," *Wall Street Journal*, September 9, 1996.

49. There have been a number of male retorts to this charge, Warren Farrell's *The Myth of Male Power* (New York: Simon and Schuster, 1993) being the fullest. Two others of many are Nicholas Davidson, *The Failure of Feminism* (Buffalo, NY: Prometheus Books, 1987), and Geoff Dench, *Transforming Men: Changing Patterns of Dependency and Dominance in Gender Relations* (New Brunswick, NJ: Transaction Publishers, 1996).

50. Frank Louis Rusciano: "The Case of West German Elections, 1949–1987," *Comparative Politics*, April 1992.

51. Gail Hareven, "The Deciding Vote," *The Jerusalem Report*, August 31, 1998.

52. Unemployment at the beginning of a work life, of course, often yields a permanent deficit.

53. Associated Press, "Rate of Teen-Age Pregnancy Increases Again," *New York Times*, October 7, 1993.

54. These have been eloquently and forcefully presented by Jean Bethke Elshtain in a review of Kristin Luker's *Dubious Conceptions: The Politics of Teen-age Pregnancy*. See "The Lost Children," *The New Republic*, October 21, 1996.

55. Arline Geronimus, "Teenage Childbearing and Social Disadvantage: Unprotected Discourse," *Family Relations* 41 (April 1992): 244–48.

56. "Tomorrow's Second Sex," *The Economist*, September 28, 1996.

57. Arline Geronimus and S. Korenman, "The Socioeconomic Consequences of Teen Childbearing Reconsidered," *Quarterly Journal of Economics*, in press.
    A. Geronimus, S. Korenman and J. Huillmier, cited in Arline Geronimus, "Teenage Childbearing and Social Disadvantage."

58. "Work Week," *Wall Street Journal*, September 24, 1996, p. 1.

59. I am grateful to Jane Lancaster, professor of anthropology at the University of New Mexico, for this information. Lancaster herself took unusually vigorous and brave action to protect the scientific value surrounding Geronimus's work and the overall issue.

60. Lionel Tiger and Joseph Shepher, *Women in the Kibbutz*.
    Louis Kern, *An Ordered Love: Sex Roles and Sexuality in Victorian Utopias; the Shakers, the Mormons, and Oneida Community* (Chapel Hill: University of North Carolina Press, 1981).
    Spencer Klaw, *Without Sin: The Life and Death of the Oneida Community* (New York: Allen Lane/The Penguin Press, 1993).
    John D'Emilio and Estelle Freedman, *Intimate Matters: A History of Sexuality in America* (New York: Harper & Row, 1988).

61. Katie Roiphe, *Last Night in Paradise: Sex and Morals at the Century's End* (New York: Little, Brown, 1997).

62. Daniel Smith, "The Long Cycle in American Illegitimacy and Prenuptial Pregnancy," in Laslett, et al., eds., *Bastardy and Its Comparative History*, p. 365.

63. John Haskey, "Lone Parenthood and Demographic Change," in M. Hardy and G. Crow, eds., *Lone Parenthood: Coping with Constraints and Making Opportunities in Single Parent Families* (Toronto: University of Toronto Press, 1993), p. 23.

Chapter Seven

1. Melissa Ludtke, "Sometimes, One Parent Is Better Than Two," *New York Times*, August 16, 1997.
2. A broad study from an economist is Gary Becker's *A Treatise on the Family* (Cambridge, MA: Harvard University Press, 1991).
3. "The War Between the Sexes," *The Economist*, March 5, 1994.
4. Natalie Angier, "The Debilitating Malady Called Boyhood: Is There a Cure?" *New York Times*, July 24, 1994.
5. Carin Rubenstein, "New Advice on How to Raise Little Boys to Be Good Men," *New York Times*, August 11, 1994.
6. Judith Shapiro, "What Women Can Teach Men," *New York Times*, November 23, 1994.
7. See Jeffrey Rosen, "Single-Sex Schools and Double Standards," *New York Times*, July 3, 1966.
8. There is a general selective principle at work here, of which the human version is a milder but persistent example. See Lee Ellis, "Dominance and Reproductive Success Among Nonhuman Animals: A Cross-Species Comparison," *Ethology and Sociobiology* 16 (1995): 257–33.
9. Ann Gibbons, "Did Neanderthals Lose an Evolutionary 'Arms' Race?" *Science* 272 (June 14, 1996): 1586–87.
10. Karen Baar, "Camps Learn to Tone Down the Competition," *New York Times*, August 14, 1997.
11. I am grateful to the Product and Services Development Department of TIAA-CREF for information on this subject. This department or TIAA-CREF is not responsible for my interpretation of the impact of gender-neutral actuarial practice for male-female equity.
12. *Pension News*, University of British Columbia, Vancouver, British Columbia, Fall 1995.

   On this point I had corresponded with then president of TIAA-CREF, Theodore Greenough who indicated that he regarded the government's demand a serious violation of responsible actuarial conduct. I raised the issue in 1976 during a panel of the Annual Judicial Conference of the Second Judicial Circuit. One panelist, professor Ruth Ginsburg, commented that my remarks "only" applied to 16 percent of the men who die early and 16 percent of the women who live long. These are, of course, large groups of human beings. The apparent principle of insurance is that those who are favored by life will help those who are not. So why penalize further those 16 percent of men who enjoy short lives by restricting their resources? And why reward very durable women? In any event, Ginsburg made no reference to other sex-based insurance, such as for automobiles, where actuarial experience results in substantially higher premiums for males than females of the same age. See *Proceedings*, Second Judicial Circuit Annual Judicial Conference, Buck Hill Falls, PA, September 1976.

13. "Sex and Death," *The Economist*, March 11, 1989.
14. Tamar Lewin, "Men Whose Wives Work Earn Less, Studies Show," *New York Times*, October 12, 1994.
15. Steven Gray, "Not Content with the Closet: Inspired by Others and Helped by Agencies, Gays Declaring Sexuality at Younger Age," *Boston Globe*, August 23, 1997.
16. Gina Maranto, "Tick-Tick-Tick-Tick-Tick: How Long Can Women Put Off Bearing Children?" *The Atlantic Monthly*, June 1995.
17. Steven Butler, "The Whopper Killed the Salmon Burger," *U.S. News & World Report*, January 20, 1997.
   "Food," *Business Week*, January 13, 1997.
   Molly O'Neill, "Check, Please. Now Let's Eat," *New York Times*, August 17, 1997. As an industry executive commented, "My granddaughter will remember that my wife did this thing called 'cooking,' the way my wife remembers that her grandmother did this thing called 'sewing.'"
18. When I talked about this issue to a large group of food industry executives, in answer to a question about foods prepared by children, I remarked that the evening before a food journalist had complained that a particular new product was too complex for her seven-year-old to prepare on his own. When I asserted that seven-year-olds should have dinner made for them, not have to make it themselves, there was a wholly unexpected and, I gather, unusual round of spontaneous applause—the only applause during the various sessions I attended. Something about touching nerves.
19. 1998KFC312F was the code in the photo for the advertisement that offered a coupon for a six-piece meal for two, among other options.
20. Yumiko Ono, "Recipe Creators' Ingredients for Success: Minimal Spice and Never, Ever Julienne," *Wall Street Journal*, December 29, 1994.
21. Yumiko Ono, "Would You Like That Rare, Medium, or Vacuum-Packed?" *Wall Street Journal*, January 6, 1997.
22. *Equal Pay for Equal Work: The Growth of the Idea in Canada* (Ottawa: Department of Labour in Canada, 1959).
   Michael Fogarty, et al., *Women and Top Jobs: An Interim Report* (London: PEP, 1967).
23. Steven Holmes, "Defining Disadvantage Up to Preserve Preferences," *New York Times*, August 24, 1997. It is also known that members of officially disadvantaged groups collude with entrepreneurs not so designated to earn contracts.
24. The extraordinary irony is that when the equal rights legislation governing race was being debated in the U.S. Congress, it seemed so self-evidently ludicrous to a representative from the South that as a joke he added "sex" to "race" as the protected category. Of course it passed. But race and sex are different in profound ways. Race is literally skin deep and has no biological significance, but sex is central in every way and has as much biological significance as any other category except "dead."

25. Benjamin Schwartz, "The Diversity Myth: America's Leading Export," *The Atlantic Monthly*, May 1995.

26. See Jeremy Tunstall's prescient *The Media Are American: Anglo-American Media in the World* (New York: Columbia University Press, 1977).
   Ferdinand Protzman, "In Germany, the Ceiling's Not Glass, It's Concrete: A Proposed Law Might Make It Easier for Women to Break Through," *New York Times*, October 17, 1993.
   World Wire, "Work Slows Japanese Births," *Wall Street Journal*, September 9, 1993.

27. B. Drummond Ayres, Jr., "Women in Washington Statehouse Lead U.S. Tide," *New York Times*, April 14, 1997.

28. Albert Wojnilower, "A Dull Forecast in an Exciting World," booklet of the First Boston Investment Management Publication, New York, 1993, p. 2.

29. Susan Gal, *op. cit.*
   Z. Taganyi, "Family, Children, and Ethical Questions of Family Planning," Institute of Sociology, The Hungarian Academy of Sciences, September 1992.

30. Bob Herbert, "America's Job Disaster," *New York Times*, December 1, 1993.

31. I am grateful for this observation to Fred Drasner whose place of business, the *New York Daily News* building, has been picketed on a number of occasions.

32. This was told to me by Richard Jerome, then an editor at *The Sciences*, published by the New York Academy of Sciences.

33. Debra Dickerson, "She's Gotta Have It: The Search for Black Men," *New Republic*, May 6, 1996.

34. Daniel Coyle, *Hardball: A Season in the Projects* (New York: Putnam's, 1993).

35. "Generation X-onomics," *The Economist*, March 19, 1994.

36. Mortimer Zuckerman, "Scary Kids Around the Corner," *U.S. News & World Report*, December 4, 1995. The demographic pattern reverses after 1997 so that there is reduced number of teenage males in the American population, which may be associated with declining rates of crime.

37. Ibid., p. 27.

38. John Haskey, *op. cit.* In Britain, one in eleven one-parent families is headed by a male, while the number of widowed single mothers has declined 30 percent. "Love Parenthood," (p. 409).

39. Margaret Usdansky, "Single Motherhood: Stereotypes vs. Statistics," *New York Times*, February 11, 1996.

40. For example, there remains controversy about the U.S. end game in the Gulf War with Iraq. Was U.S. reluctance to chase Iraqi troops to Baghdad and destroy their armament because of President Bush's unwillingness to display lethal American power on television? Or was it more the decision by Chief of Staff Powell to cease hostilities while U.S. casualties were negligible? Certainly the policy articulated most clearly by Powell of refusing military engagement without first establishing overwhelming superiority reflects deep caution about casualties. It will be interesting to observe how the one-child policy in China, in

tandem with an evident preference for male children, will affect that country's military policy. It is likely to produce a trend to a high-technology military, away from tactics based on large numbers of replaceable troops.

For a description of bias toward male Chinese children see Nicholas Kristof, "In China, Thanks to Ultrasound, It's Usually a Boy," *International Herald Tribune*, July 22, 1993.

41. Shripad Tuljapurkar, Nan Li, and Marcus Feldman, "High Sex Ratios in China's Future," *Science* (February 10, 1995).

42. Alison Gardy, "Grandparents Plan a Protest," New Jersey Weekly, *New York Times*, October 4, 1992.

43. Sandra Sugawara, "Suicides by Managers Soar as Japanese Firms Downsize," *International Herald Tribune*, July 9, 1997.

44. T. R. Insel, "Oxytocin—a Neuropeptide for Affiliation: Evidence from Behavioral, Receptor Autoradiographic, and Comparative Studies," *Psychoneuroendocrinology* 17, no. 3 (1992).

   Sue Carter and Lowell Getz, "Monogamy and the Prairie Vole," *Scientific American*, June 1993.

   Natalie Angier, "What Makes a Parent Put Up with It All?" *New York Times*, November 2, 1993.

   C. A. Petersen et al. "Oxytocin Induces Maternal Behavior in Virgin Female Rats," *Science* 216 (1992): 649–84.

45. Mortimer Zuckerman, "The Crisis of the Kids," *U.S. News & World Report*, April 12, 1993.

46. Ann Oakley, *Social Support and Motherhood* (Oxford, England, and Cambridge, MA: Blackwell, 1992), p. 5.

47. Robert McFadden, "Report Finds 20% of Students in New York City Carry Arms," *New York Times*, October 15, 1993.

48. Rick Bragg, "Children Strike Fear into Grown-Up Hearts," *New York Times*, December 2, 1994.

49. Andrew Hacker, "We All Drink the Same Water," *Transition: An International Review* 5:2 (Summer 1995). This is one essay in an issue devoted to "The Crisis of African American Gender Relations," and very useful.

50. Brent Staples, "Confronting Slaughter in the Streets," *New York Times*, November 5, 1993.

51. Hacker, "We All Drink the Same Water," p. 103.

52. For an interesting discussion of the rights and obligations of families and communities to each other, see David Haddock and Daniel Polsby, "Family as a Rational Classification," *Washington Law Quarterly* 74, no. 1 (1996).

53. Lionel Tiger, "Trump the Race Card," *Wall Street Journal*, February 23, 1996. I should apologize for using the terms black and white to refer to race, or even for using the concept of race altogether. In my opinion there is no scientific basis for the term, and it should not be a legal category, as it is so flagrantly in the United States Census. The theoretical category creates social realities, but it is a fraudulent category and its use tragically exacerbates in the long run the very problems it is invoked to solve in the short run.

54. Signithia Fordham, University of Maryland, personal communication 1993.
55. William McNeill, "Introductory Historical Commentary: The Fall of Great Powers: Peace, Stability, and Legitimacy," Conference at Norske Nobelinstitutt, Oslo, Norway, June 1993.

Chapter Eight

1. Dennis Hasselquist, Steffan Bensch, and Torbjorn von Schantz, "Correlation Between Male Song Repertoire, Extra-Pair Paternity, and Offspring Survival in the Great Reed Warbler," *Nature* 381 (May 16, 1997): 229–32. See a review of a book on bird partnerships: J. David Ligon, "Mating and Parenting," *Science* 276 (April 11, 1997): 216.
2. Roger Cowe, "Paul Raymond Still Headlines the Riches Revue," *The Guardian*, September 20, 1993. One estimate of his wealth is at least $2.26 billion.
3. "Business Travel," *New York Times*, January 1, 1997. The issue of accommodating a rapidly growing clientele of affluent female travelers has altered some hotel practices. For example, the Four Seasons Hotel chain on which I once did some brief research discovered that women did not want their room numbers shouted out to bellhops as had been the custom. So the number was never revealed, often not on the key, either. And it appears women did not choose to walk long corridors, so they were placed close to elevators unless they specifically requested otherwise. In addition, women did not favor rooms in which a business meeting was in sight of a bed. The Four Seasons management developed what they called the Junior Suite, a slightly larger than usual space in which the sleeping area was separated by doors. This proved popular and commercially successful.
4. "Cybersex: An Adult Affair; the Main Use of Many Kinds of Electronic Communication Is to Let Men Watch and Talk to Naked Women," *The Economist*, January 4, 1997.
5. Thomas E. Weber, "The X Files: For Those Who Scoff at Internet Commerce, Here's a Hot Market," *Wall Street Journal*, May 20, 1997.
6. Washington Whispers, "Room with a View?" *U.S. News & World Report*, April 14, 1997.
7. The "Mao jacket" worn by both Chinese men and women covered the body in a strict non-erotic manner. Though he wore his own eponymous garment, according to his personal physician this did not keep Mao from ample sexual consorts. "Do as I say, not as I do." Recent data from China reveals that seventy years of rigid antisexual socialization has fallen away seemingly overnight in communities such as Guangzhou and Shanghai. Men and women in these and other areas pursue sexual and sartorial agendas familiar in Euro-America.

8. Tom Kuntz, "Dancers of a Tawdry World, United: Organized Labor's Red-Light Beacon," *New York Times*, April 20, 1997.

9. I make no comment here about the morality and fairness of the industry when it involves consenting adults, nor about the disproportionate number of women involved compared with men. This is presumably a market matter: More men want to see women's bodies and behavior, and so more women take the work. In the male homosexual community, the same pattern applies, and men are the principal performers. Of course both women and men may be exploited by pornographers and audiences, and there is always special concern about the vulnerability of minors, most urgently, for example, where they are sold into prostitution by families, as in India, Thailand, and elsewhere. The committed puritanism surrounding feminist perceptions of outright and subtle pornography has been well expressed by Andrea Dworkin, Susan Brownmiller, and Catherine MacKinnon, among others. A sharp reply by a civil libertarian sympathetic to feminists is by Nadine Strossen (*Defending Pornography: Free Speech, Sex and Fight for Women's Rights* [New York: Scribner, 1995]). See also Sally Tisdale, *Talk Dirty to Me: An Intimate Philosophy of Sex* (New York: Doubleday, 1994).

   Joseph Shepher and Judith Reisman (Bat Ada), "Pornography: A Sociobiological Attempt at Understanding," *Ethology and Sociobiology* 6 (1986):2.

10. See Anne Allison, *Nightwork: Sexuality, Pleasure, and Corporate Masculinity in a Tokyo Hostess Club* (Chicago: University of Chicago Press, 1994), especially the section called "Male Bonding."

    John David Morley, *Pictures from the Water Trade: Adventures of a Westerner in Japan* (Boston: Atlantic Monthly Press, 1985).

11. John Taglibue, "Europe Enters the Big Leagues: Playing Catch-Up to the U.S., Commerce Takes the Field," *New York Times*, September 10, 1997.

12. Richard Sandomir, "Monday Football Stays on ABC; NBC Out of Game after 33 Years," *New York Times*, January 14, 1998.

13. Associated Press, *New York Times*, September 7, 1997.

14. To my knowledge the useful phrase is the coinage of the Canadian writer Barbara Moon.

15. Ed McCabe, personal communication 1997. His agency had a connection with the network's program of advertising.

16. In 1997 the U.S. Supreme Court refused to consider a Court of Appeals finding against Brown University of Rhode Island that it had violated Title 1X, a twenty-five-year-old ruling barring sex discrimination in educational institutions. This was in response to an obviously disproportionate focus on male sports, especially those generating significant revenues and alumni support such as football and basketball. To date, while attendance at women's events is increasing, there is not a substantial commercial network supporting them, and men's events remain overwhelmingly more lucrative and hence presumably more interesting to advertisers. Olympic events were an important exception in 1996, though there were complaints that U.S. coverage emphasized human interest features of the

games rather than the competitions themselves. It will remain a question how much sports activity by women in educational institutions will be propelled by legal requirements and how much by intrinsic interest among women for competitive athletics. Nevertheless, it is clear that changes in opportunity and financial support can have sharp impact on behavior. Career lines also open up. One result I have encountered among female students at Rutgers is that, like men, they juice up their musculature with steroids in order to enjoy a better shot at the benefits of athletic success. As with men, problems may also emerge with fertility and overall sexual robustness if powerful drugs are used during still-formative periods of physical development.

17. Thomas Ricks, "U.S. Infantry Surprise: It's Now Mostly White: Blacks Hold Office Jobs," Wall Street Journal, January 6, 1997.
18. For a report see Nicholas Lemann, "The Great Sorting," The Atlantic Monthly, September 1995.
19. Linda Bird Francke, Ground Zero (New York: Simon and Schuster, 1997).
20. This is a vital and exotic characteristic of contemporary industrial communities that I have discussed in some detail in The Manufacture of Evil. It is characteristic that performance on tests is treated as more salient than broader features of the life cycle often associated with sex.
21. Mary Rudie Barnaby and Jennifer Kelly, "A Pension Gap for Women," New York Times, August 31, 1997.
22. John Corry, "Dames at Sea," American Spectator, August 1996.
23. Judith Hicks Stiehm, Bring Me Men and Women: Mandated Change at the U.S. Air Force Academy (Berkeley: University of California Press, 1981).
24. Eric Schmitt, "Army Will Allow Women in 32,000 Combat Posts," New York Times, July 28, 1994.
25. Louise Leif, "Second Class in the Israeli Military: Women Are Fighting for Equality in the Ranks," U.S. News & World Report, May 22, 1995.
26. Richard J. Newman, "Can Peacemakers Make War: Americans Have Many Jobs Today—Raising Fears That They Are Less Prepared for Real Combat," U.S. News & World Report, January 19, 1998.
27. Ferdinand Protzman, "In Germany, the Ceiling's Not Glass, It's Concrete: A Proposed Law Might Make It Easier for Women to Break Through," New York Times, October 17, 1993.
    World Wire, "Work Slows Japanese Births," Wall Street Journal, September 9, 1993.
28. Laura Miller, "Feminism and the Exclusion of Army Women from Combat," Olin Institute for Strategic Studies, Working Paper No. 2, Harvard University, December 1995.
29. Linda Bird Francke, Ground Zero.
    Anna Simons, "The New Guys," Los Angeles Times Book Review, August 10, 1997.
30. See Lionel Tiger, "Sex in Uniform," Wall Street Journal, May 27, 1997.
31. Anna Simons, The Company They Keep: Life Inside the U.S. Army Special Forces (New York: The Free Press, 1997).

32. Editorial, "Rigging the Test Scores Justifiably," *New York Times*, October 14, 1996. The creators of tests usually remove any questions that reveal sex differences, on the perilously sentimental presumption they are biased. Nonetheless, differences continue to show. Many of the operations of test makers approach farce in this area.

33. For a thorough review beginning with neurocortical processes see Gillian Einstein, "Sex, Sexuality, and the Brain," in Purves et al., eds., (Andrew Smaller and Associates, 1997).

34. A senior Marine general whose identity I want to protect, personal communication, September 1996.

35. Laura Miller, "Feminism and the Exclusion of Army Women."

36. Anna Simons, "In War, Let Men Be Men: Why Combat Units Should Remain Male," *New York Times*, April 23, 1997.

37. Kirk Spitzer, "Group May Give Women a Fighting Chance at Combat: Sea, Air Warfare May Be OK'd, but Many Say Female Troops Would Disrupt Bonding," *Detroit News*, July 5, 1992.

38. See Matthew Wald, "2 Are Charged with Rapes at an Army Training Center: Dozens of Women Complain of Harassment," *New York Times*, November 8, 1996. One officer was charged, conceded that his behavior was against orders, and claimed that the encounters were consensual. The maximum penalty he faced was life in prison, but his ultimate sentence was substantially milder. Most infractions were between male and female trainees serving several weeks to several months at the base in question.

39. Jane O'Hara, "Speaking Out: Rape in the Military," *Maclean's*, June 1, 1998.

40. One military pilot told me that when he and his chums would visit bases, they would wear their flight suits all the time and "hit the bars. The suits were a babe magnet."

41. Cynthia Enloe, *Does Khaki Become You: The Militarization of Women's Lives:* (London: Pandora, 1988).

42. John Lancaster, "Reports of Sexual Assaults Add Fuel to Debate over Women in Combat," *Washington Post*, July 14, 1992.

43. In response to my question about the need for the relatively sharp distinction drawn between the officer corps and others in the military, a U.S. Air Force colonel told me, "This is an unusual job in which you may have to tell someone to go die."

44. Lionel Tiger, "Are the Harrassers in Charge?" *Journal of Contemporary Legal Issues*, October 1997.

45. Eric Schmitt, "Navy Prepares a Manual About Sexual Harassment," *New York Times*, April 10, 1994.

46. C. J. Chivers, "Yes, There Is a Double Standard," *New York Times*, November 17, 1996.

47. National Defense Research Institute, *Sexual Orientation and U.S. Military Personnel Policy: Options and Assessment* (Santa Monica, CA: RAND, 1993).
    Bernard Trainer and Eric Chase, "Keep Gays Out: They'll Cause the Military to Disintegrate," *New York Times*, March 29, 1993.

48. An informant described the arrangement at the American naval base in Subic Bay. Local prostitutes were aware in detail of the movements of the fleet, and many made agreements with men on different ships, scheduled to arrive at different times, to be their supposedly exclusive partners for a monthly fee, for example $30.

49. I was told in 1965 by a rural physician in British Columbia that during World War II practitioners were permitted to use vacuum aspirators to perform abortions that were technically illegal. After the war, the Royal Canadian Mounted Police retrieved the devices, because abortion was no longer an obvious necessity for a woman whose husband was a loyal soldier abroad. I have already referred to the same principle in commenting on U.S. Supreme Court Justice Kennedy's opinion that a married woman need not tell her husband about an abortion; that it may, in fact, protect the marriage and the family.

    During the Gulf War there were dozens of prosecutions for adultery of spouses left on bases in Germany. In the U.S. military, as more members stay longer and more are married, this looms ever larger in its judicial activities.

50. Thom Geier, "The Case of the Vanishing Priesthood. Wedding Bells Would toll a Revival," *U.S. News & World Report*, December 30, 1996.

51. Ruth Geldhill, "Church Faces Celibacy Row as Bishop Goes," *The Times* (London), September 17, 1996.

52. James Webb, "The Military Is Not a Social Program," *New York Times*, May 23, 1994.

53. Eric Schmitt, "Military Struggling to Stem an Increase in Family Violence," *New York Times*, May 23, 1994.

54. On board the carrier, an informed officer indicated that in his experience the pregnancy rate was close to 13 percent. The matter is understandably sensitive. People of goodwill and helpfulness can easily disagree even on the facts since data about human sexuality are difficult to gather under any circumstances and particularly so in the closed community of the military and the even more closed society aboard naval vessels. These may be deployed for a half year at a time, or more during crises.

    Obviously there is a special kind of reverberating consequence of "sex on board." The shipboard romance of elegant legend was acceptable and intriguing because when the vessel docked the matter was easily concluded. The partners had free choice. But in the Navy relatively detailed personnel files follow individuals through the several decades of their careers. Irreplaceable pension and other benefits attach to continued service. Even if the shipboard romance is relatively casual, it carries potentially damaging consequences.

55. Patricia Thomas, "Psychosocial and Behavioral Correlates of Pregnancy Aboard Navy Ships," Women in Uniform Conference, Women's Research and Education Institute, Washington, D.C., December 10, 1998. Thomas notes that her opinions are her own, not official views of the Department of the Navy.

56. A sample story comes from the trial of male personnel at the Aberdeen Army Base. "His accusers are habitual liars who openly yearned to have intimate

relations with him." Neil Lewis, "Sergeant's Lawyers Start Case by Accusing 2 of His Accusers," *New York Times*, April 22, 1997.

57. Again, it is worth recalling Metford Spiro's surprise that his or my description of this kibbutz failure of feminist ideology has been so sparely cited in discussions of this matter. His book was published prominently by the University of Chicago Press, perhaps the world's outstanding anthropological publisher, while mine was published by Harcourt Brace in New York and Penguin worldwide, neither of them reticent about distributing books. Our message was unpleasant and hence ignored. The U.S. military is making a similar and avoidable error by accepting an unsupportable ideology as its guide to action. In this case, however, the issue is not how children are raised but how mortal combat is conducted and people protected. See Melford Spiro, *Gender and Culture: Kibbutz Women Revisited*, (New Brunswick, NJ: Transaction Publishers, 1996).

Conclusion

1. Seymour Martin Lipset, *Political Man* (New York: Doubleday, 1963).
2. Elizabeth Olson, "U.N. Surveys Paid Leave For Mothers," *New York Times*, February 16, 1998.
3. The extreme version of this was, of course, the decision on a tennis court of a passel of French aristocrats to renounce their privileges and wealth during the tumult of the French Revolution.
4. Associated Press, *New York Times*, October 22, 1996. If nothing else, what becomes clear from this is that people are not using condoms, the most effective preventive barrier against the illnesses that these statistics document.
    Warren Leary, "Rate of Sexual Diseases in U.S. Is Highest in Developed World," *New York Times*, November 20, 1996. The underlying generalized societal idiocy and denial about sexuality is signified by the cold costs: The nation spends $1 to prevent sexually transmitted diseases and $43 on treatment.
5. Kevin MacDonald, "The Establishment and Maintenance of Socially Imposed Monogamy in Western Europe," *Politics and the Life Sciences* 14, no. 1 (February 1995).
6. Ellen Fein and Sherrie Schneider, *The Rules* (New York: Warner Books, 1995). In effect this is a deceptively breezy manual defining relatively stringent procedures of courtship against a rule-less and threatening background. In an interview, Fein noted, "Women are tired of being hurt and dumped and watching their biological futures evaporate." See also Deirdre Donahue's, " 'The Rules' to Catching Mr. Right," *USA Today*, October 3, 1996.
7. See Derek Freeman, "Paradigms in Collision: Margaret Mead's Mistake and What It Has Done to Anthropology," *Skeptic* 5, no. 3, (1997).

8. Perhaps no one tries because it is nearly useless. Not much changes. For example, in 1976 I gave a paper to a panel of judges and attorneys on discussing sex and affirmative action at the annual meeting of the Second Circuit Court of the United States. The assertion simply was that race was an unimportant human category with literally skin-deep impact but sex was profoundly and complexly important, and good legislation should not confound two utterly dissimilar categories of social analysis. It made no difference. The other speakers were Ruth Bader Ginsburg, now of the U.S. Supreme Court, Father Charles Whelan of Fordham University Law School, and Gloria Steinem who remains iconically, ceaselessly, and blithely unperturbed by evidence that contradicts her now-sentimental anguish about sex. See Lionel Tiger, "Sex Differences in Relation to Equal Opportunity and Affirmative Action," *Proceedings of the 1976 Annual Judicial Conference of the Second Circuit Court of the United States* (St. Paul, MN: West Publishing Company, 1977).

   It remains remarkable that such an easy elision is made between sex and race by social planners and managers. The principal beneficiaries of this appear to have been women, often middle class of whatever demographic classification who have attached their occupational ambitions to the effort to repair the tragedy of slavery. It seems a somewhat unseemly opportunism.

   The issue is all the more strange since the original congressional legislation designed to remedy racial prejudice did not mention sex. A representative from a southern state thought the entire effort was ridiculous and so unlikely to pass that he simply added "gender" to the language of the law as a joke. The result is a collapse of two very different social groups into one, with far-reaching consequences, many of which we have been examining.

   See the interesting essay on these matters by Tom Wolfe, "Sorry, but Your Soul Just Died," *Forbes ASAP*, December 2, 1996.

9. Editorial, "Rigging the Test Scores Justifiably," *New York Times*, October 14, 1996. Questions that discriminate between males and females are removed from the I.Q. and similar tests. Nevertheless, differences continue to emerge. I have elsewhere suggested that different responses by various groups may reflect the fact that questions revealing particular approaches to social features of sexuality are removed from the mix. Different groups display quite different notions of human sexuality, but the white-bread test systems reject such variety as factors to explore. See *The Manufacture of Evil* for a fuller discussion of the nature of test making and test taking and their links to what I call the "psychology-industrial complex."

10. Barbara Crossette, "World Is Less Crowded Than Expected, the U.N. Reports," *New York Times*, November 17, 1996.

11. Sam Dillon, "How to Scandalize a Politician: Bare a Love Affair," *New York Times*, January 22, 1997.

   Another report on Mexican birthrates suggests there is great geographical divergence and that while the rate has dropped significantly, nonetheless each year nearly two million Mexicans join the current population of ninety-two million. See Robert D. Kaplan, "History Moving North," *The Atlantic Monthly*, February 1997.

12. Marianne Jennings, "Manager's Journal," *Wall Street Journal*, July 6, 1998. The U.S. Supreme Court ruling in June 1998 said that companies are responsible for harrassment even if they don't know it is occurring unless they provide employees with material for "forethought" about the practice; this ruling will obviously abet such bizarre efforts at remedy. Jennings goes on to describe the "fear in my male colleagues' eyes that they will unwittingly offend someone and will be the subject of a career-derailing investigation." The situation is a quite remarkable victory of legality over civility and the scene of chronic low-level anxiety in everyday life.

13. I am grateful to Professor Ira Ellman of the College of Law, Arizona State University, for this datum. He is involved in acting on the boy's behalf.

14. Matthews Campbell and Jack Grimston, "Paternity tests are now available by post. But will they give birth to more unhappiness than they cure?" London *Sunday Times*, July 19, 1998.

15. For a striking vignette of one woman who sought to escape her conditions, see Mary Weaver, "India's Bandit Queen," *The Atlantic Monthly*, November 1996.

16. Nuruddin Faral, "The Women of Kiamayo: Power and Protest in Somalia," *Times Literary Supplement*, November 15, 1996.

17. Virginia Cornue, personal communication 1995. Cornue was engaged in research on contemporary Chinese women for her Rutgers dissertation and had unusual access to decision-makers as well as opportunities to perceive the goals of political insiders.

18. Nicholas Kristoff, "Do Korean Men Still Beat Their Wives? Definitely," *New York Times*, December 5, 1996.

   Sheryl WuDunn, "Korean Women Still Feel Demands to Bear a Son," *New York Times*, January 14, 1997.

19. Bob Herbert, "China's Missing Girls," *New York Times*, October 30, 1997.

20. "The Sex Industry," *The Economist*, February 14, 1998.

21. A mean-spirited but not drastically inaccurate inventory of influential feminists would likely find the great majority of them located in no more than ten postal zip codes. It's a thought.

22. Debra Dickerson, "She's Gotta Have It . . ." takes issue with some feminist writers such as Faludi who assert that women don't want to "have it all." Perhaps this is so among white women but far less among black women, according to Dickerson.

23. Quoted in Richard Zoglin, "Mad for Evita," *Time*, December 30, 1996.

24. See Michael Elliott's excellent study of this period *The Day Before Yesterday: Reconsidering America's Past, Rediscovering the Present* (New York: Simon and Schuster, 1996), especially chapter 5. A useful cognate discussion of an earlier period of prosperous social change in the United States is William Leuchtenburg's *The Perils of Prosperity, 1914–32* (Chicago: University of Chicago Press, 1958).

25. Paula Ardeheli, *Arranging Marriages in Iran*, Ph.D. thesis, Rutgers University, 1984.

26. Because of her ability with their languages, Paula Ardeheli was asked to translate marriage agreements. She has noted the very detailed adaptation of traditional ways to the commercial realities of central New Jersey with whose emigré Iranian population she was familiar.
27. Lionel Tiger, "The Male Bond," *The Observer*, June 29, 1969. It was also published in *New York Magazine* around the same time as "Male Bonding and the Exclusion of Females," a better and more honest title.
28. Diane di Mauro, "Researching Sexuality," *Items: Social Science Research Council* 50, no. 4 (December 1996). "Insufficient and erratic funding coupled with a narrowly designed research agenda that has focused primarily on a 'risk-factor' approach have contributed to a paucity of research on sexuality which, in turn, has sustained many of the social crises evident in the United States today" (p. 86).
29. As frequently happens, the Japanese case is anomalous or at least different. I've noted that the contraceptive pill has been illegal in Japan, both because of a general cultural fear of the chemistry but more likely because of the government's reluctance to do anything that may lead to a decrease in the country's already low, below-replacement birthrate. The argument about cultural fear is weak because whatever their special reservations about contraceptive medication, the Japanese have relatively little reluctance about using drugs. They are already among the planet's most medicated. This is so because doctors are able to prescribe as well as sell drugs. They have a clear economic incentive to do so. Because current contraception is inefficient, there are substantial numbers of unwanted pregnancies. They rarely end in single motherhood, as we have seen, but instead in abortion, which is legal and inexpensive. It may not be a chemical trauma like a drug, but it is clearly not a trouble-free procedure without psychological and even physical impact. As in the former U.S.S.R. it reflects both a deteriorated medical system and ramshackle family behavior.

   In late 1996 the Japanese government decided to permit the legal sale of birth control pills. It will be interesting to see the effect of this on individual behavior, social patterns, and links between men and women. See Sheryl WuDunn, "Japan May Approve the Pill, but Women May Not," *New York Times*, November 27, 1996.
30. Michael Elliott, *The Day Before Yesterday*, pp. 179–80.
31. "Holding the Baby," *The Economist*, January 31, 1998. More than one-third thought one parent could raise a child as well as two.
32. Arline Geronimus, "What Teen Mothers Know," *Human Nature: An Interdisciplinary Biosocial Perspective* 7, no. 4 (1996).
33. This position was heavily lobbied by women's organizations seeking reward for their disproportionate support of the president in the 1996. It was part of a large-scale effort to have women appointed to senior posts. One factor was the wish of the president's wife. While there appeared no evident opposition to the appointment because the candidate was a woman, there was much support for the value of appointing her because of her sex. To appreciate the emotional and political appeal of appointments of women, consider the unlikelihood of kudos accruing to an American politician for the appointment of a man *qua* male.

34. David Givens and Timothy Jablonski, "News of the Academy," *Anthropology Newsletter*, (September 1996).

35. Dina Furchtgott-Roth and Christine Stolba, *Women's Figures: The Economic Progress of Women In America* (Arlington, VA: Independent Women's Forum, 1996), p. 16.

36. Peter Passell, "Benefits Dwindle Along with Wages for the Unskilled," *New York Times*, June 14, 1998.

37. David Courtwright, *Violent Land: Single Men and Social Disorder From the Frontier to the Inner City* (Cambridge, MA: Harvard University Press, 1996).

38. Robin Fox makes the general point that socialism has not been tried skillfully enough in industrial communities, so the experiment is not over in principle. See "On Marxism," *The Nation*, 250:(19) 1990, 664–666.

39. The argument on which these announcements are made is given more fully in *The Manufacture of Evil: Ethics, Evolution, and the Industrial System* (New York: Harper and Row, 1987).

   See also Robert Wright, *The Moral Animal* (New York: Random House, 1992), which is more about evolutionary psychology than economics; and Matt Ridley, *The Origins of Virtue* (New York: Penguin, 1997).

40. "Social Science and the Citizen," *Society* 34, no. 2 (January-February 1997).

41. Barbara Crossette, "A Manual on Rights of Women Under Islam," *New York Times*, December 29, 1996.

42. Alessandra Stanley, "New Face of Russian Capitalism: Avon and Mary Kay Create Opportunities for Women," *New York Times*, August 14, 1996.

43. Karl Mannheim, *Ideology and Utopia: An Introduction to the Sociology of Knowledge*, trans. by Louis Wirth and Edward Shils (New York: Harcourt, Brace and Company, 1936).

44. "Social Science and the Citizen," *Society* (July-August 1998), p. 5.

45. Eric Jones, "The People Next Door: Australia and the Asian Crisis," *The National Interest* 52 (Summer 1998).

46. Kathy Evans, "UAE to Ban Marriage to Foreigners," *Guardian Weekly*, December 1, 1996. Eighty percent of people in the United Arab Emirates are foreigners at work. Marrying them, now illegal, was one way to avoid all the costs and kinship obligations that men must sustain if they marry local women. It is not unusual for a wedding, with appropriate gifts of jewelry, to cost $75,000.

47. Bagehot, *The Economist*, December 14–20, 1996. Presumably, male politicians already in service had to be set aside.

48. My employer, Rutgers University, has an especially vigorous program of women's studies and advocacy, but it is nonetheless reflective of the broad pattern. For one very common example, the Rutgers Institute for Research on Women proposes a "Celebration of Our Work Conference" each year. For the fifteenth, in 1997, an array of themes was proposed by the organizers, including grassroots and community activism; politics and/as activism; local/global activism; student activism; women's health activism (for example, breast cancer, AIDS/HIV); cultural production and criticism as activism; feminist organizing and organiza-

tions; mobilizing theory; feminist activism and identity/difference: race, ethnicity, class, sexuality; pedagogical activism ("Making the classroom count"); theories of activism; "The Personal is political" revisited; activism in the schools; scholar activists; activist scholars and so on.

It is inconceivable that a comparable male program would ever emerge, let alone find university approval, funding, and supporters. There is room for much argument about whether or not such deliberately activist agendas are appropriate for scholarly institutions, especially those supported by public money. For an especially excoriating critique see Daphne Patai and Noretta Koerge, *Professing Feminism: Cautionary Tales from the Strange World of Women's Studies* (New York: Basic Books, 1994). I have already referred to Christina Somers's essay.

There appears to be a communally justified female lobby for virtually any thinkable cause. For example, there exists "The Women's National Book Association" with representatives who appear on national U.S. television. There is, of course, no comparable male organization. Perhaps at one time it could have been argued that all book publishing was the Men's Book Association, but now there are so many powerful, accomplished, and decisively influential women in the industry in all its phases that a remedial argument is weak.

49. My Rutgers colleague Robert Trivers has made the telling and fundamental comment about interactions between animals, including humans, that subdominant animals succeed by deceiving the dominants and that dominant animals fail by deceiving themselves. This is precisely the process under way in the sociosexual arena. Neither side of the dialogue need know with any precision what they are doing and why. Nevertheless, the elements in the system may well produce a change in the relations of power. See Robert Trivers, "Deceit and Self-Deception: The Relationship Between Communication and Consciousness," in Michael Robinson and Tiger, *Man and Beast Revisited*, pp. 175–92.

50. Warren Cohen, "Kid Looks Like the Mailman? Genetic Labs Boom as the Nation Wonders Who's Daddy," *U.S. News & World Report*, January 27, 1997.

51. Ibid. One of the successful companies providing this test erected a Houston billboard reading: WHO'S THE FATHER? CALL 1–800-DNA-TYPE. Its president, Caroline Caskey, wasted no words: "In developing a market that didn't exist before, we've tried to plant a seed of doubt in people's minds. Most people are too shy to ask anyone about something so extremely personal, but given a number, a lot of people will go ahead and call."

52. The number of men who raise children while their wives work is tiny, though as a gesture or ideal it is much appreciated in public discussion. Also, relatively few men take advantage of parental leave opportunities when they receive no money during their time off. There also appear to be informal understandings among parents of young children that mothers prefer that their husbands not care for them.

Gail Sheehy notes that "the fastest-growing family structure in America today is the devoted single dad" and that 5 percent of fathers are heads of families. See Gail Sheehy, *Understanding Men's Passages* (New York: Random House, 1998), p. 164.

53. Cathy Tempelsman, "Dear Mom, Clear My Calendar," *Wall Street Journal*, August 20, 1993.

54. Eric Schmitt, "Day-Care Quandary: A Nation at War with Itself," *New York Times*, January 11, 1998.

55. Magnus Linklater, "Grilled at interview? Not likely," *Times of London*, July 23, 1998. "To ask even the mildest of personal questions is to invite immediate outrage and possible legal repercussions."

56. Kirk Johnson, *op.cit.*, 1996. Accepting a stranger into European family life where au pair arrangements were common on an ongoing basis was apparently somewhat easier when the young women—often of the same social class or better as their employers—were only temporarily in that position. They used it as a way of traveling, learning a language, and so forth. But also the presence of a young female in domestic closeness was not without some threat to the family overall. When Desmond Morris wrote *The Naked Ape* in 1966, he enthusiastically described the "pair-bond" as the durable basis of marriage. I threatened to write a parody called "The Au Paire Bond." I should have.

57. In his deeply flawed book on the kibbutz system, *Children of the Dream*, the now-exposed poseur Bruno Bettelheim proposed a psycho-Viennese reason that kibbutz women had about four children each. It was to get back at their own mothers. Shepher and I studied some of the same people Bettelheim had and learned that they quickly discovered he was interested solely in his own opinions and told him nothing to contradict them. They also isolated him in a remote cabin far from the action. They told us they had four children because they wanted them and love them.

58. Amitai Etzioni, "Beware of Rain Dancers at the Fed," *New York Times*, June 28, 1998.

59. At a meeting of the Wellesley Center in New York the sociologist Cynthia Fuch Epstein offered the dazzling fatuity that women who remained home while their husbands worked long hours were single mothers and that their husbands were merely sperm donors and automatic teller machines. Half the audience considered this an amusing analysis.

60. Kathy Evans, "UAE to Ban Marriage to Foreigners."

61. Melford E. Spiro, *Gender and Culture: Kibbutz Women Revisted*, (New Brunswick, NJ: Transaction Publishers, 1996), p. ix.

Additional References

Katie Roiphe, *The Morning After: Sex, Fear, and Feminism*, Little, Brown, New York, 1994.

Vernon Reynolds and R.E. Tanner, *The Social Ecology of Religion*, Oxford University Press, New York, 1995.

Katha Pollitt, *Reasonable Creatures*, Knopf, New York, 1994.

Andrea Dworkin, *Intercourse*, Free Press, New York, 1987.

Juliet Schor, *The Overworked American*, Basic Books, New York, 1993.

Benjamin Barber, *Jihad vs. McWorld*, Times Books, New York, 1995.

Edward Jay Epstein, *The Rise and Fall of Diamonds: The Shattering of a Brilliant Illusion*, Simon and Schuster, New York, 1985.

Guido Ruggiero, *The Boundaries of Eros: Sex, Crime, and Sexuality in Renaissance Venice*, Oxford University Press, New York, 1985.

Thanks

To realize how many things are involved with producing a book, think of how many combinations of words, paragraphs, chapters, ideas, and facts, and of the strategy, and point of the entire excursion. Though the author signs off on the finished work, a host of people play a constructive and prudential role in the professional and personal process of planning, research, and writing. In books I've published before, I've included the appropriate "Acknowledgments" section but now I think that word is too cool and formal. So I want here to thank various people, some specifically, most generally, for the much-welcomed array of contributions they made to this project.

Amanda Urban of International Creative Management was skillfully, deftly, and warmly on my side throughout the life of this book and I am extraordinarily grateful to her. Robert Asahina saw the point of the endeavor at its outset when he was at Simon and Schuster and has been a supportive and thoughtful manager of the project as Editor and Publisher. Meredith Greene provided fair and wonderfully incisive editorial intelligence during its final drafting. Cassie Jones of Golden Books capably translated all those letters and words into the volume at hand. David and Catherine Graham were always cordially and generously hospitable to a writer with a laptop, and their friendship has been a bustling joy. Travel master Charlie Graham made it easy to be in the best place at the best time. Andrew Marshall has been a remarkable intellectual stimulant and a wise friend. Rogers Masters and Michael McGuire have been especially helpful fellow scholars in an ongoing adventure. I always owe more than is on paper to Robin Fox with whom it was at once reassuring and stimulating to write a new introduction, after thirty years, to the third incarnation of our *The Imperial Animal.*

Lives are rich processes blessed with affection along the way. Occasionally the result of the process is a product such as this book. Lest this become another chapter, to signal my gratitude to them, I am happy simply to list the names of many friends, colleagues, and fellow-writers. I hope they know how genuinely grateful I am to them for help with my knitting: Benjamin Barber, Janet Bascom, Ann Charney, Robert Caro, Barbaralee Diamonstein-Spielvogel, The Honorable Richard Danzig, Gerti Dieker, Robert Deutsch, Irven DeVore, Jaymie Durnan, Ira Ellman, Andy and Robin Fisher, Helen Fisher, Richard Foley, Gordon Getty, Wendy Gimbel, Amy Gross, Margaret Gruter, David Hale, Jack Harris, Molly Haskell, Sarah Blaffer Hrdy, Jane Lancaster, John and Jackie Leo, Robert Jay Lifton, Ed McCabe, Wallace Mooncai, Sidney Offit, David Popenoe, Peter Prescott, Rose Ravid, James Roche, Steven Peter Rosen, Alexander Sanger, Judd Shanklin, Abram Shulsky, Elizabeth Stein, Catherine Stimpson, Sebastian Tiger, Robert Trivers, Michelle Urry, Edward O. Wilson, and Albert Wojnilower.

Index